W0035931

SAGE was founded in 1965 by Sara Miller McCune to support the dissemination of usable knowledge by publishing innovative and high-quality research and teaching content. Today, we publish over 900 journals, including those of more than 400 learned societies, more than 800 new books per year, and a growing range of library products including archives, data, case studies, reports, and video. SAGE remains majority-owned by our founder, and after Sara's lifetime will become owned by a charitable trust that secures our continued independence.

Los Angeles | London | New Delhi | Singapore | Washington DC | Melbourne

LITERACY *in* ACTION

Thank you for choosing a SAGE product!
If you have any comment, observation or feedback,
I would like to personally hear from you.

Please write to me at **contactceo@sagepub.in**

Vivek Mehra, Managing Director and CEO, SAGE India.

Bulk Sales

SAGE India offers special discounts
for purchase of books in bulk.
We also make available special imprints
and excerpts from our books on demand.

For orders and enquiries, write to us at

Marketing Department
SAGE Publications India Pvt Ltd
B1/I-1, Mohan Cooperative Industrial Area
Mathura Road, Post Bag 7
New Delhi 110044, India

E-mail us at **marketing@sagepub.in**

Subscribe to our mailing list
Write to **marketing@sagepub.in**

This book is also available as an e-book.

LITERACY
in ACTION

Challenges in the Adult Education System in India

C. KRISHNA MOHAN RAO

Los Angeles | London | New Delhi
Singapore | Washington DC | Melbourne

First published in 2019 by

SAGE Publications India Pvt Ltd
B1/I-1 Mohan Cooperative Industrial Area
Mathura Road, New Delhi 110 044, India
www.sagepub.in

SAGE Publications Inc
2455 Teller Road
Thousand Oaks, California 91320, USA

SAGE Publications Ltd
1 Oliver's Yard, 55 City Road
London EC1Y 1SP, United Kingdom

SAGE Publications Asia-Pacific Pte Ltd
18 Cross Street #10-10/11/12
China Square Central
Singapore 048423

Published by Vivek Mehra for SAGE Publications India Pvt Ltd, typeset in 10.5/13 pt Berkeley by Zaza Eunice, Hosur, Tamil Nadu, India.

Library of Congress Cataloging-in-Publication Data Available

ISBN: 978-93-532-8308-7 (HB)

SAGE Team: Abhijit Baroi, Alekha Chandra Jena, Kumar Indra Mishra and Ritu Chopra

CONTENTS

LIST OF TABLES

LIST OF ABBREVIATIONS

AECs	adult education centres
AMP	Akshara Mahila programme
AS	Akshara Sangham
ASP	Akshara Sankranti programme
ASPBAE	Asia South Pacific Association for Basic and Adult Education
BGVS	Bharat Gyan Vigyan Samiti
CBFL	computer-based functional literacy
CBOs	community-based organizations
CEC	Continuing Education Centre
CEP	continuing education programme
CONFINTEA	International Conferences on Adult Education
CSR	corporate social responsibility
DAE	Directorate of Adult Education
DWCRA	Development of Women and Children in Rural Areas
EWLP	Experimental World Literacy Programme
FFLP	Farmers' Functional Literacy Programme
GoI	Government of India
GSM	Gram Shikshan Mohim
ICDS	Integrated Child Development Services
ICTs	information and communications technologies
IPCL	Improved Pace and Contents of Learning
JSNs	Jana Sikshan Nilayams
JSS	Zilla Saksharta Samiti

KRP	key resource person
LAMP	Literacy Assessment and Monitoring Programme
LSK	Lok Shiksha Samiti
M&E	monitoring and evaluation
MHRD	Ministry of Human Resource Development
MIS	management information system
MLA	Member of Legislative Assembly
MLO	mandal literacy organizer
MP	Member of Parliament
MTs	master trainers
NAEP	National Adult Education Programme
NCFAE	National Curriculum Framework for Adult Education
NFE	Non-Formal Education
NFEMIS	non-formal education management information system
NGO	non-governmental organization
NICHD	National Institute of Child Health and Human Development
NLM	National Literacy Mission
NLMA	National Literacy Mission Authority
NPA	National Policy on Education
NPAE	National Programme of Adult Education
PGAS	Paschima Godavari Akshara Samiti
PL&CE	Post-Literacy and Continuing Education
PRIs	Panchayati Raj Institutions
RFLP	Rural Functional Literacy Project
SB	Saakshar Bharat
SBP	Saakshar Bharat programme
SEP	social education programme
SHG	self-help group
SLMA	state literacy mission authority
SRC	State Resource Centre
TCS	Tata Consultancy Services
TLC	Total Literacy Campaign

UIL	UNESCO Institute of Lifelong Learning
UIS	UNESCO Institute for Statistics
UNDP	United Nations Development Programme
WePMIS	Web-based Planning and Monitoring Information System
WSHG	women self-help group

FOREWORD

Literacy and education have invariably been seen as vital forces in all the discourses on development at national and global levels. Particularly, adult literacy and adult education have been recognized as having a great potential to make an immediate and dramatic impact on development and thereby in the socioeconomic and political transformation of the society. They are also seen as powerful tools of empowering the oppressed populations. Accordingly, adult literacy and education are also considered as important components of poverty reduction strategies, and as core goals in the Education for All programme (EFA) and other global and national agendas, including Millennium Development Goals and Sustainable Development Goals. However, adult education has not received as much attention as it deserves in national planning in India and in many other developing countries. Today, about 770 million adults in the world are illiterate, and, among them, more than one-third live in India, calling for serious attention and search for innovative methods of improving adult literacy.

During the post-Independence period, India has adopted a variety of methods to raise the literacy levels of the population, important among which include the citizenship/social education programme in the 1950s, functional literacy programmes launched in the 1960s, the National Adult Education Programme (NAEP) in 1978, Total Literacy Campaign (TLC) in 1988 and Saakshar Bharat in 2009. Many of these programmes included both post-literacy programmes and continuing education programmes. Simultaneously, it is also hoped that efforts to universalize elementary education will improve adult literacy over the years, and accordingly the focus has also been on the provision of universal elementary education. In all, the efforts have yielded mixed results.

Dr C. Krishna Mohan Rao, who has been closely associated with adult education programmes for more than three decades in different capacities, looks into divergent and often contradictory perspectives that have influenced these programmes. The contradictions in the perspectives of the State vis-à-vis the common citizens, viewing literacy as a mean for development versus perceiving literacy as development and as a human right, have impacted the conceptualization, development of the curriculum, adoption of different pedagogic methods, the design and implementation of the various programmes and schemes in literacy and adult education. Some of the contradictions have indeed contributed to the very failure of the programmes. For the literacy and adult education programmes to be effective, there is a need for better and sound understanding of different perspectives. After all, literacy is not a simple and isolated social or educational problem, which can be solved with the help of quick-fix solutions and short-term interventions. It requires a long-term vision, a strong political commitment, a consistent plan—a multi-sectoral plan—and a strong and sustained implementation mechanism, all backed by sufficient public funds. It requires a multidimensional approach, involving multiple players, rather all sections of the society.

Written in a very simple and non-technical style—easy to understand for laymen, academia, policymakers and administrators— Dr Rao's critical analysis of the shortcomings in the policy framework and loopholes in implementation of various programmes in adult education and literacy, his clear insightful views on the subject and the suggestions he makes for future will be of considerable interest to all those who are interested in literacy and national development.

Jandhyala B. G. Tilak
Former Vice Chancellor, National University of Educational
Planning and Administration
Distinguished Professor, Council for Social Development,
New Delhi

ACKNOWLEDGEMENTS

There are many who have helped me in bringing out this book, and I would like to express my gratitude to all of them, especially the following:

Dr C. Stalin, MS, my uncle, who has been a source of inspiration for all my endeavours.

Mr D. V. V. S. Varma, who taught me how to think globally and work locally, for sharing his in-depth knowledge on various socio-political issues.

Professor A. Raghuramaraju for encouraging me to write about my experiences and guiding me in the process.

Dr A. Mathew, one of the few experts in Indian adult education, for recognizing the potential after seeing the material and for his valuable feedback and advice.

Professor Jandhyala B. G. Tilak for going through the manuscript and writing the Foreword.

Dr Poonam Malakondaiah, IAS, for giving me an opportunity to take up various initiatives in literacy programmes.

Mr S. Siva Kumarappa, former Director of Adult Education, Andhra Pradesh, and a close friend, for helping me in many ways.

Mr N. C. Varadacharyulu, my constant companion in the literacy movement, for sharing his ideas and data.

Mr U. V. S. Prasad, Mr T. V. S. N. Reddy, Mr Y. V. Suryanarayana, Mr S. Siddayya, Mrs Latha and other colleagues in the Directorate for their help and feedback on the book.

Mr R. V. Harnoor for editing and suggestions on presentation.

Mrs S. Manorama, my colleague in the literacy movement in West Godavari, for her help in various initiatives.

Mr Rao Krishna Rao and Dr V. V. Nagendra Rao for sharing their perspectives on various social issues.

Professor M. Siva Raj for many years of warm friendship and guidance.

INTRODUCTION

It was in 1982, after I had joined the Adult Education Department of the then Government of Andhra Pradesh (bifurcated into Andhra Pradesh and Telangana in 2014), that I saw for the first time an adult education centre at Rampachodavaram, a tribal taluk in East Godavari district. Along with the supervisor of the area, I visited a literacy centre in Lathugadda, an interior tribal village, located at the foot of a thickly forested hill. We walked for about 2 km across the jungle to reach the village. When we reached there around 6.30 PM, the villagers were just returning from the forest after daylong work of bamboo cutting. We first met the organizer of the centre, a part-time paid worker. He was a young tribal, aged about 20 years, and had passed the seventh standard. He took us to the adult education centre, housed in a small hut in the middle of the village belonging to one of the village elders. After making us sit on a small wooden bench, he went into the village requesting the learners to come to the centre. Meanwhile, we started verifying the attendance register, which had been marked until the previous day. The average attendance was 25 out of 30 enrolled. Half an hour later, the organizer brought with him six learners—four women and two men—whom he had been able to persuade. Along with them, some children had gathered at the centre. While we were making them read the primers in the centre, which had only a dimly lit hurricane lantern, to assess their literacy level, three more learners joined the class. Of the total, five were able to read words in the third lesson of the primer 'Jana Vachakam' (people's primer) developed in the sentence method. The supervisor pulled up the organizer for the slow progress. According to the programme schedule, the learners were expected to be in the ninth lesson by that time. The writing ability of the learners was far below expectation, and most of them could only write their names on the slate, the first lesson in the primer. To get at the root of the problem, I intervened and asked the organizer and learners about the details of the regularity of classes and problems in teaching. The organizer gave a routine reply that although the classes had been running regularly, the attendance of learners was poor. The learners admitted that they had attended the classes regularly for the first three months but discontinued, as with the onset of monsoon they had to take up cultivation work. I asked them about the difficulties in learning. The organizer and the learners gave different types of replies. This was a typical literacy centre established under NAEP, the first nationwide adult education programme started in 1978. I have visited hundreds of centres functioning under NAEP and subsequent literacy programmes since then, and a majority of the centres functioned more or less in the same way. It is common to blame the field functionaries if the centre fails to achieve the desired results. The functionaries, who do not have clarity about the reasons for failure, blame the participants, poor infrastructure and facilities. At the macro level, this is reflected in the slow growth of literacy rate. As per the *EFA Global Monitoring Report* (UNESCO, 2015), India is one of the countries lagging behind in achieving EFA goals and about one-third of the world's illiterate population lives in India (Census of India, 2011).

Initially, when I joined the programme, I thought, like many others in the field, that success or failure of the literacy centre mainly depends on local factors relating to organizers or learners. I have identified some of them and examined in detail in my PhD dissertation (Rao, 1988). But, over the years, during the implementation of the adult education programmes and participation in various meetings, workshops and seminars, both as a government official (practitioner) and as an academician, I observed that there are divergent perspectives on various issues of literacy, in both policy and practice. Each of these perspectives has ideological and technical angles (Bhola, 1988), which play a critical role in the success or failure of the centre. Some of these contradictory perspectives are briefly mentioned below.

STATE AND USER PERSPECTIVES

If we look at literacy as a social activity, we find two perspectives: one is a state perspective and the other is a user perspective. Quigley (1997) used the terms 'political perspective' and 'popular perspective' in analysing the American adult education programmes. The two terms, state perspective and user perspective, are used respectively in the same sense as the terms 'political perspective' and 'popular perspective'. The state perspective focuses on macro-level policy issues based on the perceptions of government and political leadership. It highlights the purpose of literacy as that improves the nation's economy and transforms illiterates into responsible citizens. As a matter of fact, it is the responsibility of illiterates themselves to acquire literacy. In this perspective, the metaphor used is that a nation has to 'engage in battle', 'declare war' and 'fight' the enemy of illiteracy. As Kak (2000) points out, 'adult non-literates are objects, not subjects of official planning'.

The other one, the user perspective, highlights micro-level society or users' viewpoint. In this perspective, the focus is on illiterates rather than illiteracy. The purpose of literacy is to provide opportunities to the non-literates to improve their quality of life. This perspective views low literate as victim, and the responsibility of injustice is shared between an unjust society and its less-than-effective institutions, such as school system. The responsibility of supporting illiterates rests on society and the government. The metaphors used are 'social context' and 'needs and interests of individual learners'. These two perspectives present a completely different reality of literacy programmes.

LITERACY AS INDIVIDUAL DIMENSION AND SOCIAL DIMENSION

Likewise, there are contradictory perceptions of the concept of literacy. The state perspective looks at literacy from individual dimension, and, in user perspective, it is viewed from social dimension. The basic assumption in individual dimension is that literacy is a simple learned cognitive skill that can be measured independent of the context in which it is learned. It can be understood as an independent variable that produces effects—increases cognitive skills and helps to develop a critical and reflective way of thinking (McCaffery, Merrifield, & Millican, 2007).

In the user perspective, literacy is neither a state nor a technique nor a skill, because no one learns to read and write in a vacuum. It is a social process in a social context. It is not a question of first acquiring the basics and then doing something with them but a simultaneous process of learning and doing. The proponents (Street, 1984) of this model prefer to talk of 'literacy practices' and 'literacy events' as terms for the activities leading to reading and writing. Each of these perspectives has its own assumptions on various components of literacy.

LITERACY AS EDUCATION AND LITERACY AS DEVELOPMENT

Another issue in the perspectives of literacy is how we see adult literacy, whether as education or development. In the state perspective, adult literacy is seen in terms of adult schooling within the education sector. The main emphasis in this is the improvement of literacy or educational levels of the population. The focus is on higher levels of education to the population using various channels such as open schooling system and equivalency programmes. In the user perspective, adult literacy is seen as a part of development programme intended for their social and economic development. The users look at it as an opportunity to improve their standard of living. In this, the focus is on improving learners' quality of life.

The ideological differences in 'literacy as education' and 'literacy as development' approaches have influenced many aspects of literacy programmes (Rogers, 2004b). The distinction between the two is important because the emphasis changes with each perspective. If literacy is education, then schooling for adults is the obvious approach. Organization, curriculum, pedagogy and other aspects are planned in that way. The approach would be different if we view literacy as development. The focus of the programme shifts from mere literacy and education to livelihoods and other developmental issues (Daniel, 2005). In this, literacy is rooted in individual and social development.

POLICY AND IMPLEMENTATION PERSPECTIVES

Another inconsistency in adult education, which has a lot of implication for the programme, is the gap between state perspective and user perspective in terms of policy and implementation. This is mainly because there is a wide variation between policies formulated in policy documents and operational guidelines issued for the implementation of the policies. Adult education policies are mostly formulated by the national government based on overall national priorities, whereas operational guidelines are issued based on the physical and financial resources available for implementation. As a result, there are perceptional differences among people working at different levels. Policymakers look at the programme from policy perspective mentioned in policy documents, while functionaries working in implementation agencies look from operational guidelines and funding pattern. Here, policy formulation and implementation are viewed as separate activities. The hiatus between the two had influenced the programme.

I have gone through literature to see if any studies or papers have examined the assumption and contradictions in Indian adult education. I found that a major part of the research in adult education is evaluation research conducted by various universities or research institutes sponsored by the Government of India. These include about 80 studies on NAEP (National Literacy Mission [NLM], 1994), 254 on TLC, 161 on post-literacy and continuing education (PL&CE; Mohankumar & Dua, 2012), 23 on Akshara Sankranti and 5 on Saakshar Bharat programme. These are programme evaluations based on the guidelines given by the sponsoring agencies. As pointed out by Bordia (1999), often the parameters of these studies are also laid down by the official agencies, whose interest is in 'quick appraisal' rather than a profound analysis of the interplay of the factors which have a bearing on the programmes. These studies presented an overview of programme implementation in terms of inputs and outputs and not on processes and context that impact the implementation of the programme in the field (Patel, 1994). None of the studies analysed the assumptions and contradictions in perceptions in Indian adult education. Other materials available on adult education in India are the reports of many committees constituted by the government on various aspects of the programme (Shah, 1999). These reports broadly discussed macro-level issues and suggested broad guidelines. Very few studies (Bhola, 1988; Kak, 2000; Patel, 2000) did policy analysis of literacy programmes in India at the political, legislative and policy levels. Kak (2000) mentioned some of the contradictions, particularly state perspective of adult literacy, but did not elaborate it with reference to the implementation of the programme. Further, after the year 2000, books, papers and other material on adult education are rare except government documents and evaluation reports.

For adult literacy education to be successful, the assumptions or perspectives on which policies and programmes are formulated and implemented need to be understood and analysed at the operational level. The operational issues need to be traced to the policies and perspectives of the programme. The dialectical relationship between different perspectives needs to be understood properly. This is best done by practitioners with an academic background, and this book is an attempt in that direction.

The book is very much relevant in the context of revamping the Saakshar Bharat programme and launching of a new literacy programme for the eradication of illiteracy from the country with the main focus on the voluntary participation of students. It will be useful for the policymakers, administrators, students of academic disciplines and students who participate in field activity.

The book examines different issues or programme areas of adult literacy education, ranging from the concept of literacy to the funding. Theoretical and implementation perspectives are presented for each issue and analysed with reference to major literacy programmes in India since 1978—NAEP, TLCs and Saakshar Bharat. Grey areas and problems in implementation are discussed at the end of each chapter. Field-level experiences are quoted on each area of the programme to present efforts made at the local level.

In this book, the terms adult education and adult literacy are used interchangeably as it is difficult to differentiate them in the Indian context. Almost all the adult education programmes in India teaching literacy skills and imparting knowledge are combined. So it is proper to call the whole process adult literacy education. In the book, 'adult' literacy is used to mean those aged 15 years and above as used by the UNESCO and Indian adult education programmes. The book focuses on programmes in the government sector and does not include the experiences of the NGO sector. Experiences quoted in the book are mainly from the author's own experience in implementing the programme in the state of Andhra Pradesh.

The first chapter presents an overview of adult education programmes in India since Independence. Approaches and strategies followed in each programme are discussed to give a comparative picture of different programmes.

The concept of literacy and its different dimensions are analysed in the second chapter. How the concept is evolved at national and international levels over a period of time is also discussed.

The third chapter deals with literacy and development from different perspectives—literacy as education versus literacy as development. Assumptions on the benefits of literacy are examined with reference to field experiences.

The fourth chapter discusses curriculum and pedagogical issues in adult literacy and different approaches followed in different programmes in India. It examines the contradictions between curriculum and pedagogical approaches and critically analyses them from different perspectives. The author's experiences in primer development are mentioned in brief.

Motivational strategies adopted in different adult education programmes in India and the assumption underlying motivation and mobilization strategy, and the difference between social mobilization and community mobilization are highlighted in the fifth chapter. It concludes with the author's experience in community mobilization in government programmes.

Opportunities for PL&CE and their importance in sustaining literacy among the neo-literates are discussed in the sixth chapter. It explicates the underlying assumptions for the neglect of PL&CE and refers to different models of PL&CE programmes introduced in India.

At the end, the chapter discusses the field-level experiences of effective PL&CE programmes.

The seventh chapter discusses the concepts of monitoring and evaluation in literacy programmes and different approaches followed in India. Innovative approaches adopted using information and communications technologies and the experiences of international pilot project on management information system are also presented in this chapter.

The eighth chapter presents delivery mechanism of adult education programmes in India. The assumptions behind institutional setups and human resources are reviewed. The importance and problems of capacity-building in adult education are highlighted in this chapter.

The ninth chapter reviews the financial resources for adult education programmes in India. The funding pattern of different adult education programmes and its underlying assumptions and problems are discussed at length.

The tenth chapter summarizes the main findings of this book and discusses the way forward for the conduct of effective adult education programmes in Indian context.

Overview of Adult Literacy Programmes in India

Before discussing the theoretical and practical assumptions on which adult education programmes are planned and implemented in India, a brief overview of the programmes implemented since Independence is necessary to understand various approaches and strategies adopted in Indian adult education. This gives clear perspectives on policies and programmes in the present context.

After Independence, the Government of India (GoI) and state governments initiated a number of adult education programmes. Because of low literacy, adult education has been mostly confined to adult literacy although some provisions have been made for continuing education and skill development activities. Over a period of time, the concept of literacy has undergone several changes. Shah (2012) mentioned three main trends of literacy in Indian adult education during the period 1947–1987, namely, civic literacy (1948–1967), functional literacy (1968–1977) and developmental literacy (1978–1987). These concepts were operationalized into a variety of programmes, projects and schemes, namely, Social Education, Farmers Education and Functional Literacy, Rural Functional Literacy, Mass Programme of Functional Literacy, National Adult Education Programme (NAEP), Total Literacy Campaigns (TLC) and Saakshar Bharat (SB). Some of the major programmes are discussed hereunder.

SOCIAL EDUCATION PROGRAMME

In 1949, the GoI introduced a programme of adult education termed Social Education. It was in fact the first adult education programme with great emphasis on social aspects. The concept of social education was closely associated with the fundamental education at the international level. Social Education was defined as a comprehensive programme of community uplift through community action. It had three objectives: (a) the spread of literacy among grown-up illiterates, (b) the production of an educated mind in the masses in the absence of literacy education and (c) the inculcation of a lively sense of rights and duties of citizenship, as both individuals and members of a powerful nation (Rao, 1988). The programme aimed at achieving 50 per cent literacy in the 12–45 age group within a period of five years. This programme adopted the selective approach wherein a specific number of centres were established in each village in the selected community blocks to impart literacy and other adult education programmes. The implementation strategies were worked out by different state governments. The duration of the programme was 180 hours, spread over 90 days—an average of 2 hours per day. The programme was undertaken especially but not exclusively by the primary schoolteachers who were paid an honorarium of ₹10 per month and a recurring allowance of ₹25 and ₹11 per year for contingencies.

The core curriculum in Social Education included (a) health and hygiene, (b) family and community living, (c) vocations, (d) literacy and cultural activities and (e) recreational activities. Social education, when implemented along with the community development programme, emphasized developmental activities more than literacy education.

Towards the end of the Second Five Year Plan (1956–1961), the emphasis began to shift from community development to industrial development, and, as a result, the community development programme was neglected. This was reflected in the decreasing investments in social education programmes (SEPs) in the subsequent five-year plans (Bordia, 1980).

GRAM SHIKSHAN MOHIM

One of the important programmes taken up in the state of Maharashtra as a part of the SEP was the Gram Shikshan Mohim (GSM; Village Education Movement) with its mass approach to eradication of illiteracy. The GSM, introduced in 1959, was the first genuine mass campaign for literacy initiated in India after Independence. It was first introduced in one district, Satara, in 1959, and upscaled later to the whole of Maharashtra. This had a deep impact on the subsequent adult education programmes. It made a number of villages completely literate during the two years of its implementation.

The objectives of this programme were threefold: (a) eradication of illiteracy among the adults in the 14–50 age group through literacy classes, (b) retaining literacy and enriching the knowledge of neo-literates through circulating libraries and (c) bringing about all-sided development of the village through education centres. It adopted campaign approach for literacy with the village as a unit. This four-month literacy programme operated for only two years (1961–1963) but achieved substantial results in declaring many villages totally literate.

As a part of the curriculum, information was given on major topics such as sanitation, farming, village development, child development, etc. After the initial four months of the campaign were over, the programme of retraining in literacy and enriching the knowledge of neo-literates was taken up. This follow-up work was done through circulating library scheme and social education centres (Mathew, 2013). Although the campaign significantly increased the literacy rate in Maharashtra, the literacy attained during this short span was of a very low level, and, in the absence of effective and regular follow-up programmes, the neo-literates soon relapsed into illiteracy.

FARMERS' FUNCTIONAL LITERACY PROGRAMME

Another significant adult education programme was Farmers' Functional Literacy Programme (FFLP) launched in 1967–1968. The concept of functional literacy envisaged at the international level and the Experimental World Literacy Programme (EWLP) had a great influence on this programme. The main objectives of the programme were to enable the farmers to (a) read and understand labels on fertilizer bags, (b) fill up loan application forms, (c) keep a simple account of operations and (d) read and make use of simple extension bulletins, rural newspapers, etc. It aimed at training about five million farm families in 100 select districts and imparting functional literacy to one million adults at the cost of ₹90 million (GoI, 1972, cited in Shah, 2012).

This was an inter-ministerial programme in which the Ministry of Education was responsible for functional literacy, the Ministry of Agriculture for Farmers' Training and All India Radio for Farm Broadcasting. The integrated programme aimed to educate and inform illiterate farmers about high-yielding varieties of seeds and package of improved agricultural practices. The programme was initially started in three districts and later expanded to some more integrated agriculture development project districts. In respect of the focus, there was a marked shift in emphasis from the traditional 3Rs to the 3Fs—functional literacy, food production and family welfare (Dutta, 1986).

FFLP adopted a selective approach to literacy, and it was the first attempt to put educational activities directly in relation to one of the major developmental purposes. The project was conceived as a centre-based programme with an instructor to learner ratio of 1:30. The duration of functional literacy programme was one year, and it was organized in two phases of six months each. Each phase had 150 hours of effective teaching, approximately one and a half hours every day. Literacy centres were established in villages where integrated agriculture projects were taken up. The project was confined to selected districts in a state, the maximum number of centres per district was limited to 60, and they were under the charge of a project officer assisted by part-time supervisors.

NON-FORMAL EDUCATION FOR YOUTH

A major programme called Non-Formal Education (NFE) was launched in 1975–1976 for the 15–25 age group, focusing mainly on young people belonging to the weaker sections of society who did not have the benefits of formal education. The programme aimed at dealing with the social, cultural and economic needs of the learners in such a manner as to lead them to better awareness and understanding, knowledge, ability and finally to action. A significant aspect of NFE was its emphasis on locally relevant and diversified content, including science (Mathew, 1990). It also followed a selective approach with a specific number of NFE centres in the villages where the project was implemented.

The short duration programme had incorporated the latest thinking in the field of adult education, but, in practice, it was not much different from other routine literacy programmes. This programme suffered from inadequate financial outlay, poor supervisory arrangements, poor monitoring and evaluation (M&E) system (Bordia, 1980).

NATIONAL ADULT EDUCATION PROGRAMME

The experience gained in the implementation of various adult education programmes has broadened the concept and crystallized in the form of NAEP. It was the first nationwide target-oriented programme of adult education, launched on 2 October 1978, that is, Gandhi Jayanti. The Policy Document specifying the aims of NAEP, mentions,

> The objective is to organise adult education programmes, with literacy as an indispensable component, for approximately 100 million illiterate persons in the age group of 15–35 with a view to providing literacy skills for self-directed learning leading to self-reliant and active role in their own development and in the development of their environment. (Ministry of Education and Social Welfare, 1978, p. 1)

Special emphasis was given to Scheduled Castes, Scheduled Tribes, women and other weaker sections of society, which constitute the bulk of India's illiterate population. It was a mass programme covering the entire country but adopted a selective approach in establishing adult education centres (AECs) in villages. According to the policy statement of NAEP (Ministry of Education and Social Welfare, 1978), the programme was to be relevant to the environment and learners' needs, flexible regarding duration, time, location and instructional arrangements, diversified in regard to curriculum, teaching and learning material, and systematic on all aspects of organization.

NAEP was implemented by a variety of agencies, namely, state governments, voluntary agencies, universities, etc. A number of projects were sanctioned to each district on the basis of backwardness and history of social movements. A project was an administrative unit responsible for organizing the programme at the field level. The number of centres in a project varies with the organization that implements the programme. Generally, project consisting of 300 AECs, headed by a project officer, with a supervisor for every 30 AECs. The AECs conducted adult education activities and enrolled 30 learners in the age group of 15–35 years. They were taught literacy by an organizer who received an honorarium of ₹50 per month, and this was enhanced to ₹100 in 1984. Each learner was to spend about 350 hours over a period of 10 months at AEC to acquire literacy skills. Teaching materials such as a roll-up board, volunteer's guide, hurricane lantern and learning materials such as primers, writing books, slates, notebooks and pencils were supplied to the centres.

The GoI and the state governments jointly financed the projects. The responsibility of implementation lay with the state governments, which identified various agencies and constituted appropriate administrative and managerial structures. A State Resource Centre (SRC) for adult education, established under non-governmental agencies and funded by GoI, provided resource and technical support at the state level.

Some changes were made to NAEP based on National Policy on Education (NPA), 1986. It was renamed as the National Programme of Adult Education (NPAE). It aimed at covering 100 million illiterate people in a phased and time-bound manner—40 million by 1990 and 60 million by 1995. Like NAEP, the NPAE followed the project approach with the AECs as the operational unit. While there were some modifications in the management system proposed for NPAE, new stress was laid on environment creation for literacy. NPAE was closed with the launching of the National Literacy Mission (NLM) in May 1988.

NLM: TOTAL LITERACY CAMPAIGNS

On 5 May 1988, the GoI launched NLM with a view to applying technological and scientific research in the promotion of literacy. The main objectives of the mission are imparting functional literacy to 80 million illiterate persons in the 15–35 age group, 30 million by 1990 and an additional 50 million by 1995. The programme used functional literacy in a broad sense, covering both skill development for improving productivity and more radical critical literacy for understanding the causes of deprivation and moving towards organizing and participating in development. It gave a lot of importance to motivation and mobilization and worked out detailed strategies to reach people.

In 1989, after a unique experiment in Ernakulum district in Kerala, where total literacy was achieved through a 'campaign' approach with people's participation, NLM adopted it in other parts of the country. The 'campaign' mode, which has become TLCs, had become a major strategy for literacy during the next two decades.

All the major features of literacy campaigns as conducted in the world were included in the campaign strategy, but TLCs in India were different: The campaign was not taken up in the entire country at one go. The unit of campaign was a district, not the country as a whole. The campaigns were launched in districts that came forward to take up, but not on the basis of backwardness or other disadvantages. The leadership for the campaign was provided by the bureaucracy, not by the political leadership.

Three critical characteristics distinguish the TLCs from their centre-based predecessor NAEP. First, as its name suggests, the model adopted a mass campaign approach (Ministry of Human Resource Development [MHRD], 1992). Typically, the TLC has as its territorial compact, geographically administrative area. This was usually a district but sometimes a block or a municipality. It had a clearly specified target population of non-literates, usually all non-literates in the chosen area in a specified age group, such as 10–60 years, 9–45 years, and often 15–35 years. It is also time bound, the period of the entire campaign being between 12 and 18 months.

Second, TLC was based on a participatory approach, in which people at all levels were encouraged to participate actively in the campaign by joining the literacy committees at the district, block, panchayat or village levels. Third, and most important, the TLC was based fundamentally and critically on voluntarism. The entire work of imparting literacy to learners was done on a voluntary basis. All works, except that of full-time project staff, including tasks such as training, local organizing and participating in various motivational activities, were wholly voluntary.

It created a mission management structure and typically operated with a three-legged structure: One, the entire governmental machinery of the area in which the campaign was conducted; two, the full-time project staff; and three, popular literacy committees at various levels. In a district, the district collector or the chairperson of the Zila Parishad headed the literacy committee specially constituted for the campaign. There was no limit to the number of centres opened and depended on the availability of learners and volunteers. TLCs were conducted in most (about 597) of the districts in the country.

NLM also gave a lot of importance to techno-pedagogic inputs to improve the pace of learning. It clearly defined prescribed levels of literacy in definable terms. Teaching and learning process was conducted for 200 hours in a period of six months. Guidelines were framed for the preparation of primers and other reading material to Improved Pace and Contents of Learning (IPCL) approach. However, there was criticism that academic input or teaching and learning process was weak in TLC (Mathew & Rao, 1994)

SAAKSHAR BHARAT PROGRAMME

On 8 September 2009, International Literacy Day, Dr Manmohan Singh, the then prime minister of India, launched Saakshar Bharat Programme (SBP), a 'new variant of NLM'. The main assumption while initiating the programme was that 'the repositioning of the Mission would have a very positive impact on re-energizing the literacy movement' (MHRD, 2009, p. 3). SBP aimed to promote and strengthen adult education through imparting functional literacy to 70 million adults in the age group of 15 years and beyond. It is a major initiative in adult education since 1988, with the main focus on women, Scheduled Castes, Scheduled Tribes and minorities.

The mission has four broad objectives: (a) impart functional literacy and numeracy to non-literate and non-numerate adults, (b) enable the neo-literate adults to continue their learning beyond basic literacy and acquire equivalency to formal educational system, (c) impart relevant skill development programmes to non- and neo-literates to improve their earning and living conditions and (d) promote a learning society by providing opportunities to neo-literate adults for continuing education.

Although the mass campaign approach continued to be the dominant strategy, SBP scheme discounted a homogeneous approach uniformly throughout the country. Theoretically, implementing agencies can adopt any approach/model or a mix of approaches/models. This programme combined mass campaign approach and centre-based approach in that adult education centres are established in all villages, but only in selected educationally backward districts. It has paid coordinators for the centres. At the same time, services of volunteers are used to impart literacy skills in the mass campaign model.

In terms of conceptual framework, it continued NLM definition of literacy. The curriculum includes core content and locally relevant content, which are produced in the locally dominant language as per IPCL guidelines. Learners have to undergo 300 hours of tuition to reach basic literacy. Basic literacy, post-literacy and continuing education (PL&CE) programmes are integrated to form a continuum rather than sequential segments. Jan Shiksha Kendras (or AECs) are set up in each village to coordinate and manage all programmes within their territorial jurisdiction. The state governments, as against the districts in the earlier versions of TLC, are given the responsibility of implementation of the programme, and, at the local level, Panchayati Raj Institutions (PRIs) are the main instrumentalities in the execution.

LOCAL INITIATIVES

Besides the aforementioned programmes mainly implemented by the education department, a number of adult education programmes have been conducted under different agencies. They include (a) Adult Education through Students and Youth (under University Grants Commission), (b) Nehru Yuva Kendras, (c) Non-Formal Education for Women and Girls, (d) Shramik Vidyapeeths/Jan Shikshan Sansthans, (e) Central Board for Workers Education, (f) Functional Literacy for Adult Women, (g) adult education through voluntary agencies; (h) Mass Programme of Functional Literacy, etc. Some state governments initiated literacy programmes on their own. For example, Madhya Pradesh government conducted Padhana Badhana in 1999 and the Andhra Pradesh government implemented Akshara Sankranti between 2001 and 2005.

In many cases, these local initiatives have not been properly documented or discussed in academic circles. One such programme Akshara Mahila (Literate Women) which was a precursor to the Akshara Sankranti programme (ASP) is discussed in the analysis. The details of the programme are discussed in brief here.

AKSHARA MAHILA PROGRAMME

Zilla Saksharta Samiti (ZSS; District Literacy Committee) of West Godavari district conceived and implemented a group-based women literacy programme named Akshara Mahila to improve women literacy in the district. This local initiative had a major impact on thinking and brought about major changes in literacy policies of the Andhra Pradesh government. The main objective of the programme is to make all members of women self-help groups (WSHGs) literate, which would act as a catalyst in improving women literacy. It took WSHG formed under Development of Women and Children in Rural Areas (DWCRA) programme as a channel for introducing literacy among women.

AMP adopted a group-based approach, an alternative strategy for centre-based approach and campaign approach. In AMP, self-help groups (SHGs) that have already organized an economic activity are taken as the unit for literacy instruction. In TLC, the entry point is literacy whereas in AMP, literacy is introduced as one of the components for an already organized group. The programme was planned in such a way that the group would identify the learners (non-literate members) from their own group, select the volunteer (educated member) from among the group members. If no educated woman were available within the group, then they would request educated persons in the neighbourhood to teach the group members. This would also increase the pace of learning because they would adopt peer-learning techniques to motivate other non-literate members. Based on the needs and interests of learners, a new primer was developed locally to suit the local conditions. Priority was given to language learning over other components. The content of the primers is mainly related to women issues and organization of SHGs. Literacy course duration was confined to 180 hours in a 3-month period.

Taking this experience, the Andhra Pradesh government launched Akshara Sankranti, a special literacy programme for SHGs and stake-holders' associations of different development programmes. Under this programme, apart from WSHGs, literacy programmes were taken up for Srama Shakti Sangams of Mahatma Gandhi National Rural Employment Guarantee Scheme, youth clubs, forest management committees, etc. Each group was to take the responsibility of making all its members literate. Agencies or departments dealing with groups at the district level were made responsible for organizing the literacy programme for the groups. ZSSs or adult education department supplied teaching–learning material and provided training to the volunteers. District collectors coordinated the overall implementation of the programme.

From the overview of literacy and adult education programmes in India, one can see that the government has taken the major responsibility and conducted a variety of programmes to improve literacy among population. Some of the programmes could achieve good results in some aspects of the programme. Each of these programmes has adopted different approaches and strategies to reach the target population. Two main approaches adopted are selective approach and campaign approach. The two approaches mainly differed in terms of technology and approach, not in ideology. There is criticism that changes in education policy in India are essentially in the realm of technology and not in ideology (Bhola, 1988). Only technical factors played a major role in the success or failure of the programmes. The ideology is reflected to some extent in the way the concept of literacy is used in major adult education programmes in India. This issue is discussed in the next chapter that deals with the concept of literacy.

Concept of Literacy

I once attended a meeting of WSHGs at Denduluru village in West Godavari district. About 35 women in the age group of 18–60 years participated in the meeting held in a community hall. When I asked how many of them were literate, about one-third of them raised their hands. Feeling let down, I told the group leaders that only fewer than 12 members had raised their hands. On being asked the concerned members why they had not raised their hands although they were literate, they replied that had they done so I would asked them to write something and that they were not sure whether they would write that correctly. When I asked how many of them had attended primary school, even for one day, almost all of them said that they had attended school for some time. Some said that they had not learned anything at school and others said that they had forgotten whatever they had learned over the years.

During a chat, they jokingly said that they change their literacy status according to the situation. For example, members of WSHGs claim themselves to be literates while applying for loans and append their signature, but when asked to read a book or their group's ledger, they say they are illiterate. They append their signature on the minutes of the meeting but put their thumb impression when casting their vote during the elections, as they have to make way for those in the queue behind them. Similarly, those who claim to be non-literate read film posters, use mobile phones, recognize destination boards on the buses.

During the meeting, I asked what they meant by literacy or literate. The replies were wide and varied, ranging from writing one's name (to them, there was no difference between one's name and signature), recognizing alphabets, reading newspapers, ability to read the Bible, write applications, letters, getting information on various issues relating to their daily life, active participation in group activities and questioning injustice.

In official meetings as well, I found that the participants used the term literacy ambiguously. In one training programme, I asked the participants, who were full-time field functionaries of adult education, what they meant by literacy. The meanings they gave ranged from the ability to sign or write their names to reading newspapers. The same was the case with senior bureaucrats dealing with adult education. Most of them use the term vaguely to indicate some level of awareness about alphabets and some level of ability to read and write. However, when we discuss this issue with academicians in seminars and workshops, we find that they use the term in a much broader sense as a concept with different dimensions and meanings.

What is literacy? Is there a uniform meaning and definition of literacy? If not, what are the different perspectives of literacy? What 'level' can and should be defined for measurement? How did the concept of literacy evolve over a period of time? How is the concept used in Indian adult education programmes? These are among the questions that are critical for understanding literacy. Lack of conceptual clarity on the meaning of literacy has generated lots of problems in the implementation of the programme. In order to understand the concept of literacy, it is necessary to discuss some of the theoretical perspectives.

The discussion on the concept of literacy is divided into four broad areas: (a) dimensions of literacy at the theoretical level; (b) the conceptual evaluation of literacy at international and national levels; (c) conceptualization of literacy in Indian adult education programmes and (d) problems of conceptualization.

DIMENSIONS OF LITERACY

What is literacy? It seems like an extremely simple question, but, in reality, it is very difficult to answer. In fact, there is no single correct answer, and there is no consensus on the definition of literacy. The perception regarding what constitutes literacy has varied over time and across countries. It denotes different things to different people in different contexts. Its meaning ranges from reading the 'word' to reading the 'world'. People's notions of what it means to be literate or illiterate are influenced by academic research, institutional agendas, national context, cultural values and personal experiences (UNESCO, 2005). Moreover, in recent times, outside the adult education circles, the word 'literacy' has begun to be used in a much broader, metaphorical sense, to refer to skills and competencies, for example, 'computer literacy', 'legal literacy, 'media literacy'. Similarly, different programmes use different terms to indicate programmes based on clientele, objectives, contexts and methodologies (Bhola, 2010) such as women literacy programmes and rural functional literacy programmes.

If we look at literacy as a concept, we find two distinctive dimensions of literacy: One is the personal dimension and the other is social. In the first case, literacy is understood to be something that one either has or does not have. In the other approach, the emphasis is laid on the social aspects, that is, literate or not depends on the social context and the use that individuals make of literacy (Bhola, 2008). The first one defines literacy in absolute terms and the second one looks at literacy in relative terms. Each of the dimensions represents a school of thought and has philosophical and ideological connotations.

LITERACY AS AN INDIVIDUAL DIMENSION

The basic assumption in individual dimension is that literacy is a simple concept which can be understood as an independent variable and which produces effects. It is a simple learned cognitive skill that can be measured or tested independent of the context in which it is learned. Literacy increases cognitive skills and develops a critical and reflective way of thinking. Within this, there are two kinds of perceptions: literacy as a skill and literacy as a task.

Literacy as a Skill

The most common understanding of literacy, which prevailed over centuries, is that literacy is a simple, learned cognitive skill. One learned to read and write just as one learned to make baskets, kick a ball, kill a deer, or build a fire. This view of literacy has come to be referred to as 'autonomous literacy' (Street, 1984). According to this view, literacy means the ability to code and decode alphabet/symbols—recognizing and pronouncing letters, using them to form words and understanding their meanings. The skills are viewed as generic, so the skill used in one setting can be applied in another and measured through tests (McCaffery, Merrifield, & Millican, 2007). Approaches based on defining skill-based literacy are often called 'competency' approaches.

Literacy as a Task

In another perspective, literacy is viewed as the ability to perform a particular task using literacy skills. In this approach, literacy means engaging in tasks that require the written word in life and work situations. It emphasizes the application of literacy skills rather than the skill itself. This approach is generally called 'functional literacy' (McCaffery et al., 2007). In functional literacy approaches, the ability to decode text is less important than the ability to carry out life tasks defined beforehand. Initially, the 'literacy as tasks' approach focused on improvement of productivity and later incorporated a wider array of tasks in spheres beyond work, including citizenship, families and community involvement.

In this connection, the distinction between literacy and functional literacy is important. UNESCO (2005, p. 154) has clarified the distinction between the two:

> In a simple way a person is literate who can with understanding both read and write a short simple statement on his [or her] everyday life, whereas a person is functionally literate who can engage in all those activities in which literacy is required for effective functioning in his [or her] group and community and also for enabling him [or her] to continue to use reading, writing and calculation for his [or her] own and the community's development.

LITERACY AS A SOCIAL DIMENSION

In the social dimension perspective, literacy is neither a state nor a technique or a skill, because no one learns to read and write in a vacuum and the act of learning is a social act in a social context. Within the school of thought, there are a number of theories on different perspectives of social dimension. Of them, two important ones are literacy as a social practice and literacy as critical reflection.

Literacy as a Social Practice

Literacy as social practice does not see it as a generic set of technical skills, but it looks at the social dimensions of acquiring and applying literacy. It refers to the many ways in which literacy is employed throughout the life of an individual in a community or society. People acquire and apply literacy for different purposes in different situations based on culture, history, language, religion and socio-economic conditions. In this approach, literacy is not uniform, but diverse in cultural, linguistic and temporal spheres. It is shaped by social as well as educational institutions: the family, community, workplace, religious establishments and the state (UNESCO, 2004). The proponents of this approach talk of 'literacy practices' and 'literacy events' (Street, 1984) as terms to focus on activities entailed by reading and writing.

Street (1984) makes a clear distinction between autonomous and ideological notions of literacy. In his analysis, 'autonomous literacy' refers primarily to literacy as a set of cognitive skills and their generic use. In contrast, 'ideological literacy' refers to the social conceptions and uses of literacy. In this view, literacy is what society does with literacy, and society is, to some extent, what literacy brings to it.

Literacy as a Critical Reflection

Yet another view of literacy is that of critical literacy. Advocates of critical or radical literacy emphasize the empowering role that literacy plays in reshaping the world in which one lives and works (Freire, 1972). In this approach, literacy is a weapon for social change through critical reflection and action. It is the means by which people perceive, interpret and finally transform the world about them. According to proponents of this approach, the purpose of education is not to help people fit in and conform, not just to get a job or engage in economic activity, but it is to enable people to engage themselves actively in developing their communities and the world. It incorporates experiential learning, critical analysis, and problem-solving in the programme.

LIMITATIONS OF THE MODELS

There are some inherent limitations in both the models. As pointed out by Gomez (2008), individual dimension of literacy considers people as isolated subjects and not interested in understanding social interaction or intersubjective relations. Consequently, the measures they propose to overcome the problem of illiteracy always focus on the individual and on the need to improve their functional competencies. On the other hand, those who opt for the social dimension consider that functional illiteracy is a problem related not so much to individuals but rather to societies, so that the solution to the problem must also depend on the transformation of societies. This paradigm assumes that reality is much more complex than in the former approach. On this, Bhola (1991 a) clarified that literacy is both a skill and a social process. He argues that while literacy is a social process and a practice, it does not cease to be a skill and, therefore, it might be much more appropriate to describe literacy as a socio-technical process rather than merely a social process.

EVOLUTION OF CONCEPT OF LITERACY

As mentioned earlier, the concept of literacy evolved over a period of time under the influence of various agencies and governments. At the international level, UNESCO has a major influence on adult education and the evolution of its approach and strategy, especially in the Third World countries. Starting from 1949, it has organized six International Conferences on Adult Education (CONFINTEA) involving all member states. It influenced adult education in respect of all its core dimensions—objectives and contents, institutional problems and organization, methods and teaching, means of establishing international cooperation, etc. (Mathew, 2013). Based on the documents produced in these conferences, we can discern major trends in adult education at the global level.

FUNDAMENTAL EDUCATION (1950S–1960S)

The term was adopted by UNESCO at the first session of its General Conference held in 1946, centred mainly upon the skills of reading and writing. It defined a literate person as one who can, with understanding, both read and write a short simple statement on his or her everyday life (UNESCO, 2005). It aimed to help children and adults who do not have the advantage of formal schooling to understand the problems of their environment and acquire essential knowledge and skill for the improvement of their living conditions and to participate effectively in economic and social development of their community (UNESCO, 1956). The programmes designed using the concept of fundamental education gave a lot of attention to the most pressing needs and problems of the community. A variety of content was provided in these programmes, including skills of thinking and communicating, elementary vocational skills, health education, knowledge and understanding of the physical and human environment.

Fundamental education is concerned with both children for whom there is no adequate system of primary schooling and with adults deprived of educational opportunity. However, a large part of fundamental education is 'adult education' in the strict sense that it is concerned with adults. It is, however, narrower than 'adult education' in two ways. In the first place, it is concerned only with adults who 'do not have the advantage of formal schooling'. Second, it stops short of the 'further education' of adults beyond the essential minimum of knowledge and skill required as a foundation for effective living.

FUNCTIONAL LITERACY (1960S–1970S)

The World Congress of Ministers of Education on the Eradication of Illiteracy (held in Tehran, 1965) stressed for the first time the inter-relationship between literacy and development and highlighted the concept of functional literacy. The notion of functional literacy became the lynchpin of UNESCO's EWLP implemented in 11 countries. The EWLP, funded by the United Nations Development Programme (UNDP) and other agencies, aimed to provide literacy acquisition via experimentation and work-oriented learning. Although it initially focused on enhanced efficiency and productivity, the concept of functional literacy was later expanded to include broader areas of human concern and aspiration. The human capital theory, which regarded education an economic investment, was the ideology behind EWLP (UNESCO, 2005). Much effort is invested in the teaching and learning materials and methods, especially in respect of adult-centred pedagogy in every country (Mathew, 2013).

In 1978, UNESCO's General Conference adopted a definition of functional literacy—still in use today—which states,

> A person is functionally literate who can engage in all those activities in which literacy is required for effective functioning of his group and community and also for enabling him to continue to use reading, writing and calculation for his own and the community's development. (UNESCO, 2005, p. 154)

CRITICAL LITERACY (1970S)

During the 1970s, Paulo Freire's theory of 'conscientization' gained popularity in many countries and heavily influenced evolving conceptions of literacy in UNESCO and other international organizations. The theory stated, among other things, that social awareness and critical enquiry are key factors in social change. In this conception, literacy must go beyond the process of learning the skills of reading, writing and arithmetic, and contribute to the 'liberation of man' and to his full development. It is conceived that literacy creates the conditions for the acquisition of critical consciousness of the contradictions of society in which man lives. It is not an end in itself but leads to further action (UNESCO, 2005).

More benign versions of critical literacy encourage new literates to use literacy as a means for political action. By gathering appropriate information, organizing and defining specific objectives, literacy serves as a means of achieving desired ends. The literate person reflects on what is wrong in his/her world and uses the enabling power of literacy to change that world. More radical notions of critical literacy equate literacy and activism.

PLURALITY OF LITERACY (1990S–2000S)

The plurality of literacy refers to the many ways in which literacy is employed and the many things with which it is associated in a community or society. Literacy is not seen as a generic set of technical skills, but is looked at from the social dimensions of acquiring and applying it (more as a social practice). Plurality of literacy emphasizes that people acquire and apply literacy for different purposes in different situations based on their culture, history, language, religion and socio-economic conditions. It is shaped by social and educational institutions, such as the family, community and the state.

The plurality of literacy also implies that it takes both dominant and subordinate forms in every society. The dominant form is transmitted through official institutions such as schools and religious establishments. It often neglects the other forms based on historical experiences and lived realities. Such institutional domination tends to legitimize existing social structures and therewith unequal power relations. In response, individuals and groups in subordinate positions may construct their own forms of literacy in their own language(s), articulating their own (officially unacknowledged) meanings, knowledge and identity (UNESCO, 2004).

A proposed operational definition of literacy, particularly for measurement purposes was formulated during an international expert meeting in June 2003 at UNESCO. It states,

> Literacy is the ability to identify, understand, interpret, create, communicate and compute, using printed and written materials associated with varying contexts. Literacy involves a continuum of learning in enabling individuals to achieve their goals, to develop their knowledge and potential, and to participate fully in their community and wider society. (UNESCO, 2004, p. 13)

Now the international community is looking at literacy as a social practice and plurality of literacy practices contributing to broader purposes of lifelong learning.

METHODS OF ASSESSING LITERACY

Each of the concepts of literacy has its own methods of assessment, which depends on how it is defined. However, there are two major approaches followed around the world in assessment in both individual dimension and social dimension; one is an indirect approach and the other is a direct approach (UNESCO, 2017).

The indirect approach seeks to assess the literacy level of an individual by asking him, or his associates, whether they are literate or not. It is based on the perception of the individuals on their or associates' literacy status. It is mostly used in national censuses and other large-scale surveys. Within this approach, different methods are used. They include self-reporting, often as the response to a census question regarding whether the person sees himself as literate or not. Other methods include using the number of years of schooling as a proxy. For example, assuming that anyone who has completed four years of primary school is literate. These indirect methods depend on individual perceptions and give no indication whether a person can use written communication at an appropriate level in the society in which he/she lives.

The direct approach seeks to assess the level of literacy competence through a test. In its simplest form, this involves asking a survey respondent to read a short piece of text. A more nuanced method tests a respondent's familiarity in dealing with texts of different kinds, such as narrative, tables or Internet information. This method looks into how well people are able to use literacy in their everyday life. The International Adult Literacy Survey was one of the first efforts to examine literacy skills based on levels of competence. Designed and implemented by the Organisation for Economic Co-operation and Development in 23 member countries between 1994 and 1998, the survey posited three levels and three different types of literacy (prose, document and quantitative literacy). The UNESCO Institute for Statistics (UIS) drew on this approach to develop the Literacy Assessment and Monitoring Programme (LAMP), aiming to develop instruments for contexts where literacy was less widespread and there was a need to assess literacy at lower levels of competence (UIS, 2005).

CONCEPTION OF LITERACY IN INDIA

The term 'literacy' in its present use is an alien concept, which was introduced during the British period. Prior to that, reading and writing to indicate literacy was uncommon and the term 'literacy' had no meaning by itself. India has oral tradition, where even scriptures considered to be sacred are passed on orally for generations. But reading and writing in the modern meaning was confined to elite sections of society. However, each community has its own literacy (social practice). The highly skilled artisans learned particular aspects of literacy relevant to their fields. 'Studies on the Indian experience intuitively appear to represent a new kind of relationship between orality and literacy. Here the concept overlaps and share a number of characteristics' (Merh-Ashraf, 2004, p. 210). After the advent of the British, the perspective has changed. Introduction of general education on the lines of British education system and gradual adoption of technology in the daily life of people made literacy a necessity in the modern society.

Since Independence, literacy has been viewed in the individual dimension as the possession of a skill. However, there is a difference between the literacy definitions of the national census and the adult education programmes. Indian population census uses the 'skills approach' whereas adult education programmes use the 'tasks approach' to measure literacy within the individual dimension. National-level data collection agencies such as National Sample Survey Organization assessing literacy and making intra-country comparisons use the skills approach for literacy survey. In the census enumeration (Census of India, 2011), a person who can read and write with understanding in any language is classified as literate. The person may or may not have received any formal education. The census considers 7+ age group while calculating and declaring literacy rate. In measuring literacy, the population census adopts an indirect approach and does not use any test. The literacy status of the individual is recorded based on the oral self-declaration of the person or his family members or even neighbours.

There are problems in accepting oral declaration of the individual on literacy status. First, it is purely based on the perception of the individual reporting the literacy status without any objective criteria. Second, it does not consider different levels in the literacy continuum. Third, in rural areas, people equate literacy with formal education. They consider a person literate only if he/she has attended school for a certain period of time. Spratt (2004, p. 4) rightly pointed out,

> Census-based literacy statistics commonly contain some implicit assumptions. One assumption is that those who have attended school for a given number of years are literate, and that they have experienced no attrition of skills in the years since leaving school. A second, corollary assumption is that those who have not been to school are illiterate. Census-based statistics also assume that household heads are capable of judging the literacy capabilities of other household members, even if they themselves are non-literate.

CONCEPT OF LITERACY IN ADULT EDUCATION PROGRAMMES IN INDIA

In the Indian adult education programmes, the concept has undergone several significant changes over the years, especially after Independence. It is due to not only a variety of socio-economic and political developments within India but also the influence of other countries and international organizations such as UNESCO, UNICEF and UNDP (Mathew, 2014). In the major adult literacy programmes, India adopted the concept of functional literacy with slight variations. Initially, the definition of functional literacy was rooted in economic functions. However, over a period after the FFLP, the concept got widened and, with the influence of Paulo Freire (1972), a middle way functional literacy emerged. NAEP and NLM used the concept as more than mere economic skills.

NATIONAL ADULT EDUCATION PROGRAMME

NAEP used the concept of functional literacy to indicate three elements: literacy, functionality and awareness. Literacy component focuses on the skills of reading and writing. As per NAEP's definition of literacy, it includes following three aspects (Ministry of Education and Social Welfare, 1978):

- Literacy and numeracy, at a level, that would enable the learners to continue to learn in a self-reliant manner.
- Functional development, functionality being viewed as the role of an individual, as a producer and worker, as a member of the family and as a citizen in the civic and political system.
- Social awareness, including an awareness of the impediments to development of laws and government policies, and the need for the poor and non-literate to organize themselves in pursuance of their legitimate interests and for group action.

The level of literacy skill to be achieved is defined under NAEP and is given in Annexure 1. The functional component deals with economic awareness issues with the intention of not only teaching but also demonstrating economic skills through income-generating projects. The awareness component creates awareness among learners in regard to their social, cultural and political life.

NATIONAL LITERACY MISSION

Similarly, NLM used the 'task approach' to define functional literacy. As per NLM document (MHRD, 1988), functional literacy implies the following:

- Achieving self-reliance in 3Rs;
- Becoming aware of the causes of deprivation and moving towards amelioration of oppressive conditions through organization and participation in the process of development;
- Acquisition of skills to improve the economic status and general well-being; and
- Imbibing values of national integration, conservation of environment, women's equality, observance of small family norms and developing a scientific and rational temper.

However, measurement of functional literacy in NLM is confined to the 3Rs. The levels prescribed to be achieved to declare a person literate are given in Annexure 2. All the government programmes since NLM have adopted this definition of functional literacy. Now the present

SBP continues with this concept of literacy. In NAEP, some attention was paid to the assessment of the social awareness component while declaring a person literate, but the functionality component was not given much importance in measuring literacy skills. NLM programmes neglected even the social awareness component and confined only to reading, writing and arithmetic skills.

DISCUSSION ON CONCEPT OF LITERACY IN INDIA

From the discussion above, it is clear that literacy in India is looked at from state perspective as a skill possessed by an individual. It looked at literacy from the individual dimension, that is, a skill or competency possessed by an individual. The metaphor used always highlights the deficit with the slogan 'fight against illiteracy'. However, field experience shows that learners who attend literacy classes perceive literacy as a social practice, that is, learning and using skills necessary in their day-to-day life. For them, learning is a social process that helps improving their living standards and enables them to access other skills and benefits. That is why it is not surprising when they convey different literacy statuses in different social contexts.

Within this skills approach also, there is a gap in understanding between policy-makers and field functionaries, that is, policy and implementation. Policy documents claim the functionality aspect of literacy, but it is confined to traditional literacy in the field. The traditional literacy considers literacy a simple skill whereas functional literacy views literacy ability to perform specific tasks. This difference has not been explained to the field workers clearly in any of the manuals. Further, the tasks an individual is able to perform after the completion of the literacy course have not been clearly defined except for the literacy component. Consequently, there is a lot of confusion on the functionality aspect, some using for productive skills and others for performing tasks. People who have been associated with the literacy programme for decades are still confused about the meaning of functional literacy. The vague and ambiguous understanding of literacy among the functionaries of literacy programme has resulted in the dissemination of vague conception of literacy creating various myths and stereotypes on literacy in society.

As a result of the skills approach and individual dimension in adult literacy, many anomalies have occurred in practice. One such inconsistency is binary classification of literacy. The fundamental assumption here is that literacy and illiteracy stand in a dichotomous relationship with no common space between them. People are either literate or illiterate. As a policy, we have defined minimum levels of literacy to declare an individual as literate, but have not specified the levels below or above this. But in practice at the field level, it is very difficult to classify people in clear and demarcated groups of literates and illiterates. While launching literacy programmes, many times we tested the literacy levels of people who claimed themselves as non-literates and enrolled in literacy classes. We find a wide range of literacy levels. Some of them could sign their names, some could recognize letters and syllables, some could form words, some read words without vowel and consonant combinations, and some could even read simple sentences without comprehension. Some of the learners attend primary schools for some time and others are exposed to alphabets in various ways. But most of them could not read and write as fluently as prescribed by NLM to declare them literate. All of them are put together in a literacy class and start with basic literacy primers. Once all of them are put together, learners with previous exposure to literacy will pick up very fast, and those without exposure will lag behind and eventually drop out. This problem has not been addressed in any policy documents.

Illich (1971) rightly commented that binary divisions such as healthy/ill, normal/abnormal or, more pertinently, rich/poor, are like steamrollers of the mind; they level a multiform world, completely flattening anything that does not fit. The same applies to literacy. The binary classification is not only meaningless at the grassroots level but also misleading for policy-makers and planners who depend on them for designing programmes and policies. Furthermore, the dichotomy is of little help in providing more than the crudest policy direction, since there is so much variation within and across the terms literate and illiterate (Wagner, 1993).

It is very difficult to plan literacy and continuing education programmes (CEPs) without knowing the literacy levels of the participants and their learning needs. Literacy levels of learners have to be defined and measured before the commencement of literacy programme. For this, the concept of literacy has to be redefined avoiding binary classification of literacy. It has to be viewed in the literacy continuum perspective. State perspective and user perspective have to be reconciled to avoid confusion among the functionaries and beneficiaries of literacy programmes. Literacy assessment needs to adopt the direct literacy assessment method as proposed in LAMP.

At the international level, the International Adult Literacy Survey conducted in OCED countries and LAMP of UNESCO viewed literacy as a continuum and avoided dichotomous classification and defined different levels of literacy. For example, LAMP used five levels of literacy in its assessment. (UIS, 2005). The literacy levels assessed in LAMP project are given in Annexure 3.

EXPERIENCES IN LITERACY MEASUREMENT

We once made an attempt to measure the literacy levels of population in two villages on a scale instead of binary classification. At that time, we were not aware of UNESCO experiments in literacy assessment and confined our assessment to reading and writing components. In this, literacy was perceived as the existence of a range of literacy skills, which the individual possessed, to a greater or lesser degree. So, we conducted a survey adopting the direct assessment method in the year 2000 in two villages of West Godavari district: one is Kalavapudi near Bhimavaram and the other is Naidugudem near Eluru. The main aim of the survey was to assess (a) the exact literacy position among different age groups of the population and (b) the levels of literacy among neo-literates and semi-literates. The survey, it was thought, would help not only in knowing the literacy situation in the villages, but also in preparing reading material for neo-literates and semi-literates depending upon their level of literacy.

Each village had a population of about 1,500, and the entire population of the village was enumerated and all the neo-literates and semi-literates were tested to gauge their level of achievement in reading, writing and numeracy. Prepared schedules were used to collect information and test the neo-literates. All the investigators were students of degree classes aged between 18 and 21 years. Supervisors of the adult education department gave them training in survey and evaluation techniques and also guided them during the survey period.

A schedule in Telugu was developed and administered to each person above 15 years in the village. The population was categorized in three groups: literates, semi-literates and illiterates. Literate and illiterate definitions were taken from NLM and semi-literates were defined as those who cannot be classified as literates or illiterates in pure terms. They might have attended formal schools or AECs for some time but had not achieved the minimum level of literacy required to be declared as literate. Therefore, this category was shown as a separate group in the survey. Table 2.1 shows the literacy status of Kalavapudi and Naidugudem villages.

The survey revealed that in Kalavapudi village nearly 48 per cent people were literate, 37 per cent illiterate and 15 per cent semi-literate. Similarly, in Naidugudem village 48 per cent people were literate, 25 per cent semi-literate and 27 per cent illiterate. In the 1991 population census, which classified literacy into two categories, Kalavapudi had a literacy rate of 59 per cent and Naidugudem of 57 per cent. This clearly shows that there is a need to identify semi-literacy as a stage in literacy continuum and devise a separate programme for this stage.

LITERACY LEVELS AMONG SEMI-LITERATES

It is a known fact that the literacy level of semi-literates is not uniform. In fact, they are not a separate category but only a group that have not reached the literacy level to be declared literate. They are on different levels in the literacy scale and these levels have not been defined anywhere. Therefore, we made an attempt to classify semi-literates based on their competencies in reading and writing, as they need special programmes to achieve the level of literacy required to become literates. In fact, it is very difficult to know the exact level of literacy achieved by a person and more so in the case of semi-literates. Knowing the correct position of literacy level would help in preparing reading material for the learners at the different levels, which is essential for continuing education.

Table 2.1 *Literacy Status of Villages (Age and Gender Wise)*

Literacy Survey	6–11 Years				12–16 Years				17–42 Years				43 and above			Total	Total %
	M	F	T	%	M	F	T	%	M	F	T	%	M	F	T		
A. Village: Kalavapudi																	
Literate	50	53	103	63	60	59	119	63	170	148	318	45	67	60	127	667	48
Semi-Literate	21	19	40	24	12	7	19	10	51	52	103	15	26	17	43	205	15
Illiterate	10	12	22	13	25	25	50	27	138	140	278	40	73	81	154	504	37
Total	**81**	**84**	**165**	**100**	**97**	**91**	**188**	**100**	**359**	**340**	**699**	**100**	**166**	**158**	**324**	**1376**	**100**
B. Village: Naidugudem																	
Literate	64	55	119	60	60	46	106	63	203	170	373	48	83	73	156	754	48
Semi-Literate	24	26	50	25	16	14	30	18	99	120	219	28	57	41	98	397	25
Illiterate	14	15	29	15	15	16	31	19	88	100	188	24	74	90	164	412	27
Total	**102**	**96**	**198**	**100**	**91**	**76**	**167**	**100**	**390**	**390**	**780**	**100**	**214**	**204**	**418**	**1563**	**100**

Source: PGAS (2000b).

So, in this survey, an attempt has been made to classify the semi-literates based on their ability to read and write. A separate scale has been prepared using primers of ASP. The scale is given in Annexure 4. For Example, Level I in reading (Annexure 4, 2AI) means that the person can recognize all alphabets of Telugu and also numbers up to 10 but cannot read combining the letters and words. Similarly, all the three stages in reading and writing have been defined. Each person in the semi-literate category was tested with specific lessons in the primers of ASP.

Table 2.2 indicates the levels of semi-literates in reading skills and Table 2.3 for writing skills respectively. One interesting finding is that some persons, who are able to read properly, are not able to write a single word. That is why there is a difference in Tables 2.2 and 2.3. Table 2.3 shows that in Kalavapudi village 60 per cent of semi-literates are in the first level, 17 per cent in the second level and 23 per cent in the third level in respect of reading ability. In the case of Naidugudem village, 46 per cent are in the first level, 22 per cent in the second level and 32 per cent in the third level. If village-wise differences are taken into consideration, Kalavapudi has a higher percentage of semi-literates in the first level (60%) compared to Naidugudem (39%).

Similarly, in the case of writing skills, Table 2.3 reveals that in Kalavapudi 64 per cent of semi-literates are in the first level, 12 per cent are in the second level and 24 per cent are in the third level. In the case of Naidugudem, 46 per cent are in the first level, 22 per cent are in the second level and 32 per cent are in the third level. Like reading skills, in writing skills also, there is a variation between the two villages in respect of levels achieved by semi-literates. For instance, in Kalavapudi, 64 per cent of semi-literates are in the first level where as in Naidugudem the percentage is 46 only.

This has to be done on a large scale to get a clear picture of literacy status of the population. Literacy or continuing education classes have to be planned based on such surveys at both the levels society and individual. Methods of imparting literacy should be specific to each individual learner based on his/her literacy levels and competencies. Only then would impartation of literacy skills be successful.

Table 2.2 Age Group-wise Literacy Status (Reading)

Literacy Levels	6–11 Years				12–16 Years				17–42 Years				43 and above				Total %	
	M	F	T	%	M	F	T	%	M	F	T	%	M	F	T	%	T	%
A. Village: Kalavapudi																		
2A1 (Level I)	14	15	29	58	5	4	9	47	28	32	60	58	17	9	26	60	124	60
2A2 (Level II)	4	3	7	14	3	0	3	16	9	9	18	17	4	3	7	16	35	17
2A3 (Level III)	3	1	4	28	4	3	7	37	14	11	25	25	5	5	10	24	46	23
Grand Total	**21**	**19**	**40**	**100**	**12**	**7**	**19**	**100**	**51**	**52**	**103**	**100**	**26**	**17**	**43**	**100**	**205**	**100**
B. Village: Naidugudem																		
2A1 (Level I)	13	16	29	58	4	4	8	27	35	50	85	39	20	12	32	33	154	39
2A2 (Level II)	4	3	7	14	2	3	5	17	20	27	47	21	11	9	20	20	79	20
2A3 (Level III)	7	7	14	28	10	7	17	56	44	43	87	40	26	20	46	47	164	41
Grand Total	**24**	**26**	**50**	**100**	**16**	**14**	**30**	**100**	**99**	**120**	**219**	**100**	**57**	**41**	**98**	**100**	**397**	**100**

Source: PGAS (2000b).

Table 2.3 Age Group-wise Literacy Status (Writing)

Literacy Levels	6–11 Years				12–16 Years				17–42 Years				43 and above				Total %	
	M	F	T	%	M	F	T	%	M	F	T	%	M	F	T	%	T	Total %
A. Village: Kalavapudi																		
2B1 (Level I)	10	13	23	79	4	3	7	47	24	26	50	60	12	11	23	68	103	64
2B2 (Level II)	1	1	2	7	1	0	1	6	3	10	13	16	3	0	3	9	19	12
2B3 (Level III)	2	2	4	14	4	3	7	47	13	7	20	24	4	4	8	23	39	24
Grand Total	13	16	29	100	9	6	15	100	40	43	83	100	19	15	34	100	161	100
B. Village: Naidugudem																		
2B1 (Level I)	10	12	22	54	4	2	6	22	34	55	89	49	20	12	32	45	149	46
2B2 (Level II)	6	5	11	27	2	3	5	19	23	16	39	21	8	6	14	19	69	22
2B3 (Level III)	5	3	8	19	9	7	16	59	29	25	54	30	14	12	26	36	104	32
Grand Total	21	20	41	100	15	12	27	100	86	96	182	100	42	30	72	100	322	100

Source: PGAS (2000b).

Broadly, the concept of literacy, which has different dimensions, has evolved over of a period of time from traditional literacy to plurality of literacy. However, in India, it is still viewed in the traditional way as a skill and classified in binary way as literacy and illiteracy. There is a need for a paradigm shift in the perspective of literacy as a skill in individual dimension to literacy as a part of learning continuum in lifelong learning perspective. Literacy has to be understood in both individual and social dimensions. For this, clarity on the relationship between literacy and development is essential. The next chapter will discuss literacy and development in detail.

Literacy and Development

As a field functionary of the adult education department, I attended numerous meetings conducted in villages to create awareness on literacy and motivate non-literates to enrol in literacy classes. I participated in one such meeting in Gopalapuram village in West Godavari district of Andhra Pradesh. As expected, the adult education supervisor, who conducted the meeting, told the audience, consisting mainly of village elders, members of the local women's groups, and the youth club, about the importance of literacy and the high rate of illiteracy in our country, which is a shame on the nation. He explained how poverty and illiteracy are linked, how educated people get good jobs and earn more and how children of educated people get better education. He told them the aims and objectives of literacy programmes and about the opportunities to acquire formal educational qualifications through open school and open universities. He stressed the need for eradicating illiteracy and achieving total literacy in the village. The village leaders and elected representatives, who were invited to the meeting, addressed the gathering in the same language highlighting the importance and need for achieving total literacy. The participants listened quietly and nodded their heads.

Generally, we don't ask participants why they want to learn and what they want to learn. But in that meeting, I tried to elicit the views of the participants on the purpose and benefits they expect from literacy. The overwhelming majority of the participants said they wanted to learn vocational skills to earn supplementary income through the literacy programme. They considered literacy class as a platform for development. When I asked them the relation between literacy skills and vocational skills, they said that both are for development and they needed both for improving their economic condition.

This raises some fundamental questions: What is the purpose of adult literacy education? Is it to improve the literacy rate or is it for social and economic development? Which comes first? Does literacy automatically lead to development? Are the effects of literacy the same for children who acquire literacy in formal education and adults who acquire it in adult literacy programmes? These are among the questions raised in literacy circles but answered vaguely. Let us discuss some of the perceptions on literacy and development and how these aspects are viewed at international and national levels.

As in the case of literacy, there are divergent perceptions on the relationship between literacy and development. The aforementioned discussion in the meeting presents the two perspectives. In one perspective, literacy is viewed more as education, and, in another, it is perceived as a part of the development process. The contradictions in these perspectives are reflected in two approaches: literacy as education and literacy as development.

LITERACY: EDUCATION VERSUS DEVELOPMENT

There are divergent perceptions on how we look at literacy and the benefits that may be expected from it. Rogers (2004b) talks about the division in the perceptions of adult literacy in developing societies. According to him, some see adult literacy in terms of adult schooling within the education sector, while others perceive adult literacy as rooted firmly in social and economic development. The ideological differences in the two approaches—literacy as education and literacy as development—have influenced conception and pedagogy of literacy programmes. On the same lines, Daniel (2005, p. 16) points out,

> [T]he distinction between literacy as education and literacy as development is important because, how we go about it will depend on which emphasis we choose. If literacy is education then schooling for adults is the obvious approach. Organization, curriculum and aspects are planned in that way. The approach would be different if we view literacy as development. The focus of the programme shifts from mere literacy and education to livelihoods and other developmental issues.

There is an argument that education is one of the instruments through which development is achieved and the final aim of education is development only. So, there is not much difference between the two approaches. Even if we agree that the final objective of both approaches is development, which should come first? It leads to a classic debate, literacy first or development first? In other words, development through literacy or literacy through development, what would be the priority?

In the 'literacy first' approach, literacy is introduced first and development is expected to be achieved through literacy. In this approach, literacy is viewed more as education which will eventually lead to development. Further, literacy comes first and development tasks second. The 'literacy second' approach says that the development task comes first and, if the group wants to acquire literacy during the development task, literacy can be built on the development tasks, using related written materials. In this approach, literacy is viewed as a part of development and literacy skills are acquired in the process of development. Further, the programme starts with a developmental activity including literacy learning within it. The first model is adopted mostly in the government sector for major literacy programmes. Non-governmental organization (NGOs) working in the development sector adopt the second model. Generally, they introduce the literacy component after initial development activities and mostly as a part of the development process. The main thrust in these programmes is not on the basic literacy but on development.

There are some inherent advantages and disadvantages in both the models. In the 'literacy first' model, it would be difficult to motivate adult learners as they find literacy as schooling, isolated from their real life and daily concerns. Further, adult learners are mostly interested in immediate benefits of literacy and very few of them are motivated enough to attend literacy classes with long-term educational goals. Although rampant adult illiteracy is linked with the failure of the formal primary education systems, experience shows that the 'literacy first' model does not adequately address the needs of individual adults and may seem irrelevant to many adult learners who are marginalized in socio-economic terms. For adults, a relatively decontextualized literacy learning may not hold much attraction (Asia South Pacific Association for Basic and Adult Education [ASPBAE], 2006).

The 'literacy second' model has also some disadvantages. In this model, priority is given to 'development' which leads to neglect of the literacy component. The SEP implemented in the 1950s is one example where the literacy component gradually receded to the background and, over a period of time, totally removed from the scheme. The same is the case with the programmes conducted by NGOs where literacy gets neglected in the process of development activities. Naturally, people are interested in development activities, which would deal with their livelihood concerns and literacy activity gets relegated to the second level. Moreover, it is very difficult to design programmes integrating literacy and economy-related activities, as it requires intensive planning and huge financial resources. So, these programmes are likely to remain development programmes without literacy.

COMPARATIVE STUDY OF MODELS

The World Bank (Oxenham et al., 2002) conducted a study in Africa to compare and assess the effectiveness of two types of education and training programmes for poor adults: (a) programmes that have attempted to incorporate training for livelihood skills into mainly literacy instruction and (b) programmes that have incorporated literacy instruction into training for mainly livelihood skills. The findings of the study are as follows:

- Programmes that start from livelihood skills seem to stand a better chance of success. They can demonstrate immediate reasons for learning.
- Organizations that are more concerned with livelihoods and other aspects of development seem to be better at designing and delivering effective combinations of livelihoods and literacy than organizations that primarily focus on education.
- Deriving literacy content from livelihood skills and integrating it with the livelihood training from the very start seems more promising than either running the two components parallel with

each other or using standard literacy materials to prepare people to train for livelihoods.

- Livelihood-plus-literacy/numeracy programmes can greatly improve their chances of success if they incorporate training in savings, credit and business management along with actual access to credit.

- Chances of success are even greater in a programme that works with established groups of people who share common purpose rather than with individual applicants. In the absence of such groups, it would probably still be better to take time to identify promising common purposes and to work on forming new purpose-driven groups than to resign the programme to unconnected individuals.

As pointed out by Rogers (2005), it would seem best to combine the two elements (vocational skills training and literacy learning) rather than keeping them parallel—to embed acquiring literacy within the skills training by using the embedded literacies of the craft or trade as the teaching–learning materials. Thus, literacy becomes one of the skills being learned rather than something on its own.

LITERACY AND DEVELOPMENT MODELS IN INDIA

Let us discuss the perspectives of literacy and development in Indian adult education programmes and which of the aforementioned models have been adopted. In India, there is a gradual shift from literacy as development to literacy as education. In the 1950s, under the SEP, literacy was an integral part of the community development programme. The main thrust was on social development using the literacy medium. In the 1960s, the emphasis of the literacy programme shifted from civic to functional literacy which focused on improving the productivity of persons using literacy skills as the starting point. Over a period of time, the emphasis on the education component has increased gradually. There is much variation between policy highlighted in policy documents and strategies adopted for implementation of the policy at the field level.

NATIONAL ADULT EDUCATION PROGRAMME

While launching NAEP, the Ministry of Education and Social Welfare (1978) clearly stated that the thinking on adult education was based on the assumptions that (a) illiteracy is a serious impediment to an individual's growth and to the country's socio-economic progress, (b) education is not coterminous with schooling but takes place in work and life situations, (c) learning, working and living are inseparable and each acquires a meaning only when correlated with others, (d) the means by which people are involved in the process of development are at least as important as the ends and (e) the illiterate and the poor can rise to their own liberation through literacy, dialogue and action.

Elaborating the approach, the document stated that the problems of poverty and illiteracy are two aspects of the same stupendous problem, and the struggle to overcome one without waging a fight against the other at the same time is certain to result in aberrations and disappointments. For this reason, NAEP is visualized as a means to bring about a fundamental change in the process of socio-economic development, from a situation in which the poor remain passive spectators to being at its centre as active participants. The learning process involves emphasis on literacy but stresses the importance of functional upgradation and of raising the level of awareness regarding their predicament among the poor and the illiterate.

Theoretically, NAEP policy document clearly analysed the link between literacy and development and presented the programme in a development perspective. It was stated in the policy document (Ministry of Education and Social Welfare, 1978, p. 3) that 'NAEP is not a literacy programme but should be considered as a part of a development programme, that is, an educational programme in development strategy'.

Here, there is a wide gap between policy and implementation. As per policy, NAEP is a comprehensive adult education programme, linking literacy and development. But in implementation, the main thrust of the programme remained on the literacy component. The content and pedagogy that were supposed to be in the development perspective are confined to mere topics on development programmes. Literacy is not linked to any social or economic development programmes. Nor were skill development activities introduced as a part of the programme.

TOTAL LITERACY CAMPAIGN

The emphasis on education is much more prominent in NLM, which was launched in 1988, based on the NPA, 1986. In the introduction to NLM document (MHRD, 1988, p. 5), it was stated, 'Literacy is an indispensable component of human resource development. It is an essential tool for communication and learning, for acquiring and sharing of knowledge and information, a precondition for an individual's evaluation and growth and for national development'. NLM, however, enlarged the definition of functional literacy to include development perspective besides the 3Rs. As per the document, functional literacy includes (a) being aware of the causes of deprivation and moving towards amelioration of oppressive conditions through organization and participation in the process of development, (b) acquiring skills to improve the economic status and general well-being and (c) imbibing values of national integration, conservation of environment, women's equality, observance of small family norms and developing a scientific and rational temper (p. 14). Further, it acknowledged the fact that 'adults participate in literacy programmes if they are already engaged in political action, or some socio-economic programmes, and they perceive literacy as a part of the total development process' (p. 22).

As the name suggests, the main thrust of NLM was on literacy. Under NLM, TLCs were organized with district as a unit. Since it was a mass campaign, it was not possible to link literacy to development activities on a large scale. Further, literacy classes were conducted by volunteers who were not familiar with development activities or skill development programmes. Therefore, the focus of the programme remained literacy, and it was viewed in the 'literacy as education' perspective.

SAAKSHAR BHARAT

Another major adult education programme is SB which aims at achieving 80 per cent literacy with the primary focus on women. It did not go into literacy and development linkages but confined itself to the empowerment angle of literacy. The SB document mentioned the empowerment value of literacy, especially among women:

> Literacy would be its key programme instrument for emancipation and empowerment of women. Efforts of the Government to give an impetus to school education, health, nutrition, skill development and women empowerment in general are impeded by the continuance of female illiteracy. The Government expects increase in female literacy to become a force multiplier for all other social development programmes. However, this is only the instrumental value of female literacy. Its intrinsic value is in emancipating the Indian woman through the creation of critical consciousness to take charge of her environment where she faces multiple deprivations and disabilities on the basis of class, caste and gender. (MHRD, 2009, p. 2)

But this vision has not been highlighted in the objectives of the programmes. The objectives of SBP (MHRD, 2009) are (a) to impart functional literacy and numeracy to non-literate and non-numerate adults, (b) to enable the neo-literate adults to continue their learning beyond basic literacy and acquire equivalency to formal educational system, (c) to impart non- and neo-literates relevant skill development programmes to improve their earning and living conditions and (d) to promote a learning society by providing opportunities to neo-literate adults for continuing education. The objectives clearly indicate the focus of education over development.

The objectives of SB included four major components: basic literacy, basic education, continuing education and skill development. Of the four objectives, funds are provided only for three components: basic literacy, continuing education and in some cases to basic education. Although skill development is part of Saakshar Bharat as a policy, funds have not been provided and this component has not been implemented anywhere in India. While policy papers and policy discussions include the skill development component in Saakshar Bharat, operational guidelines and funding do not talk about it.

Since NAEP was launched, it is common to show that Jan Shikshan Sansthans are established to provide skill training as a part of adult education programmes in India. It is a fact that there is a provision for skill trainings through Jan Shikshan Sansthans which are funded by GoI and implemented through NGOs. But there are two problems that have not been resolved at the policy level. One is the lack of convergence between Jan Shikshan Sansthans under the NGO sector and literacy programmes implemented by government agencies. Even if there is convergence between the two agencies, the coverage of Jan Shikshan Sansthans is very limited, ranging from 3,000 to 4,000 people in a district, whereas the coverage under literacy is 3–4 lakh in a district. With this gap, it is not possible to integrate literacy and skill trainings.

The perception of literacy as education is much more predominant at the field level. Most of the field functionaries of adult education programmes consider literacy as education. There are many reasons for that assumption. One is that they are employed by the education department; so, their main job is educating people. Another one is that there is no provision for taking up individual development programmes or integrating literacy and development under adult literacy schemes. The funding pattern of the programmes in the last two decades is confined to literacy aspects, although skill development is mentioned as one of the objectives in literacy programmes. Thus, there is a wide gap between the visions envisaged in policy documents and implementation guidelines.

Balasubramanian (2005, p. 57), while discussing literacy in the Indian context at an international expert meeting on literacy and livelihoods in Commonwealth of Learning, pointed out,

> For a long time literacy programmes (in India) were treated as a part of welfare programmes and were not considered an integral part of the development perspective.... While NLM had better theoretical perspectives in perceiving literacy and education as components of development, it had only a limited framework for putting the perspectives into practice.

The main perplexity in Indian adult education programmes is the gap between policy and implementation in terms of objectives and outcomes of literacy. Policy statements of adult education programmes conceive literacy as a part of development; whereas, in practice, literacy is viewed as an isolated phenomenon without any convergence with development. Notwithstanding policy statements, the State viewed literacy as education for human resource development and the purpose of literacy is improvement of the literacy rate. The same view percolated down to field functionaries. However, users looked at literacy in the development perspective. For them, the aim of literacy is the improvement of quality of life and they expect it to be socially and culturally relevant to them in their day-to-day life. This contradiction has a major impact on enrolment and retention of people in literacy programmes and their overall success.

IMPACT OF LITERACY ON DEVELOPMENT

Whatever the perspective, the ultimate aim of literacy in both state and user perspectives is development. Does literacy automatically lead to development? What is the impact of literacy on individual and social development? These are the questions commonly raised in literacy circles. There are a number of assumptions regarding the impact and benefits of literacy. We find two different perspectives here as well. Those who see literacy as education see cases of individuals acquiring literacy skills in adult literacy classes and continuing their education through open schooling system. The others, who look at it as development, look at benefits accrued to individuals, like higher income and better quality of life. They show its impact on their health, children's education and awareness on economic opportunities.

EFA Global Monitoring Report 2006 listed the benefits of literacy based on the research studies and other evidence available the world over (UNESCO, 2005). The *EFA Report 2006* mentioned the following types of benefits of literacy:

• *Human benefits:* Human benefits are related to factors such as improved self-esteem, empowerment, creativity and critical reflection that participation in adult literacy programmes may produce.

- *Political benefits:* Participation in adult literacy programmes is also correlated with increased participation in trade unions, community action and national political life and thus contributes to the quality of public policies and to democracy.
- *Cultural benefits:* Cultural benefits of adult literacy are at two levels—cultural transmission and cultural transformation. Adult literacy programmes facilitate the transmission of certain values, attitudes and behaviour. In some cases, adult literacy programmes can help cultural transformation by challenging existing attitudes and behavioural patterns.
- *Economic benefits:* Literacy has a positive impact on earnings beyond the impact of quality of schooling. However, studies on the impact of literacy on economic growth at individual or national level are rare.
- *Social benefits:* Improved literacy levels have potentially large social benefits and can be instrumental in people's achievement of a range of capabilities such as maintaining good health and living longer, learning throughout life, controlling reproductive behaviour, raising healthy children and educating them.
- *Children„s education:* Literacy has important educational benefits; particularly, if parents are educated, whether through schooling or adult literacy programmes, are more likely to send their children to school.

LIMITATIONS IN RESEARCH EVIDENCE

UNESCO (2005, p. 138) acknowledged the limitations of research evidence on the benefits of literacy:

> Providing an evidence-based account of these is not straightforward. Providing systematic, evidence-based account of the benefits of literacy is not easy for several reasons. Most of the research has not separated the benefits of literacy per se from those of attending school or participating in adult literacy programmes.

The report mentioned the following points on the limitations:

- Little research has been devoted to adult literacy programmes (as opposed to formal schooling) and existing studies focus mainly on women. The benefits of acquiring literacy in adulthood are thus less clearly established in comparison to those of acquiring cognitive skills through education in childhood.

- Research has focused on the impact of literacy on the individual: Few authors have examined the impact at the family/household, community, national and international level.
- Some effects of literacy, for example, those of culture, are intrinsically difficult to define and measure.
- Benefits such as political awareness, empowerment and critical reflection, moreover, are intrinsically difficult to measure.
- Literacy is not defined consistently across studies and literacy data is frequently flawed.
- There have been few rigorous assessments of the latter in terms of cognitive achievement and lasting effects.
- Most of the research findings are based on the self-reporting of individuals than on the objective observation criteria.

A World Bank study (Abadzi, 2003a), which reviewed the implementation of 32 adult literacy experiences, pointed out that social outcomes such as self-confidence and empowerment are typically assessed only once and through self-reports, so long-term effects cannot be ascertained. Only willingness by literacy participants to send their own children to school is constantly documented in many projects.

Scribner and Cole (1981) questioned the assumption that literacy automatically contributed to cognitive development across content domains and learning contexts. He cautioned the error of equating school effects with literacy effects and mentioned that such equations make invalid assumptions as to the quality, effects and consequences of schooling across all contexts. Prinsloo (2005), while agreeing that there are quantitative correlations of adult literacy with other social indicators such as economic productivity, fertility rates, children's health, nutrition levels and success in school, pointed out that such correlations have distracted the field from paying attention to what and how, under what conditions, adults' reading and writing can contribute to such broad social indicators.

SOCIAL CONTEXT OF LITERACY BENEFITS

It is not easy to explain the impact or benefits of literacy in adult literacy programmes. Benefits of literacy depend on the social context in which it is located. A number of factors, such as approach to literacy, the context in which literacy is imparted, expectations of beneficiaries, etc., influence the extent and relevance of benefits. It is difficult to measure them. Field experience shows that literacy benefits are indirect and mostly help in improving the quality of life of the participants. When we ask persons, who had completed the basic literacy course, what benefit they got from the literacy course, they enumerate the benefits that are told to them such as ability to know things about self-help and banking, development, etc. They also tell about their personal experience of reading the destination board of a bus and film posters (Paschima Godavari Akshara Samiti [PGAS], 2000).

In many motivational meetings, adult education functionaries quote the example of how difficult it is for illiterates to travel on bus/train. They say that the difference between literacy and illiteracy is that literates can travel on their own and illiterates cannot and depend on others. However, in real life, all illiterates travel, the only difference is that illiterates ask someone at a bus stand about the destination of a bus before boarding it and literates board the bus after seeing the board. So naturally, literates enter the bus first and occupy good seats. The illiterates enter later after ascertaining the details of bus and have to sit on available seats, mostly back seats or have to travel standing if the bus is full. It is the difference in quality of travel which is difficult to measure.

Adult literacy programmes measure only literacy skills acquired by individuals in the literacy classes. Other aspects such as awareness generated in the course of teaching and functional usages in applying literacy skills are not assessed. For instance, a literacy campaign in Nellore district of Andhra Pradesh in the early 1990s may not have been successful in terms of literacy achievements, but, in terms of social awareness, it is one of the most successful campaigns. As pointed out in the study of Nellore TLC, George (2000, p. 111) commented,

Increasing self-assertion of women has been the main achievement of the literacy movement in Nellore. The anti-arrack/liquor movement and the thrift movement reflected it. There has been an increase in literacy. But in Nellore, the impact of literacy has out-measured the attainment of literacy itself. Much of this social impact has come from the non-literacy inputs provided to the learners through discussions in which all could participate. Literacy itself acted as a helpful base to this process.

Further, the benefits of literacy ensue only when broader rights and development frameworks are in place and are operating effectively. Individual benefits, for example, accrue only when written material is available to the newly literate person, and overall economic benefits only when other conditions and suitable development policies. Similarly, certain benefits, such as women empowerment, will result only if the socio-cultural environment is accommodating of them (UNESCO, 2005). The report of the expert group (known as Arun Ghosh Committee) on evaluation of literacy campaigns in India clarified this issue. It said,

> We are not sure that greater literacy per se leads necessarily to greater and better socio-economic development. There is no direct causal relationship between literacy and development. Literacy is a training or skill whose purpose and value is contingent upon the availability of opportunities for its use, and upon benefits, economic, political, social and cultural, to be derived from its use. (NLM, 1994, p. 25)

Further, the report elaborated the relationship saying that socio-economic development has both an individual and a collective/social dimension because it is a problem not only for the individual but also for society as a whole. Greater literacy in some cases may mean greater/ better opportunities for socio-economic improvement in individual lives/families, without much impact on other factors. The report says that mass poverty cannot be resolved by treating it as a sum of individual problems to be resolved individually. It must be seen as a collective problem requiring collective solutions. Mass literacy, on the other hand, may set off certain chain reactions on the socio-economic and political structures, but it cannot itself resolve the collective problem of mass scale impoverishment (NLM, 1994). Further, the economic and social benefits of literacy do not spring from acquiring literacy skills but from using them. Virtually no one has benefited from acquiring literacy skills; people only benefit from using them to achieve some purpose (Rogers, 2004b).

The CONFINTEA V discussed this and pointed out that the social, economic and cultural context of the learner is more important than literacy alone. For example, it is important to recognize that it is not just illiteracy that is keeping women or marginal groups powerless, but a whole range of factors, such as resources and uneven land distribution. Literacy needs to be seen in this context (UNESCO Institute of Education, 1997).

The benefits of literacy do not automatically lead to development. It depends on the social context in which literacy skills are imparted. The dialectical relationship between literacy and development has to be clearly articulated and embedded into the programme guidelines in their true spirit of policy statements.

LITERACY PROGRAMMES AND GROWTH OF LITERACY RATE: SOME EXPERIENCES

Theoretically, the outcome of any literacy programme is improvement in the literacy rate. Policy documents on literacy express a similar assumption. This assumption percolates from the highest international level to the village level. How far these assumptions are valid in the Indian context with reference to the field experience is to be discussed to give a better understanding on the benefits of literacy.

In the year 2012, two paradoxical things happened on the literacy front in undivided Andhra Pradesh. One, in the 2011 census, the rank of Andhra Pradesh in literacy status among all the states and union territories fell from the 28th position to the 31st position. Two, the Andhra Pradesh State Literacy Mission got the National Award for best implementation of adult literacy programmes in the country. After the announcement of census data of 2011, there was a hue and cry on the performance of Andhra Pradesh on the literacy front. State's overall literacy rate at 67.02 per cent was much lower than the national average of 73.0 per cent. This trend is reflected in both male and female literacy rates. The first reaction in education circles was that adult literacy programmes failed to achieve their goals, and this is one of the main causes of low progress in literacy. How far is this true?

The target fixed for the major adult literacy programmes since their inception in 1978 has been the people of 15–35 age group. The focus of the programme has always been on the young adults who are in productive and reproductive age group. The target has always been in absolute numbers, not percentages and literacy rates. The same trend continued even during NLM's TLC approach. In most of the TLCs, the target age group was 14–35/40. Nowhere was the total non-literate population in all age groups taken as the target. Only in SBP, introduced in 2009, was the total population above 15 years taken as the target for the first time. It was also for the first time to link literacy programmes with the literacy rate. It is another matter that people over 40 years are rarely enthusiastic about attending literacy classes, and it is very difficult to motivate them. Moreover, they need reading glasses and other support to acquire literacy and there is no provision in SBP to give such equipment.

So, the literacy programmes in the last decade (until 2010) mainly focused on the 15–35 age group which is only around 35 per cent of the population. Even if a majority of them become literate, the improvement in the literacy rate would be marginal. This can be seen in the growth of the literacy rate in West Godavari and Krishna districts during the 1990s. The literacy rate of West Godavari which was 53.38 per cent in 1991 improved to 73.53 per cent in 2001; whereas, in Krishna district, the literacy rate which was 53.16 in 1991 increased to 68.85 per cent in 2001. The increase in literacy growth of 4.46 per cent in West Godavari compared to Krishna can be attributed to the successful literacy campaign conducted during the period in West Godavari.

Further, none of the states, such as Uttar Pradesh, Jammu & Kashmir, which were below the rank of Andhra Pradesh in the 2001 census and jumped to higher rank in 2011 census, conducted any major literacy campaign during the last decade, that is, 2001–2011. Some of these states did not even start SBP launched in 2010. Only in Andhra Pradesh were some state-sponsored literacy programmes conducted during 2001–2011. How then is the jump in literacy rate in these states higher than that of Andhra Pradesh?

One plausible reason may be the difference in the perception of literacy between northern states and southern states. An NLM consultant who visited many states for the evaluation of literacy programmes observed that perception of literacy is different in different states. For example, in Andhra Pradesh, people consider those who complete primary education as literate, and, in UP and Bihar, people who attended school for one year and who are able to recognize alphabets are considered literate.

Venkatanarayana and Chaganti (2012) analysed the percentage of those who became literates (acquired literacy skills) through informal ways, non-formal educational programmes or adult literacy programmes to the total literates in the country and found that the impact is very marginal (below one per cent among 7+ years age literates), although it increased marginally while moving to subsequent older cohorts. The percentage is higher (around 4.6%) among the older age groups (60+ years age population). It indicates that adult literacy programmes implemented in India have become ineffective in raising adult literacy rates particularly in the recent past. Premchand (2014) in his study on the impact of adult literacy programmes on literacy estimated that the contribution of adult literacy programmes works out to around 15 million additional literates and to an increase of about 2 percentage points in the adult literacy rate during the decade 2001–2011. Even EFA Global Monitoring Report (UNESCO, 2015, p. 135) highlighted, 'Progress in adult literacy rates may be the consequence of younger, better-educated people replacing older, less educated ones and not due to the implementation of effective literacy programmes'.

Adult literacy programmes create a literate environment in the society and facilitate enrolment of school-age children in schools. Many studies on the impact of adult literacy showed educational progress of the children whose parents are attending literacy classes. It does not automatically reflect on the literacy rate. It is supplementary to the formal education system and not an independent variable in improving the literacy rate.

From the discussion in this chapter, it is clear that the assumption that literacy programmes improve literacy rate is doubtful on two counts. One, a very few participants of literacy programmes are interested in literacy for education's sake and a majority of the participants are interested in literacy for development, so the majority of the participants do not claim literate status. Two, there is no clear-cut evidence to show that literacy programmes substantially improve the literacy rate as shown in the population census. Therefore, the State should rethink the policy of looking at literacy as an educational programme and make it a part of development programmes.

The content and pedagogy of a literacy programme decide and reflect the perspectives—whether as education or as development. The next chapter will discuss the content and pedagogy of literacy programmes and their perspectives.

Curriculum and Pedagogy

I once listened to an interesting discussion at an AEC in Lakkavaram village of West Godavari district (Andhra Pradesh) when I had gone there to participate in the centre's opening function. Of the 30 non-literates enrolled, 27 attended the class on the first day. I asked the volunteer, who was about 18 and had studied up to the 10th standard, to begin the class. He started teaching the very first lesson 'Avasaralu' (which means needs) in the adult literacy Telugu primer prepared by the SRC, Hyderabad, as per NLM guidelines.

In accordance with the volunteers training manual, he began speaking on the needs of individuals and families. Holding out to the class an illustration in the book, which showed, on one side, a very poor family living in an unclean house with the children in soiled clothes. Alongside, the illustration showed another family living in a neat and tidy house with the children in neat clothes ready to go to school. The volunteer asked the learners the reasons for the difference in the two families. They gave many reasons, such as ill health and unemployment, for the abject poverty of one family.

Not happy with their replies, the volunteer told them that lack of education and the family not availing the benefits of development programmes were the reasons for their plight. The learners did not agree with him and started mentioning reasons such as insufficient resources and corruption in welfare and development programmes. The volunteer who was younger than some of the learners could not pacify them and told to stop the discussion and go for acquiring literacy skills. He wrote on the blackboard the heading of the lesson and started teaching the alphabets in the title.

The learners asked him several questions: 'Is it possible to impart literacy (reading and writing) without introducing the alphabets in the sequential order?' 'Can writing be practised without using a slate?' 'Can an illiterate person copy and write the text in the workbook?' The volunteer tried his best to convince the learners on the new method, but they did not agree with him.

Finally, he told them that that was how he had been trained by the officials during the training programme. Some of the learners refused to start with sentences and insisted that they be taught the alphabet first on slates. Unable to persuade the learners, the volunteer started teaching the alphabet by writing the letters on the board.

This is a typical scene in most of the literacy centres on the first day of the literacy course. Most of the learners question the assumptions on which primers are developed and ask for teaching in alphabet method and supply of slates. They believe that education starts with writing of the alphabet on the slate, whereas curriculum and pedagogy in literacy programmes use different methods.

What is the best curriculum and pedagogy for adult literacy in the Indian context? What is the best approach for primer development? How far is the existing IPCL method adopted in literacy programmes effective? These are some of the critical issues for curriculum and pedagogy in Indian adult literacy programmes. As mentioned in the introduction, teaching and learning in the literacy class is influenced by many factors: the way adult learning is understood, content and pedagogy adopted, approach to literacy material, etc. These issues have to be understood for any good teaching and learning activity. Let us discuss some of the theoretical aspects on the acquisition of literacy before examining the curriculum and pedagogy in Indian literacy programmes.

LITERACY CURRICULUM

Generally, the term curriculum refers to the lessons and academic content taught in a school or a specific course. There are different understandings of the term 'curriculum' and different approaches to defining a curriculum. At one end of the spectrum, the definition of a curriculum involves a detailed specification of the content to be covered or outcomes to be achieved. At the other end, it means explaining the processes undertaken by learners and tutors to identify, plan, carry out and review learning programmes for individual learners (Scottish Executive, 2003).

In most of the literacy programmes, the content or outcome to be achieved is defined as curriculum. Most often the term 'content' is used as synonymous to the term 'curriculum'. How we look at the curriculum or content mostly depends on the conception of literacy adopted in a particular programme, that is, skill or task or process or critical reflection. The curriculum models can broadly be specified in four different ways (McCaffery et al., 2007).

- *The content model:* In this, the body of knowledge to be transmitted is defined. It is mostly used if literacy is viewed as a skill.
- *The product model:* This model defines goals to be achieved in a course. The product model fits well when literacy is viewed as performing a task (functional approach).
- *The process model:* It lists the series of activities to be taken up in the literacy course. This model is ideal when literacy is viewed as a social practice.
- *The praxis model:* This model is adopted when literacy is committed for radical change. It has a strong link with the concept of literacy as critical reflection.

In the first two models, the content is predetermined and what is to be achieved is fixed in advance without any consultation with potential learners, and both are more or less similar. On the other hand, the process model sees learning as active and dynamic and is less concerned with determining its content. In that, literacy is not defined as a single set of skills to be acquired but a social practice. The praxis model leads the facilitator and learners to question and reflect on both their values and their practices. There are many similarities between the process and praxis approaches in terms of their flexibility, intention to be relevant to local context. Each of the models has a specific pedagogical approach.

PEDAGOGY

Pedagogy basically deals with the theory and practice of teaching. It is concerned with the values and principles that influence an approach to learning, teaching and assessment. Different pedagogical approaches are adopted in different courses based on the content of the course. In adult literacy, each of the curriculum model follows a different pedagogical approach to reach the content to the learner. This also depends on the difference in literacy acquisition between children and adults, which is another critical issue in adult education.

PEDAGOGY VERSUS ANDRAGOGY

There has been a lot of debate whether learning as an adult is similar to learning as a child. Knowles (1980) and others argue that adult learning is quite different from child learning. They used the term 'andragogy' to represent the adult learning process instead of pedagogy that reflects the child learning process. For Knowles, andragogy is premised on at least four crucial assumptions about the characteristics of adult learners that are different from the assumptions about child learners. These are as follows:

1. Move from dependency to self-directedness.
2. Draw upon their reservoir of experience for learning.
3. Ready to learn when they assume new roles.
4. Want to solve problems and apply new knowledge immediately.

A comparison of the assumptions of pedagogy and andragogy following Knowles (Jarvis, 1985, p. 51) is shown in Table 4.1.

However, some authors argue that the only difference between pedagogy and andragogy is the difference in pedagogical approaches. They (Perfetti & Marron, 1995) believe that the process of learning to read as an adult follows the same principles that govern a child's reading acquisition. However, there are important contextual factors, including social and emotional, that exert a strong influence on the course of learning. They point out that adults come to a literacy programme from different backgrounds, sometimes motivated by specific

Table 4.1 *Comparison of the Assumptions of Pedagogy and Andragogy*

	Pedagogy	Andragogy
The Learner	Dependent. Teacher directs what, when and how a subject is learned and tests that it has been learned.	Moves towards independence. Self-directing. Teacher encourages and nurtures this movement.
The Learner's Experience	Of little worth. Hence, teaching methods are didactic.	A rich resource for learning. Hence teaching methods include discussion, problem-solving, etc.
Readiness to Learn	People learn what society expects them to, so that the curriculum is standardized.	People learn what they need to know, so that learning programmes organized around life application.
Orientation to Learning	Acquisition of subject matter. Curriculum organized by subjects.	Learning experiences should be based on experiences, since people are performance-centred in their learning

personal and occupational goals, and other times merely complying with some requirements imposed by others. One advantage that some adults appear to have over children is a clear sense of purpose. If the value of reading is not clear to a child, it is clear, in one form or another, to many adults who participate in an adult literacy programme. Adults approach such programmes not only with different goals and motivations but also with different skills.

PEDAGOGY: KEY ELEMENTS OF ACQUIRING LITERACY

There are some core principles for learning to read and write. American research has identified key elements of learning to read and write that may be relevant to anyone learning to read for the first time, whether child or adult (National Institute of Child Health and Human Development [NICHD], 2000).

Learning Reading

There are three key components for learning reading. These are as follows:

- *Alphabetics:* Alphabetics is the correspondence between letter/symbol and sound that is the basis for text. Reading and writing require an understanding of the relationship between sound and symbol. Readers need to be able to 'decode' and turn a symbol into its equivalent sound (a phoneme, the smallest unit of spoken speech). Writers need to 'encode' and turn a sound (phoneme) into a symbol. Alphabetics is the process through which people understand and manipulate the system in their language for linking letter or symbol with sound. In adult literacy, learners are familiar with sounds, but they have learnt symbols and their corresponding sounds.
- *Fluency:* It is the ease, accuracy and speed of reading. Reading fluency helps the reader to remember the words and relate the ideas to existing knowledge. Practice is very important for reading fluency. Research suggests that some kinds of practice are more effective than others (NICHD, 2000). Cognitive science research shows that reading must become automatic, fast, effortless and accurate in order to be useful. The short-term memory (working memory) needed to store the deciphered material is exceedingly brief. In educated people, it lasts about 12 seconds and holds about 7 items, and in illiterates it may last even less. If the information in short-term memory is not rehearsed or transferred to long-term memory, it gets wiped out. Neo-literates must read a word in about 1–1.5 second (45–60 words per minute) in order to understand a sentence within 12 seconds. If they take longer, they forget by the end of the sentence what they read at the beginning (Abadzi, 2003b).
- *Comprehension:* Comprehension is the active process of interacting with a text in order to interpret or make sense of it. As with fluency, features of the text and their degree of familiarity to the reader affect the process of understanding. The vocabulary,

content, structure and style of the text may be familiar or unfamiliar to the reader, and unfamiliar texts are harder to comprehend. Teaching comprehension explicitly can help students with skills to use when they come up against barriers to understanding what they are reading.

Learning to Write

Much less research has been conducted into how people learn to write than into how they learn to read. It involves coding and recording of a sound. Writing is not a language but a form of technology involving more of motor skills. Early ideas of writing as a 'product' gave way to understanding writing as a 'process' of planning, writing and revising (McCaffery et al., 2007).

APPROACH TO ADULT LITERACY PRIMERS

Most adult literacy programmes that adopt content and product models of curriculum follow primer-based approaches to impart literacy skills. A primer is a main tool designed to teach reading and writing with reading exercises and ruled lines with letters, words and sentences for learners to copy. Primers are a key resource for teachers and learners, because they organize content into elements that can be taught in different lessons. There are mainly three approaches in the development of primers in language learning: synthetic (popularly known as alphabetic method), analytic (sentence method) and eclectic approach, which implies a combination of synthetic and analytic methods (Hamadache & Martin, 1986).

Synthetic Method

The synthetic method is based on the principle that in order to learn to read, the student must first know the components of the word—letters or syllables. Once he acquires these, the next step is the synthesis of words that are then combined into phrases. There are three synthetic methods and they are by far the oldest.

1. *The alphabetic method:* It consists of teaching first the name of the letters in alphabetical order and pronouncing combinations of two or more letters and words. Then making of sentences is taught by joining the words.
2. *The phonetic method:* In this this method, the first step consists of teaching the sound of the letters, and the order in which letters are introduced generally depends on the frequency with which they recur in the language concerned.

    Some authors have introduced variations with a view to making the study of sound and letters more interesting. Laubach, for example, used the 'key words' technique whereby the letter is graphically associated with a picture of the object identified by the key word.
3. *The syllabic method:* As in the case of the first two methods, this is also a synthetic method but having the syllables as its basis. Syllables are used in preference to letters because so many consonants can only be correctly pronounced in combination with vowels. This method is suitable for certain vernacular languages.

Analytic Method

This method is the reverse of the synthetic method. In this method, the participants are taught the sentence or phrase first, then the words used in it are analysed and, after that, letters are taught. One of the techniques used in this method is the story technique in which the sentences used in the story are taught and later the letters and words used in the sentences are taught.

Eclectic Method

This is not a separate method but a blend of the above two methods. Here, after analysing the sentences and words into letters, a build-up process is started, leading to the formation of new words, phrases and sentences.

Now let us examine what type of content and pedagogy is used in Indian adult literacy programmes with reference to the models mentioned above.

CURRICULUM AND PEDAGOGY IN INDIAN LITERACY PROGRAMMES

Since Independence, literacy in government programmes is conceived as 'literacy as skill' and 'literacy as task' (functional literacy). In congruence with this conception, adult education programmes in India adopted content and product model and followed a primer-based approach in adult literacy. The GoI, which formulates the adult education policy, decides the curriculum of adult literacy programmes and gives detailed guidelines in terms of content and methodology. After the establishment of SRCs in 1978, primer development in local languages has been entrusted to them. SRCs design the primers and other material on the basis of parameters set by the GoI and the material produced at the state level is approved at the national level before printing and distribution.

NATIONAL ADULT EDUCATION PROGRAMME

The teaching content of any educational programme is determined by the objectives of that programme. Since the main objectives of NAEP were development of literacy skills, functionality and social awareness, the curriculum framework of NAEP was concretized by emphasizing three aspects of the content (Bordia, 1982, p. 26):

- Literacy and numeracy, of a sufficient level, to enable the learners to continue learning further in a self-reliant manner.
- Functional development wherein functionality is viewed as the role of an individual as a producer and worker, as a member of the family and as a citizen in a civic and political system.
- Social awareness, including an awareness about the impediments to development, about laws and government policies, and the need for the poor and illiterate to organize themselves for pursuit of their legitimate interests and for group action.

As per the policy document (Ministry of Education and Social Welfare, 1978, p. 2), adult education, while emphasizing acquisition of literacy skills, should also be

- relevant to the environment and learners' needs;
- flexible regarding duration, time, location, instructional arrangements, etc.;
- diversified in regard to curriculum, teaching and learning material and methods; and
- systematic in all aspects or organization.

NAEP followed a primer-based approach for literacy impartation. Most of the primers developed have followed either the analytic method or the eclectic method. Take for example, Andhra Pradesh, where the primer called *Janavachakam* for reading, a workbook for writing and two supplementary books on health and sanitation were used in NAEP. The primer was developed by a team headed by Professor B. Krishna Murthy, a well-known linguist. It borrowed concepts from Paulo Friere's critical literacy and developed lessons based on themes. The sentence method using the analytical approach of teaching was followed in the primer. Each lesson is named with commonly used proverbs or common sayings in Telugu. It is designed in such a way that frequently used letters in Telugu come first. It started with the signature of the learner to give him confidence and see his own name in writing. Each lesson consists of a sentence with a theme along with an illustration of the theme. The core content of the primer consists of health and hygiene, small family norm, environment, agriculture, specially the importance of manures and fertilizers, cooperatives and credit, one's own village, inflation, parenting, national integrity, etc. The list of subjects covered in the primer is given in Annexure 5. Functionaries of adult education programme who worked in NAEP consider it as the best primer as it effectively combines literacy skills and awareness using proverbs.

Regarding the methods used in AECs to create social awareness, in a majority of centres, the lecture method is adopted for creating awareness among the learners although the guidelines suggest the discussion method. No clarity was given regarding the functionality and it was assumed that incorporating lessons on themes relating to the individual and social development would automatically lead to functional literacy.

TOTAL LITERACY CAMPAIGNS

In TLC, the concept of functional literacy was adopted and the primer-based approach continued with some modifications. Functional literacy has been defined to imply self-reliance in the 3Rs, becoming aware of the causes of deprivation and moving towards amelioration of their condition by participating in the development process, skill improvement to improve economic status and general well-being, imbibing values of national integration, conservation of environment, women's equality and observance of small family norm (MHRD, 1988). The aforementioned definition of functional literacy itself clearly indicated the curriculum of the programme.

IPCL APPROACH

A major innovation in pedagogy during TLC was the introduction of IPCL approach. It is a pedagogical approach that aims at improving the pace of learning of adult learners and ensures the achievement of expected levels of literacy in 200 hours (Directorate of Adult Education [DAE], 2003a). It was assumed that IPCL approach would be better and faster if certain conditions were fulfilled, such as heightened motivation of instructors, short and intensive courses, improved material to sustain the motivation of the learners and joyfulness of learning. With these conditions, the learners would be able to acquire the expected levels of literacy in about 200 hours.

Some of the characteristics of IPCL approach are as follows:

- There are three sets of primers corresponding to three levels of NLM norms, each primer being an improvement on the other in terms of progression.
- Each primer is an integrated one in the sense that it combines workbook, exercise book, tools of evaluation of learning outcome, certification, etc.
- There are exercises at the end of every lesson and three tests in each primer.
- The entire exercise is based on the principle of self-evaluation and confidence-oriented evaluation.

- The tests are intended to be simple, non-threatening and partici-
pative; every learner is free to attain the desired level according to
his/her leisure and convenience.
- It is expected that a learner should be able to complete all the three
primers within the duration of 200 hours spread over 6–8 months.
- The numeracy content is integrated with the lesson and not treated
as a separate unit/lesson.
- There is emphasis on both, the core content and the locally relevant content.
- The content is to be presented following the principle of simple
to complex.

The IPCL curriculum, based on the programme goals set by NLM,
focused on FANV, which stands for functionality, awareness and
national values. It has two types of content, namely, core content and
locally relevant content. The core content includes national values
such as the following:

- National integration
- Women's equality
- Population education
- Conservation of environment
- Development of scientific temper

The local content is decided at the state or district level. The core
content in the primers used in Telugu during the TLC period is given
in Annexure 6. At the state level, SRCs prepared teaching learning
material based on the IPCL pattern. However, if materials required
modification or adaptation to be more district-specific, such changes
were made by the ZSSs in consultation with SRCs.

SAAKSHAR BHARAT PROGRAMME

Saakshar Bharat followed the same curriculum and pedagogy as TLC
since it is only a new variant of NLM. It continued with the concept
of functional literacy and the IPCL approach for primer development. The content/themes of the lessons used in SBP are presented in

Annexure 7. They are more or less similar to the content used in earlier literacy programmes. SB document (MHRD, 2009) for the first time discussed core curriculum framework for adult literacy and proposed to develop such a framework. It also highlighted the need for high-quality teaching and learning material and augmenting the quality of teaching and learning process. One important addition to this programme is that the assessment of learning achievement is standardized and the National Institute of Open Schooling is roped in to conduct summative assessment and issue certificates to successful learners. However, the National Curriculum Framework for Adult Education (NCFAE) proposed to be developed has not been published so far.

DISCUSSION ON CURRICULUM AND PEDAGOGY IN INDIAN LITERACY PROGRAMMES

It can be seen from the above details that adult education programmes in India followed the content and product model of curriculum and primer-based approaches covering a wide range of subjects to not only impart functional literacy skills but also to generate awareness on various development issues. Primers mostly adopted the analytical method (theme-based sentence method) to teach reading and writing. Many field functionaries believe that complicated curriculum and pedagogy introduced in adult literacy programmes is one of the main reasons for the low success rate in adult literacy. There is a lot of criticism on curriculum and pedagogy in Indian literacy programmes on various grounds. The criticism ranged from content for its ideological bias to unsuitability of teaching and learning methods to Indian languages. Let us discuss some of the critical aspects of curriculum and pedagogy in Indian adult education.

MISMATCH BETWEEN STATE AND USER PERCEPTIONS

There is a mismatch between the state perspective and the user perspective on the basis of content of literacy programmes. Policy-makers look at literacy programmes as a channel to reach education and development goals of the State. So, the content and instruction goals of literacy programmes are oriented towards the development needs as perceived by the policy-makers. As discussed in the previous chapter, there is divergence in perception of State and users on the purpose and benefits of literacy. The State intends to impart skills for achieving long-term educational and development goals, whereas learners are interested in satisfying immediate felt needs. On many occasions, during discussions, learners said that they want immediate use of literacy acquired in the course in their day-to-day life. They are more interested in satisfying their felt needs using literacy skills. The content of literacy programmes failed to balance the felt needs of the learners and the development needs of the State. This mismatch has affected the literacy programme.

Further, the literacy programmes are designed at national and state levels, and naturally, they focused on broad general issues applicable to all sections of the population in a geographical area. Although there is scope for inclusion of locally relevant content in primers, it is not possible because different sections of population have different requirements and needs. So, the primers are confined to broad general issues. But learners want literacy content that is relevant and applicable to their immediate environment and work. This contradiction has not been sorted out in Indian literacy programmes.

CONTENT OF PRIMERS

Another major criticism of the content of literacy programmes is that it shows a biased approach. According to Kumar (1989), the gist of narratives in the primer is that a man can change his economic conditions by dropping a set of backward and disabling characteristics and adopting an alternative set of characteristics that are modern and healthy. It focuses on what people lack rather than on what they have and emphasizes their deficits, not their strengths. All the problems of the individuals are seen as the outcome of a disorganized, unthinking, ignorant personality whose salvation lies in new knowledge and skills (including literacy) and self-control. Further, he pointed out that the primers adopted a 'Pseudo-Freirean' perspective that operates in adult education through the following steps:

- Labelling the central problem as 'poverty' rather than as 'oppression'.
- Identifying the cause of poverty as the self-inflicted deficiency of the poor rather than oppression.
- Proposing, as treatment, to change the behaviour of the poor through transmission of information and skills.
- Converting Freire's method into a 'neutral' classroom technique without 'politics'.
- Defining 'action' as coping activity.

An analysis of literacy primers in use in six states of India (Dighe, 1996) showed how certain recurring patterns ran through each of the literacy primers in use in different languages. In all these primers, the overall approach was to treat the adults as those with 'empty minds' who had to be sermonized about the manner in which their lives could improve. The basic thrust was 'victim blame' and not 'system blame'. Such individual blaming perspective did not attempt to link the development problems with the structural reality of the poor. Such a top-down approach reinforces the dominance of the viewpoint of the 'progressive' protagonist while depicting the learners as passive recipients of development messages (Dighe, 2005a).

CRITIQUE OF IPCL APPROACH

NLM introduced the IPCL guidelines for primer development and pedagogy during the TLC, and they became sacrosanct for primer development. As far as it is known, IPCL guidelines are not based on any concrete research findings but finalized on the assumptions of the educational experts, a majority of whom are not acquainted with field reality. As pointed out by Daswani (2000), there is no research evidence to support the implicit assumption that the TLC curriculum can be acquired within the stipulated time period. He adds that it is well known that children require at least three to four years to acquire independent reading skills. Although adults are believed to have certain advantages of cognitive maturity, it is also believed that they do not necessarily acquire basic reading skills at a more rapid pace. Bharat Gyan Vigyan Samiti (BGVS, 1993) also commented that reduction in the duration of the course from 300 hours in NAEP to 200 hours in TLC is based only on hunch, and there is no research backing for this. SRCs that prepare a final prototype of primers based on IPCL guidelines have not tested them by teaching the prototype primer for a specific period but only tested familiarity of the vocabulary.

Further, the IPCL primers do not emphasize fluency of reading that is necessary for a reader to comprehend sentences faster. It is assumed that learners acquire literacy skills in 200 hours if the environment is made conducive. As pointed out in many world reports (Abadzi, 2003b), a person must read a word in about 1–1.5 second (45–60 words per minute) in order to understand a sentence. Fluency practice is the key to retain literacy skills and this aspect has not been given importance in literacy primers. Lack of importance to fluency has resulted in poor learning of literacy skills, difficulty in their use and consequent relapse.

UNSUITABILITY OF ANALYTICAL METHOD TO INDIAN LANGUAGES

Some authors such as Ranganayakamma (1995) and Varma (1999) have criticized the use of the analytical method (sentence or word method) in literacy primers as letters in the Telugu language, for that matter for most Indian languages, has a natural sequence and they have to be taught in that sequence alone. The analytic method in imparting literacy skills is not suitable for phonetic Indian languages. These languages have syllable pairs that have to be taught in a certain sequence. Since the analytic method does not follow the syllable sequence but uses frequently used words or thematic words, it is not appropriate in the Indian context. Further, a majority of the fieldworkers say that adult learners do not accept the analytical method, as they are well aware that literacy language learning starts with letters and insist on teaching letters. Volunteers or instructors who learned literacy skills through the alphabet method prefer to teach letters first. Most of the volunteer/instructors are either 10th class (matriculation) pass or fail and are trained only for two or three days, and so they are not in a position to teach theme-based analytical method that requires a higher level of understanding of issues and methods. Generally, they use literacy primers to start a discussion on a theme but teach letters and syllables in the traditional alphabet method.

CLASSROOM PRACTICES IN ADULT LITERACY

One of the neglected areas in pedagogy of adult education in India is classroom practices. It is assumed that literacy classes are conducted in the same way as the classes in a school. It is assumed that all the learners attend the class at the same time and are in the same lesson. But in adult education, it is far from true. All learners rarely attend the class together, they attend according to their convenience and a majority of them are not regular as they go to the centre after completing the day's work and family responsibilities. In fact, in adult literacy classes, teaching and learning take place at different levels and the assumption that the entire group learns a single lesson or discusses a common theme is untenable. Teaching takes place in the one-on-one instruction method. This important point has never been highlighted in the training sessions of volunteers. The same is the case with discussion on themes of the lessons. They never take place in a systematic way as suggested in the teacher's guide. Most of the volunteers simply follow the lecture method and speak briefly on the topic instead of linking literacy component with the topic.

Classroom practices of adult education have to be studied scientifically and appropriate methods adopted to suit the learning context and conditions of the learners. Unofficial and informal usage of multilevel and one-on-one instructions need to be channelized. Proper guidelines have to be developed on multilevel teaching and they have to be included in the volunteers' training.

LACK OF CLARITY ON FUNCTIONALITY

Functionality was another difficult concept, although it was given as much importance as literacy. Many field functionaries never understood what functionality is. It has not even been defined (BGVS, 1993).

People mean different things by these terms. Some understood it as the ability of the learner to perform a particular task in day-to-day life using literacy and other skills acquired in literacy classes such as filling an application form or writing a letter. Most of the field functionaries understand functionality as training in vocational skills. NLM used the term vaguely to mean both. So, proper instrumentality was not developed to transform the objective of creating developing functional skills into learning system. Pedagogical aspects of functionality are completely neglected in adult education programmes. Patel (1996) commented that despite the inclusion of functionality and awareness in the definition of adult education, NLM's focus continued to be on imparting cognitive literacy skills.

UNIFORM CONTENT AND METHODS

Even though India never has the NCFAE in place, all major adult education programmes in the country have adopted a uniform curriculum and pedagogy in the name of national programmes. The guidelines on curriculum and pedagogy formulated at the national level are applied to the local languages in developing primers by SRCs at the state level. National commitment for literacy is important, but it should not be translated into uniform content and methods for the entire country. Dighe (2005a) rightly pointed out that one of the problems with the existing adult literacy programmes is that the diverse learning needs of diverse groups of learners are not recognized. As a result, there is a tendency to offer a narrowly focused 'one size fits all' educational programme. Diverse needs and interests of learners from diverse backgrounds are not given the importance they deserve while preparing primers.

The SB policy document (MHRD, 2009) highlighted the importance of NCFAE and an Expert Group on NCFAE deliberated on the issue in a series of meetings, but no NCFAE has been announced so far. Lack of the framework and prescription of the content and methods at the national level and their routine application for diverse languages have made literacy acquisition much more complex.

CONTRADICTIONS BETWEEN CONTENT AND PEDAGOGY

If we look closely at content and pedagogy in adult literacy pro-grammes in India, we will notice an inherent contradiction between content and pedagogy in the government programmes. The curriculum basically adopted 'content' and 'product' models and confined itself to literacy skills. It focused on the development needs of the country and dissemination of information on welfare and development pro-grammes. It aims at bringing about behavioural change at the indi-vidual level. However, when it came to pedagogy, it adopted advanced pedagogical methods used in Paulo Freire's 'critical literacy', that is, the praxis model to impart the content of the product model. These critical literacy methods, widely used in Latin American countries in a revolutionary context, are directly applied in the Indian context. For any good education, the content and pedagogy should have unity and be based on the same ideological and theoretical basis. However, in India, there is a contradiction between the two. The ideology of the curriculum is totally different from the ideology of pedagogy. The former viewed literacy as a skill or task and the latter perceived lit-eracy as a critical reflection. Further, critical pedagogical methods are introduced in a non-revolutionary context, and some of the techniques used are not culturally suitable in the Indian context. This has created a lot of confusion among the functionaries and resulted in the wastage of large quantities of teaching and learning material.

Take for example, the first lesson in Telugu primer developed by SRC, Hyderabad as per NLM guidelines. The content of the lesson and illustrations show different needs of a person—food, house, clothing, etc. The lesson suggests that a person should work hard and develop good habits to satisfy the needs. This content has to be taught in the dialogue and discussion method followed in the Freirean approach, which is, in fact, followed to encourage the participants to question the existing structures which do not allow equal distribution of resources, a basic cause of non-fulfilment of the needs of all the people. Teaching a conformist content in a revolutionary methodology is very difficult, especially for volunteers who are mostly rural youths with bare minimum education. They had neither the competencies nor the training to reconcile the contradictions in the curriculum and pedagogy. As pointed out by Dighe (2005a), the problem relates to the difficulty of the process of conscientization taking place in bureaucratically organized education systems, while a Freire-style response requires something much closer to a political movement.

The contradiction between curriculum and pedagogy needs to be reconciled for any successful literacy programme. It is not easy to teach a conformist content and revolutionary pedagogy, especially by underqualified and semi-trained volunteers. Pedagogy is not a simple teaching technique, and it should be in tune with the objectives and content of the programme.

There are a number of attempts at the local level to overcome the deficiencies discussed above and also to develop primers in consonance with the local needs and interests, as it was felt that the primers used by NLM are not suitable to the local needs. Some of the author's experiences in dealing with curriculum and pedagogy are discussed here.

EXPERIENCE OF PRIMERS IN WEST GODAVARI DISTRICT

As discussed, during the visit to the literacy centres, it was observed that there was a huge gap between what the learner expects and what is taught in the primer. Learners expected letters as a starting point, but literacy classes started with sentences on themes. It has also been observed in the field that the most difficult part in teaching Telugu language is pairs, aspersions and vowel clusters. In Telugu, and many Indian languages, the alphabets have a natural sequence, but this aspect was not taken into consideration in the primers. So, an attempt was made in West Godavari district of Andhra Pradesh, to develop a primer in the alphabetic method. I was closely associated in the development, and it was an interesting experience. The primer was used in Akshara Mahila programme (AMP) and some of the salient features of these primers are discussed further.

Emphasis on Reading Skills

The main emphasis in the primer is to impart literacy competencies—reading, writing and numeracy skills—in the shortest possible period. Literacy was conceived as a skill and confined to teaching skills without any contradiction between content and pedagogy. The primers are designed in such a way as to give importance to a specific set of cognitive skills such as recognition of letters and combining letters into words. The lessons mainly consist of practice of recognition of letters and combining them to make words. As many words as possible with practised letters are incorporated in each lesson. Writing was introduced after a gap of one month when learners felt comfortable in recognizing letters and reading small words.

Natural Sequence of Letters

The primer and the workbook are prepared taking into consideration the specific features of the Telugu language. Telugu is a phonetic language with 56 vowels and consonants. Combination of vowels with consonants gives different phonetic sounds used in the language. Further, Telugu has letters in pairs such as 'A' and 'AA', 'E' and 'EE', etc. Therefore, these letters have to be taught together for easy learning. Hence, all these letters are given in the primer in a sequential order. However, some of the letters that are not used frequently are given in the boxes. The intention is to introduce these letters to give the learner an idea of the letter. But the learners are not asked to practise them thoroughly. Initially, only 29 letters are taught in detail and later 6 more letters are introduced.

Planning of Lessons

The lessons are planned in such a way that simple vowels and consonants are introduced in the first five lessons with more than 500 words to practise these letters. The next five lessons in the primer dealt with combining vowels with consonants. Here as well, the main thrust is on understanding how different phonetic sounds are generated when different vowels are combined with different consonants.

After the tenth lesson, a short story, 'Damayanthi Katha' is given. The story narrated by one learner (Damayanthi) deals with many important developmental issues such as small family norm, savings, WSHGs, etc. (the story became very popular during the AMP and every learner was able to read and tell the story.) The story used already covered letters and combinations. Again, Lessons 11–15 covered letters having a consonant combined with the same consonant (*Vathulu* in Telugu) and consonants combined with other consonants are given. In these lessons as well, the main focus is on exercises and practice.

After the completion of all the 15 lessons, some important topics are given in brief for reading and discussion. They are time measurement (number of seconds per minute, number of minutes per hour in writing form), names of days in a week, names of months, issues of clean and green, women's rights and WSHGs.

Workbook

Workbook followed a totally different approach. In this programme, since writing is introduced after reading, there is no direct relationship between the lessons in the primer and those in the workbook. Lessons in the latter are based on the shape of the letter and emphasized psychomotor skills. For example, the first lesson in the workbook is drawing full circles and half circles which are critical for writing letters in Telugu. Workbook has 14 lessons, mainly exercises. Another five lessons in the workbook covered numerical skills.

Use of Teaching Aids

One important addition in using this methodology was development of low-cost teaching and learning material in the AEC itself. It was made part of centre-based activity, and volunteers were trained in the preparation of teaching aids. They were prepared at the centre and used very effectively, as they had prepared themselves. An exhibition of teaching and learning aids, which was considered very rare, was conducted in Eluru to showcase how local volunteers can design teaching aids with locally available material.

Different Primers

Over a period of time, the primers were improved with additions and deletions. The Akshara Mahila primer was primarily developed for WSHGs. New primers were developed when literacy programmes were taken up for new groups. In two years, the District Literacy Committee has generated five primers, sometimes, refining, redefining the context, process and thrust. The primers developed in West Godavari are as follows:

- *Chaduvadaaniki Vachakam* (1998)
- *Chaduvu Vachakam* (1999)
- *Akshara Yuva Shakti* (1999)
- *Akshara Mahila* (2000)
- *Akshara Deeksha* (2001)

In the last named primer, reading and writing were not separated, but writing was introduced a little later. This is because it was observed during the AMP that learners were not taking much interest in the writing aspect and were focusing only on reading. A person cannot be considered literate unless he is able to read and write and make calculations with understanding. So, reading and writing are introduced in the same primer even though the pace of learning was a bit slow. The basic approach followed in all the primers was initial *Chaduvu Vachakam* and the focus in all the primers was on literacy skills.

EXPERIENCE OF A SCHOOLTEACHER

The above discussion might give the impression that one method, in this case, the synthetic method, is superior to other methods. It is not the superiority of the method but only suitability of a particular method in a particular context. The suitability depends on many factors such as age, cultural background of the learners and capabilities of the instructor. In the case of a capable and committed instructor, the importance of the method gets reduced.

For example, when I visited a literacy centre in K. Kota village in West Godavari, where a schoolteacher was voluntarily running a literacy centre during Akshara Sankranti and found that he taught the learners with the help of school textbooks, instead of primers developed by us. When reviewed the progress of the learners, I was pleasantly surprised to see that almost all the learners had achieved the same level of literacy level and some even a higher level in 3–4 months. I understood that the teaching capabilities of the instructor are more important than the actual method used in the primer. Therefore, it is difficult to conclude that one method is superior to another, and a lot of research has to be done to develop a suitable method for adult education in the Indian context.

USE OF ICTS AND TEACHING AIDS IN ADULT LITERACY

Whenever we attend meetings with political authorities of the state and very senior officers of the state administration, they ask one question: Why don't you use ICT to disseminate literacy among the mass of illiterates? They say that total literacy can never be achieved in a short period with traditional methods of imparting literacy and tell us to use innovative methods developed by various institutions such as TCS, HP or IIM Ahmedabad.

A number of attempts are being made to introduce information and communications technologies (ICTs) in teaching and learning in literacy classes to improve the pace of learning and achieve total literacy in the shortest possible period. Tata Consultancy Services (TCS) tried to introduce teaching using computers in many states through their Adult Literacy Programme as a part of their corporate social responsibility (CSR). They developed software to impart literacy skills in computer-based functional literacy (CBFL). They supplied refurbished computers to select centres where, using CBFL method, they conducted literacy classes for adults. CBFL method used animated graphics and a voiceover to explain how individual alphabets combine to give structure and meaning to various words (www.tatalitercy.com). TCS claimed that about 11,141 adults were imparted literacy skills during 2011–2012 in their *Corporate Sustainability Report 2011fi2012*. I visited one such centre in Bandlaguda village in Medak district in 2004. When I asked the local volunteers about the success of the method, they were hesitant to claim success or failure of the programme. The centre had not showed any difference from regular AEC conducted by government agencies. Initially CBFL confined to reading skills, but later introduced writing skills using notebooks and pencils. However, the government changed the primer on which the software is developed, and TCS has not yet developed the software for the new primer.

In the 1990s, a similar effort was made by Hewlett-Packard in three centres of the Kuppam Constituency, Andhra Pradesh, from where Chief Minister Chandrababu Naidu got elected twice. They provided touchscreen computers for reading and writing. A learner's progress can be assessed using the question bank embedded in the system and a certificate can be issued as well. The Hewlett-Packard experiment gained publicity as it was done in a high-profile constituency.

Another method known as Same Language Subtitling was developed by Professor Brij Kothari and others at IIM Ahmedabad. In this approach, the mainstream TV content is subtitled in the 'same' language as the one in the audio. In other words, one reads what he hears. IIM Ahmedabad claims that this method was very successful in improving the quality of reading skills among the weak readers. Although the Government of Andhra Pradesh insisted on implementing this method, it is not suitable for non-literates and can be used by neo-literates and school dropouts for reading practice.

My colleagues and I found it difficult to organize literacy programmes based on these methods. We felt that they could be used in experimental classes but not in large-scale programmes. Among the many reasons for this, one is that the introduction of ICTs in literacy classes requires huge infrastructure and funding. This is not possible in a programme that is basically run on a voluntary basis in rural areas. Two, imparting literacy skills using these methods is not possible because literacy includes reading and writing, and computer-based methods help only in imparting reading skills. Further, they only supplement the teaching process and are not an alternative to instructor-based teaching. These issues have never been discussed properly in any of the meetings, and adult educators are often blamed as conservative and interested in maintaining status quo of teaching.

I once discussed with the learners the usefulness of computers in acquiring literacy skills. They said that they were not comfortable with these machines and that they need the instructor's help whenever they want to use them. They are at ease with the traditional methods of teaching using slate and pencil as they can take help from family members or educated persons in the locality. They say that the computers have not improved the pace of learning; in fact, they need more time to get acquainted with the new method. Further, they firmly believe that they are not going to use computers in the near future and that it is a waste of energy and time. They requested us to use computers for teaching their children. This is the user perspective of ICTs in literacy.

Curriculum and pedagogy in adult literacy is one area that is riddled with assumptions and biases. No systematic research has been conducted in India on the adult learning process, especially on acquiring literacy. It is mostly based on the assumptions of the experts and instructors. Consequently, adult illiterates face a combination of instructional and cognitive obstacles, which together prevent many from attending classes or mastering literacy skills. These obstacles have not been studied through a valid experimental or quasi-experimental research. To understand their importance separately and in combination, a systematic study of the process of literacy acquisition, dropout and relapse into illiteracy has to be conducted (Patel, 1994, 1996). For this, research on adult education has to be strengthened and funded. The curriculum or content should be based on the needs and interests of learners in the local context, as this will motivate the learners to attend literacy classes. Motivation and mobilization play an important role in literacy programmes. The next chapter deals with these components of literacy.

Motivation and Mobilization

In 1983, I visited the literacy centre in Devipatnam village of East Godavari district, Andhra Pradesh, along with the adult education supervisor of the area. The centre was open but nobody, not even the instructor of the class, was there. We asked people sitting nearby about the instructor. They told us that he had gone to motivate and enrol learners. We went to the street to meet him. We found him sitting on the veranda of a village elder's house and talking to two non-literates, who were standing. The instructor was telling them about the benefits of literacy, and asking them to join the literacy class. We went to the next house with him and met the inmates. The instructor and supervisor repeated the process of telling them the importance of literacy and requested them to enrol for the literacy class. The village elders who came with us also made speeches on the importance of education. Some of the members we met agreed to join the literacy class and promised to come there the next day. This was the common practice to motivate adult non-literates.

In 1991, during the TLC in West Godavari, we organized *kala jathas* (a team of artists visiting villages and performing a series of cultural programmes) to motivate and mobilize people for literacy. I had the chance to witness many such performances. The cultural artists, most of them teachers in the district, were trained by BGVS, an NGO well known for its activities in the area of science, communication, education, health and environment, gave performances with songs and drama skits. A large number of people, sometimes the entire villages, turned up to watch the programmes. The performances were excellent and highly motivational. The themes of these performances included how illiterate people got cheated by moneylenders and other people, how difficult it was for them to travel, and how difficult it is to guide their children in their education, etc. It created a kind of positive and enthusiastic atmosphere for literacy among the people and literacy activists. After the conclusion of the performances, village elders and literacy functionaries gave speeches, thanked the district administration for organizing such a motivating performance in the villages and requested the non-literates to join the literacy classes. This was another kind of motivation strategy followed in literacy campaigns.

Motivating non-literates to participate in the literacy programme is one of the most challenging tasks every adult educator always faces everywhere. Different countries and different programmes have adopted different motivational strategies depending on the type and objectives of the programme and the socio-cultural context in which the programme is sought to be implemented. Each motivational strategy has its own theoretical and practical assumptions.

What are the motivational strategies adopted in literacy programmes and what are the assumptions made in each of the motivational strategies? What kind of motivational strategies are followed in Indian adult education programmes? What are the problems/limitations of motivational strategies in India? These are some of the issues that need to be understood to develop any effective motivational strategy in literacy programmes. Some of these issues are discussed in detail.

APPROACHES TO MOTIVATIONAL STRATEGY

Approach to motivation of a particular programme depends on many factors such as the concept of literacy, strategy of the programme like selective or mass campaign, etc. Different literacy programmes adopt different motivational strategies, which can be broadly classified into two categories: (a) those focusing on the individual learner and (b) those emphasizing social mobilization. One is approaching individual learner and the other one is appealing to the community/ society as a whole. The two experiences mentioned above represent the two models of motivational strategies.

The main thrust in the first strategy is to motivate the individual to participate in a literacy programme. The common practice is that volunteers or instructors of adult literacy programmes meet the potential learners, tell them the importance of literacy and persuade them to enrol in the literacy class. This is very suitable in small-scale literacy programmes following selective approach. It identifies the needs, interests and personal profiles of learners to motivate them. In the case of the second strategy, the stress is on social mobilization of the community and society as a whole to build up social pressure, generally with patriotic appeal. In this model, a massive publicity campaign is conducted involving different sections of society and using a wide variety of media to create a positive and conducive atmosphere for literacy and mobilize people for literacy activity. This is used in large-scale mass literacy campaigns.

INDIVIDUAL MOTIVATION THEORIES

One of the most cited of motivation theories is probably Abraham Maslow's hierarchy of needs (Maslow, 1987). In this theory, behaviour is partially motivated by external factors, but more by innate human needs. These are intrinsic and common to all humans, and hierarchically ordered. These are as follows:

- *Physiological needs:* Breathing, food, water, sex, sleep, homeostasis, excretion
- *Safety needs:* Security of body, employment, resources, morality, the family, health, property
- *Love/belonging:* Friendship, family, sexual intimacy
- *Esteem:* Self-esteem, confidence, achievement, respect for others, getting respect from others
- *Self-actualization:* Morality, creativity, spontaneity, problem solving, lack of prejudice, acceptance of facts

According to Maslow, the more basic levels must be relatively well satisfied before the individual is able to function on a higher level. It implies that any adult education programme should be implemented in such a way that it fulfils the immediate needs of the learners, rather than the long-term needs. For this, the first formula is to classify adult educational programmes according to the individual needs that they attempt to satisfy and to ensure that the correct balance is struck in each community setting. The second one is to divide the particular constituency into target groups related to a hierarchy of needs (Selvaraj, 1986). Further, motivation depends either on extrinsic or on intrinsic factors. Extrinsic factors are external incentives or pressures, such as attendance requirements, external rewards and punishments or examinations. These, if internalized, create an intention to engage in the learning process. Intrinsic motivation consists of a series of inner pressures and rational decisions that create a desire for learning. For example, the desire to learn a particular subject or achieve a life goal is an intrinsic motive.

FOUR GROUPS OF MOTIVATION

Alan Rogers (2004a) studied the motivation of learners in different countries and, based on his experience, identified four major groups of motivation for participation in literacy programmes.

1. *Symbolic reasons:* Some adults join a literacy class not because they want to use their literacy skills but because they want to join 'the literacy set'. In other words, they want to join a literacy class to enhance their social status. They know that literates are respected in society, and they want to be considered as literates and respected. 'Literacy' for them is not a tool to be used but a badge that identifies them as belonging to a particular group; it has in other words symbolic value.
2. *Instrumental reasons:* Some want to acquire literacy skills because they want to accomplish some literacy task. Some aspire to read the Bible or the Quran. Some want to write letters to their kin, and some others want to keep accounts. Literacy classes set within an existing WSHG see these tasks within the context of that group's activity. These people often come to classes with clearly set stages and end goals in their minds. They normally learn fast when they see the work of the literacy learning programme as directly helping them with their desired literacy uses.

3. *Opportunities:* Some adults join literacy classes, not to acquire literacy skills for use but for the opportunities the course will give them subsequently. For example, getting some benefit or other from the government or obtaining a loan that is dependent on their being literate. These participants generally do not intend to use their literacy skills after the end of the course. Their goal, however, is more specific than that of the symbolic participants. They aspire to obtain very real benefits after the completion of the learning course. Their goal, like that of the symbolic participants, is distant. Keeping them going through the entire course will be difficult.

4. *Access:* The main motivation for some adults to attend literacy classes is to be able to go into a formal or non-formal educational programme; it provides access to further learning. This is a kind of opportunity motivation—the end of the literacy programme will open the doors of education to them—but it is also an instrumental motivation, for the literacy skills will be learned for use. They hope to use their literacy as an entry point into second stage education, for example, to get into a school through their adult literacy classes.

SOCIAL MOBILIZATION

The second motivational approach followed mostly is social mobilization. It is a process that raises awareness and motivates people to demand change. It aims at mobilizing public opinion on a particular issue and creates the atmosphere for community participation. It uses different forms of mobilization strategies such as mass media campaigns, cultural forms and, in most cases, the process of social mobilization takes place in public places, such as processions, demonstrations, marches and mass meetings. Social mobilization is also used by organizations to facilitate change.

UNICEF defines social mobilization as

[A] process that engages and motivates a wide range of partners and allies at national and local levels to raise awareness of and demand for a particular development objective through dialogue. Members of institutions, community networks, civic and religious groups and others work in a coordinated way to reach specific groups of people for dialogue with planned messages. In other words, social mobilization seeks to facilitate change through a range of players engaged in interrelated and complementary efforts. (www.unicef.org/cbsc/index_42347.html)

In literacy, social mobilization has dual aim of reducing the resistance to literacy and of creating an environment conducive to articulate literacy course participants' potential/talents. It also aims at building the morale, and securing the commitment of volunteers and other personnel involved in literacy movement. It is intended to generate demand for literacy, motivate the individual learners to participate in literacy programmes. Thus, creating a strong and intense motivation in society.

COMMUNITY MOBILIZATION

In adult literacy programmes, there is a good deal of confusion between social mobilization and community mobilization, and the two terms are used interchangeably. There is a subtle difference between these two terms. Social mobilization is a broad term used to refer to mobilization of the entire society. In this, the focus is on creating social pressure to motivate individuals for a particular cause. On the other hand, community mobilization mostly confines itself to small communities or villages, and the main focus would be on motivating individuals towards a particular issue or a task. Here emphasis is on moving towards an action. Community mobilization is important for seeking community support and promoting its involvement in development activities that affect the lives of its members. Community mobilization promotes consideration of the needs of specific populations and localities. In particular, underprivileged populations can be reached more effectively through community mobilization. This mobilization also leads to greater sustainability, as communities are empowered and capable of addressing their own needs.

Community mobilization is extremely important for initiating a literacy programme in any community, especially in rural and tribal areas. The community mobilization cycle is composed of eight steps and can regularly be used to enable the community to solve their own problems and initiate their own projects (Facilicom Consult, 2003). The following steps are part of building up the cycle:

1. Getting to know the community, provide information and create an interest
2. Analysis and identification of problems, solutions and resources
3. Decision-making and selection of leaders by community
4. Identification of stakeholders
5. Planning and selection of implementing leaders
6. Project implementation by community
7. Follow-up and monitoring
8. Evaluation

Within community mobilization, when every member of a community has the chance, directly or through representation, to participate in the design, implementation and monitoring of community-level initiatives, there is a higher likelihood that the programme accurately reflects their real needs and interests. An analysis of projects that have failed in the past (UNESCO, 2006) shows that failure occurred because (a) the people concerned were not involved in the planning, implementation and monitoring of programmes which affected their lives and (b) there was an insufficient level of participation of the beneficiaries.

People's participation can take a number of forms. At one end of the spectrum is 'passive participation' in which community members participate by being informed about something that will happen or has already happened. At the other end of the spectrum is 'self-mobilization', when communities organize and take initiative independent of any external actors. There are seven levels of participation (Mercy Corps, 2009): (a) passive participation, (b) participation in information giving, (c) participation by consultation, (d) participation for material incentives, (e) functional participation, (f) interactive participation and (g) self-mobilization. The higher the level of participation, the better would be the success of community mobilization.

Let us examine what motivational strategies have been adopted in Indian adult education programmes.

MOTIVATION AND MOBILIZATION STRATEGIES IN INDIAN ADULT EDUCATION

National Adult Education Programme

Motivational aspects have not been given much importance in pre-NAEP literacy programmes in India. Although NAEP document high-lighted the importance of motivation in literacy programmes, it has not evolved any clear-cut motivational strategy. It only followed individual motivation strategy on the assumption that the organizers would moti-vate the learners and the motivated learners would attend the literacy classes on their own. In this strategy, instructors meet potential learners individually explaining to them the importance of literacy and enrol them in literacy classes. Another strategy is door-to-door campaign, in which a group of people visit the potential learners at their homes and persuade them to participate in the literacy programme.

Since NAEP was not a massive campaign and adopted only a selec-tive approach at the project level, not all the non-literates need to be motivated at one go. Only those interested would attend the literacy classes. It was expected that organizers would interact with the learners and identify all those who were genuinely interested and enrol them in the literacy class. As the number of learners to be enrolled at each literacy centre was only 30, it was not found difficult when there were a large number of non-literates available in the villages.

However, during the later years of the implementation of the pro-gramme, the importance of social mobilization was realized. Since 1987, some provision was made for mobilization activities. (An amount of ₹60,000 was provided for each project under the centrally sponsored scheme of Rural Functional Literacy Programme.) This amount was spent on the conduct of cultural programmes, public meetings and publicity campaigns to motivate the learners and to create a positive atmosphere for literacy in society. This was the first time in India that some provision was made for motivation and envi-ronment building in literacy programmes.

However, not much attention was paid to community mobilization, and there was no clear-cut strategy on this. As a part of community participation, advisory committees at various levels were constituted to take the help of the various sections of population. However, in most of the cases, the advisory committees were only on paper, and it was expected that the government functionaries would take the support of the village leaders in implementing the programme.

NAEP was criticized for lack of motivational and mobilization approach and its primary dependence on paid workers. In the absence of a serious effort to involve the community, the task of starting and sustaining AEC thus became a 'job' to be performed by a hierarchy of salaried employees. This was inherently a difficult situation, and, in many cases, the young and poorly paid instructor was unable to mobilize enough local support and participation to ensure enrolment and retention of adult learners at the AEC. Its strategy was based on the mistaken notion that if AECs are open, they will automatically attract adult learners (Athreya & Chunkath, 1996).

TLC: Major Focus on Social Mobilization

Of all the adult education programmes in India, TLC gave the highest priority to motivation and mobilization aspects. TLC has to mobilize not only learners but also volunteers, who have to teach the learners voluntarily, to participate in the literacy programme. The main thrust was on social mobilization with patriotic appeal (Dighe, 2000).

The motivation and mobilization strategy of TLC aimed at the following:

- Mobilizing public opinion for and creating community participation in literacy efforts
- Sensitizing the educated sections of society so that they participate as volunteer instructors
- Mobilizing learners as individuals and as a group to demand literacy for themselves and their children
- Enthusing teachers to step up efforts to enrol, retain and teach children
- Minimizing dropouts from among the cadre of volunteer-instructors and learners

In TLC, all kinds of media and art forms were utilized for dissemination of the message that literacy is the foundation for the development of society. Many of the tools of social mobilization discussed above were used in the campaigns. The two main methods used are (a) direct contact forms such as *padayatras* (walks), kala jathas, *kala melas* (art fairs), group songs, *nukkad nataks* (street plays) and (b) publicity using various print and visual media such as posters, banners, hoardings, wall writings, cinema slides and newspaper articles. The most important tool used for motivation in literacy campaign during the period was kala jatha. The kala jatha is an exciting form of street theatre. It is a simple form of drama. The teams were trained before they set out for kala jatha, mostly by BGVS. They presented the themes in a powerful manner.

As a policy, TLC envisaged community mobilization and people's participation through village-level committees constituted as a part of the campaign. They had to assume ownership of the campaign at village/community level. The committees constituted on an ad hoc basis by the local administration under the leadership of village president with the involvement of different sections of population, development functionaries and local activists. Although the nominated committees as a whole did not function effectively, activists using the name of the committees did extremely good work in TLC.

The main criticism of TLC strategy was that though the strategy succeeded in creating a positive climate in society for literacy, it failed to focus on individual learners and was weak in sustaining learners' motivation over a period of time. In the critics' view, TLCs were more 'campaigns for literacy' than 'literacy campaigns' (Mathew & Rao, 1994). Further, TLC was envisaged as a short duration campaign and did not give importance to long-term sustainability and community ownership of the programme over a period of time.

Saakshar Bharat

SB has some characters of a selective approach similar to NAEP and some features of mass campaign of TLC as well. It depended on the paid workers—village coordinators (*preraks*)—to motivate the non-literates and volunteers. At the same time, however, provision is made for awareness and publicity campaigns for social mobilization, but the scale of these activities is restricted because of the limited funding for motivation and mobilization activities. Wall writings, public meetings and cultural activities are conducted in specific areas to motivate and mobilize non-literates and volunteers. The main thrust remained on individual motivation.

SB identified low community participation as one of the main weaknesses of earlier literacy programmes and in order to overcome the problem of low community participation, it envisaged involvement of PRIs through committees constituted at village, mandal and district levels. The Gram Panchayat Lok Shiksha Samiti at the village level, Mandal Lok Shiksha Samiti at the mandal level and Zilla Lok Shiksha Samiti at the district level are headed by the chairpersons of local PRIs at respective levels. The responsibility of the implementation of the programme has been entrusted to these committees along with necessary funds and powers. The effectiveness of this strategy is questioned by many field functionaries. They argue that the involvement of PRIs in SB is very limited. One reason for the lacklustre response for this model is that panchayat-level committees are constituted by the government with fixed categories of people headed by village president, and it has not evolved at the village level. Being an ad hoc committee like the TLC, it neither belongs to the local body nor is it an institution by itself.

DISCUSSION ON MOTIVATION AND MOBILIZATION IN ADULT LITERACY

If we look at motivational strategies in major adult education programmes in India, we find that each of them focused either on individual motivational strategy or on social mobilization strategy. Although they are different in their approach, we observe that they have some common underlying assumptions at the field level, which are discussed below.

Motivation Is an Easy and Simple Job

A common assumption, mainly in the state perspective, is that motivating a non-literate to join literacy class is an easy and simple job. Any educated person by interacting with non-literates and telling them the importance of literacy can convince and motivate them to participate in a literacy programme. Volunteers, mostly high school students, who are not even adults in the true sense, can also motivate the adults to participate in the programme. The basic assumption is that non-literates by virtue of being illiterate are ignorant and do not know the benefits of literacy. Once somebody tells them, they realize the value of literacy and attend the literacy class. Further, it is believed that the non-literates are different and afraid of change, and if confidence is created in them, they certainly would participate in the literacy programme.

In reality, however, this assumption is not valid. Motivation is not a simple task; it is a complex phenomenon that requires a multidimensional approach. It is not correct to say that learners do not know the benefits of literacy. In fact, they know the benefits of literacy or at least the disadvantages of being illiterate better than school-educated persons. They faced the problems of illiteracy in their own life. Motivation is not simply explaining the benefits of literacy or creating or inspiring for it, but removing the bottlenecks in attending literacy classes. Intention is not sufficient to make this happen. A support system has to be created for each learner as has been done in the case of family planning. Many eligible couples may have the intention to undergo family planning operation, but they are hesitant to go to the doctor. Therefore, a system is created wherein the local paramedical worker or volunteer will personally take the person to the doctor and help him in getting operated. This kind of system is needed for literacy.

UNIFORM NEEDS AND INTERESTS OF LEARNERS

Another assumption while planning motivational strategy is that all the learners have similar needs and interests and the same outlook. This assumption is more predominant in TLC. It is believed that mass media campaign invariably leads to the motivation of learners, and the same motivational strategy applies to all adult learners. However, we know for sure that each individual is unique, although, at the same time, he is a member of a group. Each person has his own needs and interests as an individual and as a group member. These needs and interests have to be satisfied to motivate him to perform a task. For this, we need action in both individual and social spaces. These two are very important because creating social pressure and conducive environment is as important as motivating persons at a personal level. For this, individual motivation and social mobilization are necessary. Some programmes, such as AIDS control, water and sanitation, have designed well-conceived motivational plans for different categories of clientele. Such a strategy has not been evolved for literacy programmes.

SUSTAINABILITY OF MOTIVATION

Another critical area in adult literacy is sustaining motivation. In major literacy campaigns, motivational campaign was taken up as a single shot dose although the policy papers emphasize the importance of continuous motivation. It is believed that once an individual is motivated to attend a literacy class, he will continue to attend classes until he completes the course. It is assumed that other factors such as content and teaching methods have little relevance for motivation.

This assumption is not true in practice. Motivation is not a one-time affair, and it should be continuous. In fact, the literacy class itself should be converted into a motivational institution. Many adults enrol in literacy classes enthusiastically but dropout in one or two months. There are many reasons for this. One is the gap between what they expected at the time of joining the literacy class and what is actually taught in the class through curriculum and content. The other one is the teaching methods followed in the classroom. If the instructors don't follow effective teaching methods, the class would become dull and monotonous, which adults don't like. Further, the learning curve of adults reaches a plateau in one or two months and learning becomes slow. More attention has to be paid to these issues. Besides, activities in the class play a dominant role in motivating learners to attend literacy classes.

BARRIERS OF MOTIVATION

While formulating motivational strategies, not enough importance is given to barriers of motivation in Indian adult education. Researchers (Ahl, 2006) usually categorize three different types of barriers of motivation:

1. Situational barriers that arise from one's situation in life such as lack of time, lack of interest, lack of expected results, etc.
2. Institutional barriers are practices and procedures that hinder participation such as lack of educational opportunities, lack of finance, course timings, etc.
3. Dispositional barriers are attitudes and dispositions towards learning such as insufficient self-confidence, negative early experiences, etc.

These issues have not been given sufficient importance in planning and implementation of the programme. For example, many adults who are over 40 years of age require reading glasses. But nowhere in the policy or planning was this issue discussed while including 35+ age group in SBP. Similarly, other kinds of barriers for motivation are also not taken into consideration in implementation of the programmes.

As Rogers (2004a) rightly pointed out, the area of motivation of adult literacy learning (as with other forms of adult learning) is still under researched. It is of course highly localized, and we need much more localized research into the real aims of those who attend, and also the aspirations of those who do not attend. There are very few research studies in India to identify the reasons for participation or non-participation of potential learners in adult education programmes. Constraints in participation have also not been studied systematically.

GAP BETWEEN POLICY AND IMPLEMENTATION

There is a wide gap between policy and implementation in motivational policies in Indian adult education. The importance of motivation is highlighted in policy documents. But this importance is not reflected in operationalizing the programme at the field level. While launching NLM, the policy document stated that adults participate in literacy programmes if they are already engaged in political action or some socio-economic programmes, and they perceive literacy as a part of the total development process (MHRD, 1988). However, in implementation, no such attempt has been made and only social mobilization using mass media campaign was implemented to motivate the learners. Policy documents made excellent suggestions, but, in reality, the same stereotyped assumptions are made. There is no advocacy policy on literacy.

COMMUNITY MOBILIZATION A NEGLECTED STRATEGY

Community mobilization is an important motivational strategy adopted in many countries in adult literacy and community development projects. This strategy is very effective for people's participation and community ownership of the programme, which are essential for success. But this strategy has not been effectively used in Indian adult education programmes. Formal organizational structures or advisory committees have been constituted to seek community participation. In SB, PRIs have been involved for community mobilization. These kind of formal structures are not able to create a conducive atmosphere for community participation in its true sense. The experiences of some states like Andhra Pradesh, which made innovative efforts in this direction, also failed due to other factors such as the transient nature of the programme. The experience of Andhra Pradesh is presented here to highlight the efforts made and the difficulties encountered in community mobilization in government programmes.

In this connection, it is also relevant to mention some experiences in adopting different motivation and mobilization strategies in West Godavari district to present an overview of the efforts made in government programmes.

EXPERIENCE OF MOTIVATION AND MOBILIZATION IN WEST GODAVARI

The experiences of West Godavari district reveal quite interesting facets of motivation and mobilization. There are three types of experiences in adopting three models of motivational strategies. All the three important strategies, that is, individual motivation, social mobilization and community mobilization, were put into practice in the literacy programmes of the district during a period of 10 years, between 1991 and 2001. Many aspects of the motivational strategy adopted in Akshara Mahila and ASP are similar to TLC, but the way they were planned and linking literacy motivation with the cultural life of the people is innovative and shows how motivation and mobilization strategy evolved locally, understanding the socio-cultural ethos of people would be effective.

SOCIAL MOBILIZATION

Akshara Padayatra (Literacy Walk)

One important aspect of social mobilization in Akshara Mahila and Akshara Sankranti in West Godavari district was a padayatra, conducted between 25 and 31 October 2000 for popularizing the idea of literacy among the public. The idea was mooted during the discussions of the District Literacy Committee, where it was suggested that a major event would be necessary to draw the attention of the public towards the literacy campaign. Kala jathas played such a role during the TLC in the early 1990s. They were not feasible because of the financial limitations of the programme and partial effectiveness in attracting public second time. Therefore, a padayatra to reach out to 200 major villages, covering a total distance of 500 kilometres in the district was planned. It was flagged off by the then education minister, Government of Andhra Pradesh, in the presence of other ministers and Members of Legislative Assembly (MLAs) belonging to the district on 25 October 2000. The padayatra went on non-stop, through day and night, for 9 days, until it returned to its starting point. One vehicle—Literacy Chariot—decorated with items depicting the values of literacy, the disadvantages of illiteracy and the need to become literate, accompanied the padayatra. Cultural troupes performing plays, songs and the traditional art form of Burra Katha, etc., also formed part of the padayatra. The literacy flag leading the padayatra was carried with great honour and respect by the president of the village until he/she handed it over to the president of the next village. The whole thing acquired a religious fervour.

The schedule of Akshara Padayatra was given wide publicity so that advance intimation reached the village about the date and time of the padayatra's arrival. People of the villages through which it passed were asked to receive it and keep the literacy flag high with honour and walk along with the vehicle (Ratham) to their village limits. The flag was to be handed over to the next villagers in a relay fashion. The literates of the village were exhorted to sign in the white cloth bale as a pledge to achieve total literacy. The district collector personally participated in the padayatra in tribal areas two nights from 1:00 AM to 3:00 AM when the participation of the public would normally be poor. This galvanized the entire district administration with officials, from the lowest to highest, participating in it. This motivated the elected representatives including Members of Parliament (MPs), MLAs and Mandal Presidents to participate in the padayatra. Some of them walked 10–15 km in a day. (One minister of the state cabinet, hailing from the district, Mr Kothapalli Subbarayudu, showed me his swollen legs as a result of walking more than 20 km.) People who participated in the padayatra still remember it as a touching event. As the media covering the procession put it, 'In 216 hours in 9 days, the Akshara Padayatra was able to conquer the hearts of hundreds of thousands of people of the district' (*Eenadu*, 20 October 2000).

The padayatra created an extremely positive climate for literacy in the district, and people started talking about it and officials took it as an important programme. The village-level workers and volunteers who took part in the padayatra felt proud when they saw news items of the padayatra in their village.

Creating a Visual Environment: Banners and Slogans

To make literacy activities more visible to sustain the motivation and morale of everyone involved in the programme, literacy environment was created in West Godavari through banners, slogan, wall writings, etc. A festive look was perceived essential, and where the literacy programme was run like a mass campaign, it needed to keep the public support, voluntarism and involvement. Dr A. Mathew, Fellow of the National Institute of Adult Education, New Delhi, who visited the district during that period, was surprised to see literacy banners hanging outside every shop, office and establishment in villages and asked us how we had made it possible to involve so many people. Village-level functionaries of the literacy programme went to every establishment in the village and requested them to display the literacy banner on their shop with the name of the shop. They got literacy banners prepared with blank space below to accommodate the shop's name. Once the shop owner agreed to contribute ₹200 per banner, they got the shop's name painted on the banner and gave it to the shopkeeper. Almost all the shopkeepers willingly took the banners and put them up on their establishments. Interestingly, there was news item about a wine shop in Undi village that had put up a literacy banner. Schools and government offices also contributed for the banners and wall writings. This created much needed visual impact and social pressure for literacy.

Literacy Flags, Badges and Pledges

Another environment-building strategy followed was using literacy flags, badges and pledges. Each mandal prepared badges on Akshara Sankranti, depicting adult literacy logo and the name of the mandal. These were supplied to all the volunteers and primary- and secondary-level motivators. The district-level officers and the nodal officers were given identity cards by the district collector. Wearing badges and identity cards was also useful in reminding them of the task ahead of them. The participants took the pledge before government meetings to re-dedicate themselves to the cause of literacy. The idea was to make the people understand the importance given to literacy by the district administration.

SUSTAINING INDIVIDUAL MOTIVATION

A major problem in many literacy programmes is motivating the individual learner and sustaining it until the completion of the course. This problem has never been addressed properly in any of the adult education programmes in India. The motivational strategy of AMP focused on this issue.

In Akshara Mahila and ASP, we have evolved a strategy to motivate the individual learner to participate in the literacy class. For this, SHGs acted as catalysts. Each group had been requested to take the responsibility of motivating non-literate members of the group. So, group members naturally motivated the non-literates through personal interaction. A series of activities were conducted in the centres to sustain the motivation of the learners. In planning these activities, literacy is linked with the traditions and cultural life. For example, Diwali, the festival of lights, and Ugadi (Gudi Padwa), Telugu New Year, are celebrated in the centres as literacy festival of lights and literacy new year.

Some of the activities include the following:

1. *Akshara Parentam:* The practice of going to the learner's house, applying 'tilak' on her forehead and accompanying her to the literacy class in a traditional procession.
2. *Akshara Kankanam:* Tying bands to the wrist of the learner as is done on Raksha Bandhan. Volunteers and learners tying Akshara Kankanam on each other or village elders, officials and literacy functionaries, and political leaders becoming active participants in the drive was a major event.
3. *Akshara Jyothulu:* Lighting literacy lamps.
4. *Akshara Mehendi:* Painting literacy emblem on the palms.

All these activities were planned keeping in mind the villager's daily routine. These motivational activities made literacy a part of their socio-cultural life. People used to celebrate every festive occasion combining with literacy programme. This attracted the learners to the centres throughout the literacy course.

EXPERIENCE OF COMMUNITY MOBILIZATION IN CONTINUING EDUCATION

This experience is prior to Akshara Mahila and Akshara Sankranti in West Godavari. In 1986, the GoI introduced CEP in the country and

West Godavari was one of the first few districts where the programme was sanctioned. The main aim of CEP was to provide continuing education opportunities to all the neo-literates and school dropouts. As per the plan, NLM would fund the scheme for the first three years and state government would share 50 per cent for the next two years, and it was envisioned that the community would take over the programme after five years. GoI suggested that new organizational structures might be developed at the grassroots level keeping in view the need to provide institutionalized framework for implementation of CEP with the active involvement of people's participatory structures (NLM, 1998). NLM left it to the state governments to work out the modalities of implementation of the scheme.

The then education secretary, Government of Andhra Pradesh, conducted a brainstorming session at the Andhra Pradesh Academy of Rural Development in June 1986 to design a model for the implementation of CEP in the state. He suggested that CEP should be designed in a new model, different from the existing programmes, which should be owned by the community and sustained over a period of time. Then I presented a model that I had seen in a small village, Raghavapuram, in Chintalapudi Mandal in West Godavari district, where they were running a library without any support from the government. During my visit to the literacy centre in the village, I was told that there was a library in the village and people read newspapers and magazines there. As a member of the district library committee, I knew that there was no sanctioned library in the village and wanted to see how they had established one. I went to the old school building where it was located and discussed with the members of the committee. They told me that about 30 people had formed an association and each one was contributing ₹25 per month which comes to ₹750 per month. They had employed one person paying him ₹500 per month and his main job was to go to the Branch Library in Chintalapudi once a week and get books from there, using the cards of the members. He would rotate the books in the village among the members. Newspapers and magazines are bought from the balance amount of ₹250 besides collecting some from local persons and Panchayat office. They told me that they had been successfully running the library for the last one year. I suggested that the same model be adopted in CEP: people running the programme and government supporting it with funds to some extent. In other words, it would be a joint venture of the community and ZSS, which is a government agency. The education secretary and others agreed that this would be the ideal model for the implementation of CEP. Although there were no policy guidelines in the form of government order, the then education secretary, Andhra Pradesh, wrote demi official letters to the Collectors and chairpersons of all ZSSs to adopt this model, which was introduced as the Andhra Pradesh model of CEP.

In this model, it was envisaged that the scheme would be implemented jointly by the government and people in equal partnership. People (neo-literates and other interested persons) would form an association and take up CEP on its own, and the government would provide grant and other technical and administrative support. The government also proposed that people's committees would manage the scheme at the village level and over a period of time, after say five years take over the programme as their own without any financial support from the government. For long-run sustainability, a system of corpus fund was intended to be raised in each Continuing Education Centre (CEC). The committees were asked to deposit this amount in banks on its name for five years and utilize it along with membership collected every year for running the programme after government funding stopped.

The model was implemented in its true spirit in West Godavari. The ZSS with the support of Jatiya Vedika, an NGO headed by Mr D. V. V. S. Varma, and social activists, mainly schoolteachers and college lecturers, made a sincere effort to implement the model. It was thought that in order to make CEP a people-owned programme, a mass awareness campaign would be necessary to motivate the people and mobilize all sections of society. A series of sensitization programmes were conducted first for government officials concerned with the programme and then to resource persons, village coordinators. In the second stage, people's representatives and other opinion leaders were sensitized. Core groups were constituted in each village with people interested in the cause of literacy and social development. Core groups were entrusted with the responsibility of organizing pre-launch activities in the village, such as collection of membership and corpus fund, and formation of association. A campaign was taken up to generate awareness on CEP and people's participation. In each village, one rally was organized with core groups, teachers and students. Village-level conventions were held. Posters depicting the concepts were pasted at important places; pamphlets and brochures related to the programme were widely distributed. To give a special thrust to the scheme, continuing education week was celebrated from 25 to 31 July 1997 in the district. Local newspapers and district editions of main papers carried news items on pre-launch activities of CEP between 10 July 1997 and 15 August 1997. The entire campaign could give momentum to the programme, and the concept of people's participation was disseminated at the village level.

CONVERSION OF MOMENTUM INTO ACTION

The enthusiasm generated by the mass campaign was institutionalized in the following manner:

- Core groups enrolled neo-literates and those interested in further education as members by collecting a membership fee of ₹10. A minimum membership of 250 was prescribed for the formation of Akshara Sangham (AS), an association for literacy. In some villages, membership exceeded 600. On an average, it ranged between 250 and 500. The entire process was completed in a short span of 15 days. Nearly 170,000 people in the district enrolled as members, paying a total of ₹1,700,000.
- The general body of AS elected executive committees consisting of nine members, of whom five were neo-literates and four were women. ZSS only issued guidelines for elections and did not interfere in any manner. Some committees elected sarpanches as presidents, and, in other cases, local leaders were elected. In general, most of the members of the committee were members of core groups and others who are active in membership, enrolment and collections of corpus fund. These committees selected and appointed preraks on their own. ZSS gave only guidelines per selection of preraks and they were designated as ex-officio secretary

to AS which appointed a prerak of their own choice. It has all the components of a people's managed body. CECs were sanctioned to these bodies.

- ASs were asked to raise corpus fund with a minimum of ₹10,000 from the donors in the village. The intention behind the corpus fund was to provide long-term sustainability. It was made clear that AS should not collect the funds from a single donor and name the CEC after any donor. In the first phase, 300 ASs collected ₹10,000 each. But later on, the amount was reduced to ₹3,000 in SC/ST localities. Some ASs collected more than ₹10,000. There are excellent examples of people's innovativeness and initiative in collection of corpus fund. In some villages, ₹100 was collected from each household, and, in some other villages, amount was collected after the sale of paddy at the local market. In some villages, entire amount was donated from common community fund. The amount collected in the entire district totalled ₹60.18 lakh, the highest amount collected for literacy or continuing education anywhere in India. ASs deposited corpus fund and membership fee in local banks. ZSS granted CECs to those ASs that fulfilled all the pre-requisites, that is, enrolment of members, formation of AS and EC, and collection of corpus fund, and applied for the sanction.

POSITIVE INITIATIVES FOR PEOPLE'S MANAGEMENT

Immediately after all the norms were fulfilled, CECs were sanctioned to the ASs. Along with the sanction order, a cheque for ₹6,000 was given to each CEC in the name of the president, AS. This gave tremendous confidence to the committees. The grant amount was kept in a joint account operated by the president, AS, and convener who is a headmaster of the local primary school. Detailed guidelines were given on the management and accounting. This funding and power to incur expenditure, though on selected items, pushed the programme forward and led to local initiatives.

CEC openings were celebrated in a big way in the villages. Ministers, MLAs, MPs and Mandal Presidents were invited, and the entire expenditure for the opening function was met by local people.

Nowhere was any opening function organized by ZSS. Most of the opening ceremonies were published in local newspapers. ASs collected donations for acquiring various items at CECs. Some people donated buildings, sites, equipment, and some others donated books, subscribed to periodicals and newspapers.

All these donations were reported in Akshara Deeksha, a fortnightly magazine brought out by ZSS. This helped in motivating other CECs to take up such activities. Preraks and presidents wrote letters to the magazine about the activities organized at CEC. Such letters are received in huge numbers—on an average, 100 per fortnight. Most of the letters are published in brief. A glance at the broadsheet over this period reflects the enthusiasm and vibrancy of CECs during this period.

With all this, a positive climate for people's participation was created and all the ingredients for people's management are also provided, even though there are some regulatory and administrative controls in the implementation of the programme.

SLOWING DOWN OF THE PROCESS

Local initiatives cannot sustain for long unless they are supported by necessary inputs at every stage. Simultaneously, the government should relax its control to make people's committees more autonomous. As expected, CECs were not able to rise to their full potential. One contributing factor for this was the release of partial grant. Initially, the government had promised that it would give ₹20,000 in the first year and ₹10,000 each year as per the funding pattern of GoI. But, when it came to actual releases, only one half of the first-year grant was released. This in turn resulted in limited grant for infrastructure. Proper atmosphere cannot be created at CEC with incomplete infrastructure, which was actually limited to purchasing one rack at a cost of ₹3,000. No other facilities were provided as promised because of the partial grant.

Other contributing factor for the decrease in interest is the small number of books available in CECs. People expected that CEC would evolve into a library and information centre, as detailed in the scheme of continuing education. But, in reality, very few booklets published by SRC and ZSSs were kept in the centres. Because of the restrictions that only SRC and ZSS books have to be purchased, purchase of other books was not allowed. Limited number of books at CECs has made them unattractive to those interested in reading.

Skill development and other target-specific programmes propagated as the major activity of CEP, as proposed in CEP document, could not materialize due to lack of budget provision at the CEC level. Women's groups that mobilized for formation of ASs got disillusioned.

In 1998, the Government of Andhra Pradesh passed a legislation called the Andhra Pradesh School Education (Community Participation) Act, 1998, constituting school committees by election from among the stakeholders. The Act defines CEC as a school and accordingly elections were conducted to all the CECs by the education department along with schools. According to the Act, the school committee consists of four members, including the president. Of them, two should be women and one from the SC/ST community. Earlier bodies, that is, executive committees of AS, formed with nine members on voluntary basis were dismantled and new bodies constituted statutorily.

These official bodies have limited representation and there was no place for those activists, who voluntarily worked for the establishment of CECs in official committees. Naturally, they distanced themselves. A voluntary informal group essential for people's participation in the non-formal sector has been replaced by officially elected statutory bodies.

These factors contributed to the process of transition from voluntary people-owned and managed programme supported by government towards government-administered and structured programme with people's participation. Instead of strengthening the people's confidence in their management, this transition created doubts about the future of CEP and the role of ASs.

Non-release of grants by NLM to ZSS and in turn from ZSS to CECs, even after two and a half years, has further curtailed the activities of CECs. The meagre funds available were sufficient only to meet prerak's salary and payment to newspapers. All other activities that involve financial commitment have become impracticable. Delays in the release of grants over a long period and limited activities at CECs disappointed committees, and members stopped taking any interest in CEC activities. Finally, the GoI closed the programme permanently from September 2009.

In planning social programmes like CEP, the sponsoring agency should have a clear-cut idea about the role of people in people-owned programmes. If they want to design such a programme, it should be done in such a way that necessary inputs are provided in time to sustain the people's interest. Centralized top-down approach is not suitable for people management. Administration should play the facilitator's role. Only then is the people's participation possible. Any attempt to infuse people's participation in a government-managed, centrally structured programme would be futile.

From our experience, we can say that if a sincere effort is made, it is possible to succeed in short-term social mobilization activities in the government sector. But it is very difficult to succeed in long-term community mobilization activities which require sustained government support, both at the policy level and resource level.

Even though everybody, who worked in adult literacy, agrees that motivation of non-literates to attend literacy classes is one of the most difficult tasks, the issue has not been given the importance it deserves in literacy programmes. A clear-cut motivation and mobilization strategy has not been evolved in India. Indian adult education mainly followed two approaches for motivation: one is individual motivation and the other is social mobilization. Each programme focused on one or the other. In fact, adult education requires all the three approaches. Sustaining motivation to continue their education beyond literacy during PL&CE phases is yet another major issue. This will be discussed in the next chapter.

Post-literacy and Continuing Education

6

As mentioned in the previous chapter, the CECs were established through community participation, and each centre conducted a number of activities. I visited one such centre in Ballipadu village of Palakollu mandal in West Godavari district in 1987. The CEC, located in a spacious building donated by the villagers, was bustling with activities: a lecture was going on, and some people were sitting in the hall and quite a few were standing outside. I inquired what was happening there. They said that a lecture on chicken diseases prevalent in that area was going on and that vaccination of chicken had been organized. I went inside and saw a retired veterinary doctor addressing a gathering of about 50 people on various diseases of chickens, and the precautions to be taken. A lively discussion was taking place, and the participants were asking him questions on why chicken diseases had become widespread this time of the year. They also distributed a pamphlet published by the animal husbandry department to the participants. After the meeting, one person wrote the names of the persons who had brought chickens for vaccination and collected from them ₹5 for an injection. About 100 got their chickens vaccinated on that particular day. It was one of the best activities in a CEC which attracted people because it has activity and awareness components. The Ballipadu CEC was one of the first CECs started in West Godavari with community participation. A village committee was constituted to maintain the CEC. About ₹20,000 was collected as corpus fund and a building was allotted—the old panchayat office, which was renovated. A number of villagers donated furniture and books to the centre. Since the village did not have a library, they made the CEC a library-cum-reading room and organized many activities inviting locally available resource persons.

On 1 October 2009, a report appeared in the newspapers that CEP in Andhra Pradesh had been closed with effect from 30 September. All the 20,000-odd CECs functioning in Andhra Pradesh for more than a decade were permanently closed. The CEP, which has been started as a people's programme with active involvement of stakeholders and village committees, ended abruptly. The newspaper report said that the CEP had been closed because GoI was going to launch a new literacy programme called 'Saakshar Bharat'. All those people, activists and local leaders, who had worked for the establishment of CECs and making them people's institutions with community mobilizations, were very upset and felt let down by the announcement.

This is not the first time that PL&CE were closed abruptly. In the 1980s, the post-literacy programme, started as a part of NAEP, was closed before NLM was launched. After a gap of nearly a decade, in the early 1990s, CEP was launched in the districts where TLC and post-literacy programmes had been completed. This programme was closed before launching SB. Although SB is confined to low-literacy districts, the CEP was closed in all the districts where it had been in operation.

Why is this happening? What is PL&CE and why is it important to have these programmes as a part of the literacy mission? What are the perspectives of PL&CE and how were these programmes implemented in India? Before discussing the policy issues of post-literacy programmes, let us discuss some of the basic concepts of PL&CE at the international level.

WHY POST-LITERACY

Forgetfulness is a common problem all human beings face if they don't use whatever they have learnt. So is the case with literacy. Relapse into illiteracy, that is, the loss of the ability to read and write, resulting from a lack of practice and insufficient upkeep, is one of the most serious threats to literacy anywhere. It is a threat for two reasons: first, it is very widespread and affects a significant portion of the benefits of literacy, and, second, it leaves the victims more destitute and less motivated. In view of the damage caused by relapse into illiteracy, Dumont (1990) argues that there is no doubt that literacy limited to the basic mechanics of reading, writing and arithmetic, with no follow-up could prove to be globally more harmful than useful, and that literacy and post-literacy form an indissociable whole.

A number of studies on the regression of literacy skills shows that there is considerable relapse among the neo-literates after a gap. An analysis of adult literacy in 21 countries in sub-Saharan Africa (Carlsen, 2010) showed that 22–24-year olds with five years of education had a 40 per cent probability of being illiterate. People with seven years of education had a 20 per cent chance of becoming illiterate. These figures point not just to an enormous waste of human potential and restricted opportunity but also to a failure of investment in education to deliver results. This is much more severe in adult literacy where the duration of the course is very short, sometimes as low as 100 days, and the regression of literacy is faster. The joke in the field is that people who acquire literacy in 100 days relapse into illiteracy in 100 days. The solution is systematic post-literacy and follow-up programmes.

POST-LITERACY

The term 'post-literacy' has come to have different meanings in various educational systems. In some countries, the term is used loosely to include all forms of education that follow after the achievement of basic literacy. In some other countries, post-literacy is defined more narrowly to simply consolidate basic literacy skills to a level equivalent to the completion of formal primary school. In this definition, post-literacy is considered as a 'bridge' between primary schooling or its equivalent and further study.

According to UNESCO (1993a), the word 'post-literacy' suggests all the means and activities that allow persons who have recently become literate to make use of their skills and to increase and deepen the knowledge acquired, after literacy. Post-literacy programmes are defined as 'programmes which aim to maintain and enhance basic literacy, numeracy and problem-solving skills, giving individuals sufficient general basic work skills enabling them to function effectively in their societies' (UNESCO, 1993a, p. 6).

The broad aim of post-literacy programmes is to consolidate the basic literacy skills of speaking, reading, writing, numeracy and problem-solving while, at the same time, overtly or covertly transforming the learner into an educated 'whole person' who is a productive socio-economic asset to the community—able to participate actively and productively in nation's process of development (UNESCO, 1993b).

Different models of post-literacy are followed in different countries, some of them are run as independent programmes and some are integrated with literacy or continuing education. Similarly, different programmes within a country followed different approaches for post-literacy, depending upon the objectives of the programme and the context in which it is implemented. Whatever the usage, post-literacy is closely linked to continuing education.

CONTINUING EDUCATION

UNESCO and some international agencies view 'post-literacy' as a type of continuing education. Some countries consider continuing education a separate phase after post-literacy. Even within a single country, various programmes, academicians and literacy activists have their own understanding of continuing education. It is difficult to define the concept of continuing education because of its sheer complexity and contextual specificity. Each country understands the concept based on its own vision and indigenous requirements. There are two primary reasons for this multiplicity of views. The first can be called normative, in as much as the area of continuing education is inchoate. The second is formal, in the sense that the content and style of the programme is determined by the context of its implementation (NLM, 1998).

Continuing education goes beyond post-literacy. In continuing education, human resource development becomes the focus of attention. Thus, it is also an essential extension of literacy to promote human resource development. Continuing education is defined as a 'broad concept which includes all of the learning opportunities all people want or need outside of basic literacy education and primary education' (UNESCO, 1993a, p. 2). The definition implies the following:

1. Continuing education is for literate youth and adults.
2. It is responsive to needs and wants.
3. It can include experiences provided by the formal, non-formal and informal education sub-sector.
4. It is defined in terms of "opportunity" to engage in lifelong learning after the conclusion of primary schooling or its equivalent.

There are different types of CEPs based on the objectives, activities and clientele.

TYPES OF CONTINUING EDUCATION PROGRAMMES

UNESCO (1993a) classified six categories of continuing education activities according to their aims.

1. *Post-literacy programmes:* These aim to maintain and enhance basic literacy, numeracy and problem-solving skills, giving individuals sufficient general basic work skills enabling them to function effectively in their societies.
2. *Equivalency programmes:* These are designed as alternative education programmes equivalent to existing formal general or vocational education.
3. *Income-generating programmes:* These help the participants acquire or upgrade vocational skills and enable them to conduct income-generating activities.
4. *Quality of life improvement programmes:* These aim to equip learners and the community with that essential knowledge, attitudes, values and skills to enable them to improve the quality of life as individuals and as members of the community.
5. *Individual interest promotion programmes:* These provide opportunity for individuals to participate in and learn about their chosen social, cultural, spiritual, health, physical and artistic interests.
6. *Future-oriented programmes:* These give workers, professionals, regional and national community leaders, villagers, businessmen and planners new skills, knowledge and techniques to adapt themselves and their organizations to growing social and technological changes.

Continuing education is often confused with lifelong education and lifelong learning. In most of the adult education literature, these terms are used synonymously.

LIFELONG EDUCATION AND LIFELONG LEARNING

The difference between continuing education, lifelong education and lifelong learning should be understood, as there is considerable confusion and overlap between these different terms. Continuing education is post-initial education, but that is not synonymous with lifelong education. Lifelong education, mainly promoted by UNESCO, views education as lifelong process—begins in childhood and continues throughout the lifespan. Dave (1976, p. 34) regarded lifelong education as 'a process of accomplishing personal, social and professional development throughout the lifespan of individuals and collectives'. Lifelong education does not distinguish between initial and post-initial education, whereas continuing education refers only to the latter part of lifelong education.

The term 'lifelong learning' is used to refer to lifelong education in learner perspective. Both, lifelong education and lifelong learning, can be understood as individual processes which continue throughout life that includes all forms of education—formal, non-formal and informal. However, there is a subtle difference between these two concepts. Lifelong education broadly focuses on the supply side of learning, that is, learning opportunity and accessibility whereas in lifelong learning, the main thrust is on the demand side and combines individual learning and institutionalized learning. As pointed out by Torres (2002), between lifelong education and lifelong learning, there are typical tensions between supply and demand, the social and the individual, institutionalized form of learning and more open form of learning, right versus opportunity.

Lifelong education is seen as a mechanism for establishing a learning society. The idea of learning society was first advanced by UNESCO in its famous report *Learning to Be* (Faure et al., 1972). According to this report, a learning society is one in which all agencies of a society are education providers, not just those whose primary responsibility is education (for example, schools, colleges, etc.). For example, while the primary responsibility of a factory is not education but the manufacturing of goods, it can and should have an educational role as well. It can provide training for its employees and educate the general public about its processes and products, its environmental policies and its societal contributions. Another aspect of a learning society is that all citizens should be engaged in learning, taking full advantage of the opportunities provided by a learning society.

Let us see how these concepts are adopted in Indian adult education.

PL&CE IN INDIA

The concept of post-literacy has entered adult education rather late. Although almost every important policy document since the 1930s mentions the necessity of post-literacy and follow-up, most do not seem to have spelt it out with clarity. The Kothari Commission, which made the strongest plea for taking up a massive, nationwide programme for tackling illiteracy, suggested effective PL&CE. It further stated that the follow-up programme should not be different from a literacy programme. The essential elements of the 'follow-up' work should be in-built in the literacy programme itself (GoI, 1966).

Different literacy programmes in India adopted different policies and models of PL&CE. The distinction between PL&CE is rather vague. Some viewed these two as integrated programmes while some others considered them as separate programmes. So, the two concepts are discussed together.

It was the recommendations of the committee under the chairmanship of J. P. Naik that gave a concrete shape to the post-literacy in post-Independence period. The report mentioned that neglect of post-literacy and follow-up programmes can be perilous (Ministry of Education and Social Welfare, 1979). It suggested concrete steps to strengthen post-literacy and follow-up. It laid down detailed guidelines and pointed out that it would not be realistic to indicate a common system of post-literacy and follow-up programme for all parts of the country. How these programmes are implemented in India is discussed hereunder.

NATIONAL ADULT EDUCATION PROGRAMME

Post-literacy was first introduced in 1981 as a part of NAEP. Of the total NAEP's financial outlay, 20 per cent is set apart for this programme. It aims at consolidating the skills in literacy, functionality and social awareness acquired through the adult education programme. GoI gave flexibility to the states to adopt any of the six possible models for organization of post-literacy activities as recommended by the J. P. Naik Committee on post-literacy and follow-up programmes. These models are as follows:

- Model 1: Village CEC
- Model 2: Continuing Education at the AEC
- Model 3: Mobile Library and Continuing Education
- Model 4: Diversification of Existing Village Libraries
- Model 5: Need-based Continuing Education Courses
- Model 6: Follow-up Activities through Students

The first two models provide for guided learning in regular CECs. Through the third model, the learners are provided with reading material in their homes. The fourth model recommends the opening of adult education sections in the rural libraries. Model 5 offers the opportunities to prepare for certificate courses for grades V–VIII, and also need-based short-term courses. The sixth model is meant for adoption by the student community, and it visualizes a reading material service catering twice a month to the learners at their home.

Many states have adopted the first three models. Andhra Pradesh is one such state, where Models 1 and 3 were adopted in state and Central projects respectively. In the first model, a local educated person looked after the activities of the CEC on a part-time basis. For this, she/he got a monthly allowance of ₹20–30. The activities of the centre include reinforcement of literacy skills, running the library and motivating adults to appear in examinations of the formal education system. In Model 2, continuing education activities were organized through the instructor of an AEC for persons who have completed literacy training in the preceding course. For this, he got an additional allowance of ₹10 per month, besides the normal honorarium of ₹50 per month for running the literacy course. In the third model, books, periodicals and newspapers were made available to the learners as a means of continuing education. The mode of operation was to appoint mobile library instructors and put them in charge of supplying books, periodicals, etc., to neo-literates in 10–15 villages. The instructors were provided with bicycles and containers to carry the books and were paid an honorarium of ₹300 per month.

The duration of post-literacy programme in NAEP was two years. In the first phase of post-literacy, that is, the second year of the adult education programme, graded textual material was provided to the learners for a guided study with the help of an instructor. It was specifically aimed at remediation, retention and continuation of literacy and basic education. In the second phase, the learners were provided with a variety of supplementary reading material, the thematic and linguistic contents. These were expected to provide a smooth transition to general reading material available in the open market and libraries. However, in 1985, the duration of basic literacy, post-literacy and follow-up programmes from 350, 150 and 100 hours over a period of 3 years was changed to 8 months of basic literacy plus 4 months of post-literacy and 1 year of follow-up, which reduced the total period of 3 years to 2 years, keeping intact the total duration of 600 hours. This has severely affected the functioning of the programme, and further, the programme was closed in 1988 when NLM was launched.

JANA SIKSHAN NILAYAMS

After the introduction of NLM in 1988, the government decided to establish Jana Sikshan Nilayams (JSNs) all over the country in a phased manner. The intention behind establishing them was to institutionalize PL&CE (NLM, 1988). The main objectives of the scheme were as follows:

1. Provision of facilities for retention, continuing education and application of functional literacy
2. Dissemination of information on development programmes, widening and improving participation of traditionally deprived sections of society
3. Creation of awareness about national concerns such as national integration, conservation and improvement of environment, women's equality, observance of small family norm, etc., and sharing of common problems of the community
4. Improvement of economic conditions and general well-being as well as improvement of productivity
5. Recreation and healthy living

The scheme did not differentiate between PL&CE and established JSN as an institution for both. It provided for the enrolment of not only neo-literates of adult education but also school dropouts, pass outs of primary schools, pass outs of NFE and all the other members of the community so far as group activities and cultural programmes were concerned. The main activities proposed to be conducted by JSN were (a) evening class, (b) library, (c) reading rooms, (d) *charcha mandal* (discussion group), (e) training programmes of short duration, (f) sports and adventure activities, (g) recreation and cultural activities, (i) an information window and (j) a communication centre. The person in charge of running a JSN was called prerak. (The word 'prerak' is intended to connote the idea of a person who acts as a motivator or who inspires others.) The prerak was envisaged as a volunteer who has the time and inclination to serve the community with a spirit of service. He was paid an honorarium of ₹200 per month, not as remuneration for the service rendered but a symbolic honorarium (NLM, 1988). JSNs were closed in the districts where TLC was launched in the early 1990s.

TOTAL LITERACY CAMPAIGNS

PL&CE are two different phases in TLC. Post-literacy programme was sanctioned to the districts which had completed the literacy phase. It was for a period of two years and conducted in a volunteer mode.

During this phase, a course was conducted using a bridge primer, whose transaction duration was 40–50 hours in a period of two years. It was aimed for systematically moving from guided, instructor-dependent learning to more self-guided learning. During the TLC, the post-literacy aspect was very weak and the system proposed to be set up under post-literacy was not established in many districts. After the completion of the post-literacy phase, GoI sanctioned CEP to the TLC districts. However, there was a time lag of 2–5 years in many districts between the post-literacy phase and the continuing education phase.

CONTINUING EDUCATION IN TLC

The scheme of continuing education was launched by the GoI in 1995. An important aim of the programme was to consolidate the literacy acquired during TLC. Continuing education was sanctioned to the districts after TLC and PLP stages of programme were completed. A major concern was to prevent neo-literates and semi-literates from lapsing into illiteracy as the literacy skills acquired during the TLC were often fragile (Chakrabarti, 2012).

The theoretical underpinnings of the continuing education scheme as mentioned in the policy document are (NLM, 1998) as follows:

- Basic literacy, post-literacy and continuing education need not be viewed as totally separate programmes, but should be seen as forming a coherent learning continuum. This means that there should be linkage between basic literacy, post-literacy and continuing education. The three programmes must strive towards a unified programmatic, pedagogic and social perspective.
- The continuing education scheme is intended to establish a responsive, alternative structure for lifelong learning.
- The continuing education scheme should be capable of responding to the needs of all sections of society.
- Learning is not only a function of alphabets but constitutes some aspect of every method of human capacity-building.
- Learning should begin at, and be based on, the existing cultural and technical skills of the people and inculcate a sense of pride in them for their accomplishments.

As per the document, the central aim of the CEP was to ensure a comprehensive range of appropriate and effective opportunities for lifelong learning for all adults everywhere. This means that there should be ready access to all types of continuing education programmes and activities and that these should be locally available. It enables local people to learn either through individually unstructured activities or through activities of local providers. Another idea behind the establishment of CECs was to provide an institutionalized mechanism to enable the neo-literates to retain, improve and apply their basic knowledge and skills for fulfilment of their basic needs and to facilitate continued learning through a self-directed process for improvement of the quality of their life. It should be viewed not just as a place to meet and to learn the basics but as an entry point to the whole system of continuing education, which can cater for the learning needs throughout life.

The beneficiaries include (a) neo-literates who have completed functional literacy/post-literacy courses, (b) school dropouts, (c) pass outs of primary schools and NFE programme and (d) all the members of the community interested in availing opportunities for lifelong learning. Teaching–learning centre for remaining non-literates and neo-literates, including the following:

- Library and reading room
- Venue for group discussion
- Venue for vocational training programmes and skill upgradation
- Venue for extension facility of other development departments
- Promoting sports and cultural activities
- A composite information window
- Serve as a community centre

Target specific functional programmes which includes the following:

- Equivalency programmes
- Income generation programmes
- Quality of life improvement programmes
- Individual interest promotion programmes

As per the guidelines, a CEC should be established in each village to serve around 500–1,000 neo-literates in a population of about

2,000–2,500. It had to be housed in a school building, panchayat ghar or any other public building. About 8–10 CECs would form a cluster, with one of them being designated as a 'nodal CEC'. Each CEC had a part-time motivator designated as prerak who was paid an honorarium of ₹300 per month. The in charge of nodal CEC was a full-time worker who would facilitate networking with other CECs. An amount of ₹20,000 was provided for each CEC to meet the recurring costs. Conceptually, it is a systematic programme for PL&CE, although it has faced many problems in administrative and financial aspects. It is confined to providing mere reading material for neo-literates and no target-specific programme was sanctioned to any of the districts in the country.

CONTINUING EDUCATION IN SAAKSHAR BHARAT

In SBP, literacy and continuing education are made an integral part and a clear mechanism is created to start continuing education activities along with literacy programme in SBP districts. Unlike earlier programmes, it has not separated PL&CE. SB mission has four broad objectives, namely, (a) impart functional literacy and numeracy to non-literate and non-numerate adults, (b) enable the neo-literate adults to continue their learning beyond basic literacy and acquire equivalency to formal educational system, (c) impart non-and neo-literates relevant skill development programmes to improve their earning and living conditions and (d) promote a learning society by providing opportunities to neo-literate adults for continuing education.

CEP in SB is aimed at achieving the fourth objective of the scheme that is establishing a learning society by providing opportunities to neo-literates and other targeted beneficiaries for lifelong learning (MHRD, 2009). Under SB, the CEP has no fixed time frame as in the case of the other three programmes, but is being organized on a continuous basis. The approach is to create a sustainable learning environment so that learners are encouraged to continue with their literary aspirations and take advantage of the programme facilities to satiate their learning appetite.

Lok shiksha kendras (or AECs) would be set up at the gram panchayat level to provide institutional, managerial and resource support to literacy and lifelong education at the grassroots level. One AEC would be set up in a gram panchayat having a population of 5,000. An additional AEC may be set up if the population of gram panchayat is more than 5,000. The AEC would be manned by two paid coordinators (preraks) to be engaged on a contractual basis. AECs would function from buildings provided by the gram panchayat.

DISCUSSION ON PL&CE

Post-literacy programmes in India have numerous problems at different levels—problems at the conceptual level, problems of organization, and problems of pedagogy. There are many underlying assumptions on the activities of PL&CE. They include the following:

1. The perception that literacy is a static concept; once a person becomes literate, he will continue to be literate throughout his life, irrespective usage of literacy skills.
2. Post-literacy is difficult to implement as the needs and interests of neo-literates vary widely and cannot run a common course at this level.
3. PL&CE facilities require permanent kind of institutional arrangements which are not possible in non-formal literacy programmes.
4. Providing PL&CE opportunities are costlier, and literacy programme budgets does not support such provision.
5. It is difficult to measure outcomes in PL&CE programmes as the scope of the programme is wide and divergent.

These undercurrent assumptions played a dominant role in the conceptualization and implementation of PL&CE programmes in India. Some of the problems in PL&CE are discussed below.

Gap between Policy and Implementation

In CEP, the gap between policy and implementation is very wide. Policy documents of PL&CE presented the concepts in clear terms based on international thinking. But in implementation, the concept is limited to the literacy component. For example, in the policy document, the scheme of continuing education proposed a wide range of target-specific programmes to cater to the needs of different clientele groups. But no funds have been sanctioned for target-specific programmes anywhere in the country. The same is the case with SB. Of the four objectives, only two—basic literacy and lifelong learning—have been provided with funds. The other two objectives, that is, equivalency and skill development, have been left out. Only limited funding was provided to equivalency programmes for a few states during the last year of the project in 2016–2017.

Similarly, the policy document highlighted the institutionalization of PL&CE while launching JSNs and the scheme of continuing education. But they were considered temporary and sanctioned as projects with specific period of time. Accordingly, the schemes have been closed after specific period of time. The slogan of long-term sustainability remained on paper and no strategies have been worked out.

Gap between State Perspective and User Perspective

There is a wide hiatus between state and user perspectives in PL&CE. The state perspective looked it as a separate programme different from basic literacy to stabilize and improve the literacy skills of neo-literates and provide opportunities to continue their education and impart other skills beyond basic literacy. It viewed PL&CE short-term programmes to make neo-literates move from guided learning to self-directed learning. But users, that is, neo-literates, did not understand the difference between literacy and PL&CE. For them, both are literacy programmes conducted by instructors. They expected skill trainings to improve their standard of living whether it is literacy or PL&CE. The majority of government programmes such as schools or Anganwadi centres, which the users see in their daily life, are permanent in nature. So, naturally, they expect literacy programmes or PL&CE activities to continue permanently in the village.

Envisioned as Short-Duration Programme

As pointed out by Krishna Kumar (2010), one of the major weaknesses of all our adult education programmes has been the lack of long-term conceptual framework of lifelong and life-wide learning. Most of our literacy programmes have been focused on achieving higher percentages of adult literacy with post-literacy, continuing education and lifelong learning added as afterthoughts or appendages. There has been a lack of clarity about how the literacy achieved would be sustained, strengthened and taken towards the next and most important step of moving towards lifelong learning or achieving a learning society. Literacy is only the foundation, but laying the foundation cannot be the objective.

As discussed earlier, the basic assumption of those who designed PL&CE programmes seems to have been that literacy is a static concept and once a person becomes literate he/she will learn on their own. That is why these programmes have never been given the importance they deserve. Policy-makers and even adult education functionaries have been found to attribute secondary importance to this programme. There is no clarity on the academic activities that are different from literacy phase.

Academic Motivational Problems

Academic work in PL&CE is really very difficult. This phase has to make the neo-literates move from guided learning to self-directed learning. Reaching the learners and supplying reading material is a challenge because of many reasons. One among them is that motivation of the learners in this phase is generally low and they will not show much interest in attending classes that are conducted once or twice a week. Another reason is that the educational goals are too vague. No immediate reward appears to emerge. Learners are more interested in spending time on activities that are useful to them in their day-to-day life than on general education.

According to observers, a weak point is that the neo-literates find the books approved and supplied by the government uninteresting. So much so that the neo-literates seldom borrowed these books on their own. Their needs and interests are diverse and difficult to cater with the small number of books and limited activities. The programme failed to design reading material that is not only interesting and instructive, but also inexpensive. The private sector publishers did not show much interest as they considered the market too small. Besides, they felt that getting government approval was difficult.

Administrative and Monitoring Issues

In this stage, administrative and financial problems are much more severe. After the completion of TLC or a major literacy programme, the administration becomes slack and does not pay as much attention to the programme. In fact, PL&CE requires more attention and close monitoring because of low level of learner motivation and difficulty in implementation. Funding PL&CE programmes is another major problem. PL&CE programmes were never started immediately after the completion of literacy programmes and funds were never released in time. Most of the PL&CE programmes are conducted by paid workers with small honoraria, and non-payment and delayed payment adversely affect the functioning of the programme.

M&E is another complicated issue in PL&CE. No monitoring indicators were developed. One reason for this is an undercurrent feeling that post-literacy need not be as seriously monitored or evaluated as literacy. Some others feel that a continuing phase with no clear end points and a more diverse programme can inherently be much less monitored or evaluated. Monitoring indicators have not been clearly defined in any of the major PL&CE programmes, and data on enrolment and achievement is hard to come by. It is very difficult to monitor the programme in terms of learning outcomes as assessment of learners' progress is not part of programme monitoring. Further, levels of learning and achievement have not been defined for post-literacy or CEP. Since PL&CE are diversified programmes, a single parameter for assessment of learners' progress is not suitable and need a wide range of indicators/parameters of measurement.

NEED FOR LIFELONG/EDUCATION LEARNING PERSPECTIVE

It is amply clear that neither adult literacy in the limited sense of the word nor adult education in its wider sense is achievable within a short span of 1–2 years. It is a long-term project that has to be guided by a clear philosophy and conceptual framework. The old saying that there is no point in formulating an adult literacy programme if one doesn't have a very clear-cut plan for a sustainable CEP is proving absolutely correct (Kumar, 2010). It is high time we move out of the total literacy framework to a comprehensive, inclusive and integrated lifelong learning.

Realizing the importance of equipping people for future and changing needs, many developed countries adopted lifelong learning as a critical component of their educational planning. For instance, the UK released a policy paper 'Learning Age' on how learning throughout life will build human capital by encouraging the acquisition of knowledge and skills and emphasizing creativity and imagination. Lifelong education/learning is much more important in India where more than one-third of the population is non-literate and another one-third is semi-literate or having less than eight years of schooling. There are lifelong learning opportunities for persons who have completed secondary education. Others have very limited scope and opportunities of continuous learning. They need to be provided opportunities for improving their skills and knowledge.

The UNESCO (1993a) concept of lifelong learning is very much relevant in India. Here, lifelong learning means providing every individual with the conditions for learning further, learning continuously for improving his/her lot. Depending upon where one is positioned in the ladder of learning, it may mean different things to different individuals. For a non-literate, it would mean functional literacy combined with a series of learning programmes that would help him improve awareness, capability, skills, confidence and participation. To a farmer, it would mean acquisition of farming and farm management techniques. For a semi-literate rural woman, it may mean the facility to learn a new skill that would enable her to enhance the level of living of her family, or it may mean attending a short course on gender equality which would give her enough confidence to speak out against injustice.

In India, PL&CE has never been given the importance it deserves in sustaining literacy achievements or providing lifelong learning opportunities. Even though policy documents highlighted the importance, the operational guidelines treated it as a short-term project in a state perspective. However, some efforts had been made at field level to conduct various activities under PL&CE. Such experiences in West Godavari district are presented below.

WEST GODAVARI DISTRICT EXPERIENCE

Experience in organizing PL&CE programmes shows that there are two critical elements for effective implementation of continuing education programmes: (a) community ownership and (b) conduct of different types of activities to cater to the needs of different groups of people. As mentioned in the previous chapter, CEP was started in West Godavari district as a community-owned programme and an action plan was prepared to take up various activities under continuing education. Important activities conducted in CECs in West Godavari are as follows:

1. Centre-based activities
2. Family-based activities
3. Publication of broadsheet

CENTRE-BASED ACTIVITIES

The categories of programmes that were conducted in each centre (Table 6.1) are discussed in brief here.

Educational Programmes

Each CEC conducted three types of educational activity. One was organizing library and reading room facilities for the benefit of literate population with special focus on neo-literates and school dropouts. Books and newspapers were provided. Villagers were encouraged to collect books and old magazines from people. Some CECs collected a large number of books and used magazines and kept in the library. Second activity was conduct of a refresher course for semi-literates. This course was conducted occasionally to improve the reading and

Table 6.1 *Activities in Continuing Education Centres in West Godavari District*

Type of Programme	Activity	Target Group	Frequency	Strategy
Educational Programmes	Library and reading room	Literates/ neo-literates	Regular	Newspapers and books for Neo-literates/literates in the villages are provided
	Literacy class	Illiterates	Regular	A literacy class for illiterates
	Refresher course on reading	Semi-literates	Regular for one month	One-month refresher course in reading conducted periodically for semi-literates
Awareness Programmes	Vaaram Vignanam	Villagers	Weekly	Talk-cum-discussions on various development issues by officials of agencies concerned
	Publication of broadsheet	Neo-literates	Fortnightly	A broadsheet is published fortnightly and sent to all CECs
Quality of Life Improvement Programmes	Activity-based packages on food & nutrition, health & sanitation expenditure & savings	Neo-literates	Regular for one month	25 Families have been identified per CEC to monitor the food consumption, health practice and expenditure patterns; necessary inputs depending on individual needs have been provided
Skill Development Programmes	Skill development programme for SHGs	SHGs	Regular	Education/training requirements of SHGs like DWCRA, thrift group, etc., taken up in CECs
Recreational Programmes	Provides facilities and organizing games	Villagers	Regular	Games and sports material is provided in CECs; villagers play games; (mainly indoor); material for cultural activities is provided
	Conducting competitions in cultural items	Villagers	Festivals and important national days	Encourage display by organizing competitions on important days

Source: PGAS (1998).

writing skills of semi-literates. It was the first of its kind in India as no other literacy programme ever recognized semi-literacy as a category. A separate primer was designed for this course conducted for a period of one month.

Awareness Programmes

An awareness programme was conducted once a week or fortnight in each CEC on current topics relevant to the people. The list of topics that could be covered in these programmes was circulated in advance by ZSS through broadsheet. Sometimes, material on the topic, such as pamphlets or booklets published by the agencies dealing with the subject, was sent to the centres along with the broadsheet. CEC can take up the same topic or any other topic they think relevant to their context. They have to identify a resource person from the village or mandal and arrange talk-cum-discussion sessions. All these activities were published in Akshara Deeksha magazine, a fortnightly broad-sheet brought out by the ZSS. This helped in motivating other CECs to take up such activities. Preraks and presidents of ASs wrote letters to the magazine on the activities organized at the CEC. Such letters were received in large numbers—on an average 100 per fortnight. Most of the letters were published in brief. A glance at the broadsheet published during this period reflects the enthusiasm and vibrancy of CECs.

Quality of Life Improvement Programmes

Quality of life improvement programmes aim to equip learners and the community with that essential knowledge, attitudes, values and skills to enable them to improve quality of life as individuals and as members of the community. Activity-based packages (questionnaires and activities) were developed on food and nutrition, water and sanitation, savings, etc. Some agencies like Rajiv Gandhi National Drinking Water Mission and the health and family welfare depart-ment supported these programme as part of their IEC activities which are coordinated by the ZSS. In this activity, blank schedules (called interactive schedules) are given to the neo-literates and semi-literates to fill the schedules about their behaviour patterns. It not only gave information on the topics but also improved the reading habit. Besides this, various activities like giving water testing kits, nutrition charts, etc., were conducted. The change in the behaviour pattern was monitored using the filled-up schedules.

Skill Development/Income Generation Programmes

Training programmes on skill development and income generation programmes were conducted for different clientele groups based on their needs and interests. WSHGs formed under the DWCRA scheme actively participated in these programmes. Short-duration trainings such as surf- and detergent-making, candle-making, phenyl-making were conducted by the adult education staff who were trained as resource persons. Information on various trainings conducted by the DRDA and other NGOs was given through broadsheet and interested persons are recommended for these courses conducted at the district or mandal level.

Recreational Programmes

Two kinds of activities were conducted under this category. One was sports and games. Sports and games material was provided to CECs. This activity, especially indoor games like caroms and chess, attracted a large number of people to the centres. When coming to the centre, they also read or took books home. Competitions were conducted on sports and games on important national days. Similarly, competitions were conducted in songs and other local cultural forms. Response and participation of people was very good in villages where rehearsals were conducted in CEC for cultural activities. Many people interested in cultural items became part of CECs in many villages.

Each CEC committee was asked to conduct at least two programmes every month besides educational programmes that were compulsory for all the centres. Each centre has sent a report on the activities and highlights of these were printed in fortnightly broadsheet published by the ZSS.

Sustaining these activities and searching for innovative activities to generate interest is a major problem in CEP, and West Godavari experience is not different. A dedicated team of people and group of NGOs regularly worked on these issues and identified topics and activities.

FAMILY-BASED ACTIVITIES

One of the innovative activities conducted in the district during CEP was family-based literacy activities. Each centre was asked to identify 50 families in the village that are relatively poor and one of the family members was either illiterate or semi-literate. Each of the two preraks was asked to adopt 25 families and conduct a simple survey of educational, health and economic status. They contacted the families once a month and identified the activities that would help them improve their status. These activities, organized through CEC or some other agency, encouraged family members to participate in them and gave the preraks an opportunity to develop a kind of personal rapport with the families. These families showed lot of interest in health-related and vocational training programmes. This first-of-its kind programme was very interesting. It focused on family literacy instead of just adult literacy. Involvement of these families in overall development motivated them to participate in continuing education activities effectively. It is difficult to assess the impact of the activities on the families, but in three years' period in which it was implemented in 1,000 CECs, about one lakh families had actively involved themselves in the project which covered about five lakh population.

PUBLICATION OF BROADSHEET

One fortnightly broadsheet was published by the West Godavari ZSS for the benefit of neo-literates, Akshara Sangams, preraks and other functionaries of adult education. It had 4–6 pages in A5 size and printed in big type and had separate columns for each of the stakeholders of the programme. Each month, it contained one additional page, covering information on centre-based activities proposed to be conducted in the next month. Activities conducted in the previous month in different centres were published in a separate column. Letters to Editors were printed. It is interesting to note that about 100 letters were received from the public every month on a variety of issues. Another interesting item in the broadsheet was the Question and Answer column, where answers were given to the questions raised by the ASs, preraks and other grassroots functionaries on both academic and administrative issues. The broadsheet got a huge response and successfully ran for more than three years. Even people outside the programme such as NGOs and village panchayats bought this magazine. An amount of ₹200 was collected from such agencies towards the subscription. The expenditure for printing of the broadsheet was met from the recurring cost of CEC grant which was deducted from the grant to be released to the CECs with the knowledge of the committees. With the non-release of funds from GoI, running of the broadsheet became difficult and was eventually stopped. The experiences of West Godavari show that it is possible to conduct a wide variety of activities in CECs even with community support and regular resources from the government.

From the discussion, it is clear that PL&CE programmes are looked at as short-term projects and closed with every change in literacy programme. No permanent institutional set-up has been created to sustain literacy and lifelong learning activities at the village level. The programmes are perceived from the state perspective and academic and motivational problems are neglected. They have not been properly monitored and evaluated. This issue of M&E of literacy programmes is the subject matter of the next chapter.

Monitoring and Evaluation

Monthly monitoring meeting or review meeting of functionaries is a common monitoring method used in adult education in India. These meetings take place from the village level to the national level, and the format of the meeting is simple. The senior most officer in the meeting reviews the performance of units by asking for enrolment and achievement data and review from the already compiled data. One such review meeting at the state level was conducted by a senior officer of the state government education department. He started by reviewing the achievement of the previous batch and enrolment in the current batch. When he started rebuking the officers of one district, which had showed 70 per cent achievement, for not achieving one 100 per cent, the officers of other districts started claiming 90–100 per cent achievement. When the officer said that their figures were at variance with the compiled data, they claimed that what had been given to him was old data and all the non-achievers in the previous batch were taught separately and that they had all became literate. The same was the case with enrolment. When the officer asked why all the non-literates could not be enrolled in the current phase, many officers claimed that they had enrolled all of them. The senior officer then stressed the importance of literacy and directed the district officers to achieve total literacy in the districts in the shortest possible period. And the meeting ended in a positive and happy note.

A typical monitoring system in adult literacy programme consists of one or two periodical reports on enrolment, attendance and achievement of the learners at the conclusion of the course. The instructor or volunteer produces this information in the prescribed format and sends it to the higher-ups for analysis, interpretation and utilization at each successive level. The data is rarely validated, and there is always an element of suspicion on its credibility.

In March 2016, I attended a workshop conducted by SRC, Visakhapatnam, on strengthening the monitoring system in SBP. During the discussions, some members pointed out that adult education is a non-formal programme conducted by a volunteer or part-time instructor and so does not require rigid and systematic M&E. It was also argued that it was difficult to build an elaborate database and indicators for adult education as the department does not have the resources or capacity to undertake such a gigantic task. The other assumptions on monitoring are that it is a simple task of reporting and a part of supervision. There is also not much difference between M&E in as much as both report progress in terms of achievements. Of course, some others in the workshop stressed the importance of M&E in adult education. They said credible data is the key to monitoring and eventual success of the programme. Collection of such data is possible only by using participatory monitoring methods involving the community in it. These are some of the dominant perceptions on M&E of literacy programmes in India. We will now discuss some of the concepts and how they are operationalized in the Indian context.

MONITORING

There are many definitions of the term 'monitoring and evaluation' depending on the context in which it is used. Generally, in literacy programmes, monitoring is the process of gathering and analysing data on the process of ongoing programme activities and providing feedback information to the programme managers for taking corrective action if required. It is a systematic attempt to measure (a) the extent to which the programme reaches its intended target population (programme coverage) and (b) the extent to which the services being delivered to match what was intended to be delivered, that is, programme process (UNESCO, 1998).

There is a tendency to equate monitoring with evaluation and to use the two words interchangeably and synonymously. In actuality, these are two different programme components and their conceptual interface is basically in terms of the time frame. The basic difference between monitoring and evaluation, therefore, lies in their purposes— the major function of monitoring is to improve and perfect the implementation of the programme and point out gaps so that the programme managers can address them, while that of evaluation is to assess and judge programme performance. In terms of time frames, both monitoring and evaluation activities are planned before the actual programme implementation. Monitoring work commences simultaneously with the start of the programme, while evaluation work is undertaken at regular intervals sometime after the programme begins, when it ends and/or sometime after its completion (UNESCO, 1998).

M&E BASED ON OBJECTIVES OF THE PROGRAMME

Monitoring and evaluation are clearly linked to the goals and approaches of the programme. Different objectives of the programme require different M&E methods. Further, the underlying concept of literacy upon which the programme is based will require particular methods (McCaffery et al., 2007). For example,

- A skills-based programme may give priority to measuring improvements in the literacy and numeracy skills of the participants.
- A task-based programme may give priority to documenting learners' ability to accomplish tasks, whether these are everyday literacy, work-related or community-related tasks.
- A social practice programme is likely to give priority to how learners engage in their own communities of practice and what changes are taking place in their lives.
- A critical reflection programme is likely give priority to how groups use literacy to analyse and act on issues.

MONITORING PLAN

Designing a monitoring plan before the start of implementation is very important for success of the programme or project. The major elements in monitoring plan are as follows:

- Objectives
- Indicators
- Programme activities to be monitored
- Scheduled implementation period
- Expected activity outputs and dates of completion
- Critical data to be gathered
- Data gathering tools and/or techniques
- Monitors responsible for actual monitoring
- Monitoring dates
- Budget

INDICATORS

Of all the elements of monitoring, indicators are critical for designing monitoring plans. Indicators are useful tools in documenting activities and measuring changes in the programme over time. An indicator is a variable that reflects the efficient and effective performance of a programme. It provides a standard against which to measure changes brought about by programme activities. They are determined on the basis of programme objectives (UNESCO, 1998).

There are various types of monitoring indicators for literacy and CEPs and their categorization depends on their scope and purposes. They depend on the area and the level at which it is operated. The table below shows the broad areas and levels for designing indicators.

A. Area	B. Levels
Contextual data	Individuals
Inputs	Institutions
Processes	Regional/provisional, national and international
Outcomes	

Based on the above categorization, the types of indicators used in programme monitoring are mentioned here.

Qualitative indicators are intended to measure the quality of the input, process and output of the programme. They measure performance relative to some given standards and norms. The term 'quality' can mean different things depending on the context. Here, the term refers to a perceived improvement in the implementation of the literacy programme. Examples of qualitative indicators are as follows:

- Learner/teacher ratio by level
- Classrooms in good condition
- Absenteeism (learners, teachers)
- Use of multimedia teaching aids

Quantitative indicators statistically measure the amount or value of inputs or resources available. The 'quantity' reflects a numerical condition such as the number of learners, teachers, costs, facilities or textbooks at a specified time. Examples of quantitative indicators can include the following:

- Learner enrolment percentage, including females
- Costs/expenditure per learner by level and urban/rural location
- Textbooks by level and urban/rural location

Input indicators are determinants subject to policy manipulation, for example, the characteristics of learners, teachers, curriculum, textbooks, other instructional materials, facilities, equipment, learner capacity for learning and other resources.

Process indicators are determinants that reflect forms of interaction between teachers, learners, administrators, materials and technology. Process indicators refer to the procedures or techniques that determine the transition of inputs into outputs, and are thus important for evaluation.

Output indicators are results or changes readily observable upon completion of a level of education. These indicators mainly refer to student attainment and student achievement, specifically test scores that reflect the value added.

Equity indicators are used to measure the degree to which expenditure for education is provided for the population, regardless of the economic status, place of residence and intellectual capability. These also measure equality of access not only to physical facilities such as schools or learning centres but also to good quality education.

Efficiency indicators are used to monitor the attainment of one of the programme's results at the least possible cost. Cost is basically the expenditure associated with the use of resources such as personnel or equipment. Examples of efficiency indicators are promotion rates, repetition rates, dropout rates, average study time and rate of facilities use.

Outcome indicators are results and effects on individuals and society as a whole that are evident over time as a consequence of education outputs within the socio-economic context. These education outcomes are effects more distant in time after completing education and are usually more dispersed in occurrence than education outputs.

PERSPECTIVES OF MONITORING

There are two kinds of perspectives on monitoring. One is traditional or conventional monitoring and the other one is participatory monitoring. In traditional monitoring, experts measure performance against pre-set indicators, using standardized procedures and tools. Generally, the main focus is on quantitative data which can be analysed and compared at the macro level. Monitoring is considered neutral and value-free as outsiders do it objectively without any bias.

In contrast, participatory monitoring is a process through which stakeholders at various levels engage themselves in monitoring activities, share control over the content, the process and results of the activities (World Bank, n.d.). The key principles of participatory M&E are as follows:

- Local people are active participants, not just a source of information
- Community members evaluate and facilitate the process
- Community members' capacity for analysis and problem-solving is built up

Participatory monitoring mainly relies on qualitative data and indicators identified by the stakeholders. There are various levels of participatory monitoring depending on the level of stakeholders' involvement and the role of outside experts.

EVALUATION

Evaluation is the systematic process of collecting and analysing data in order to determine whether and to what degree the objectives have been or are being achieved. To evaluate is to determine the value of something. Something has value if it is necessary, desirable, useful or important. It is also of value if it can serve a purpose of cause and effect (UNESCO, 1998).

Evaluation aims to examine the project in its entirety—the context, inputs, process, output and outcome—and make recommendations that may lead to the revision of the programme design or replacing it entirely. It may also recommend changes in the future course of action for the programme. It provides dependable evidence for optimal decision-making. It consists of (a) ascertaining the magnitude and attributes of achievements, shortfalls in the achievement of objectives and (b) finding the reasons for these.

There are two basic paradigms of evaluation in literacy (Bhola, 2006). They are (a) rationalistic evaluation and (b) naturalistic evaluation.

Rationalistic Evaluation

Rationalistic paradigm assumes that reality exists 'out there' for anyone to see or experience through the senses. In other words, the rationalistic paradigm emphasizes the explicit—that which is capable of being directly and certainly affirmed. The rationalistic paradigm demands a clear definition of evaluation objectives and of variables, a sampling plan, structured instrumentation that generates quantitative data, statistical techniques in the analysis of data and generalizability of results.

Naturalistic Evaluation

The naturalistic paradigm assumes that the reality does not exist out there for everyone to see and experience in the same way, but that the world is both found (as objective reality) and made (i.e., socially constructed by each individual). The evaluator/researcher seeks to find the meaning people carry within themselves. The naturalistic paradigm suggests that human behaviour be studied as it naturally occurs, in natural settings and within its total context. In other words, the naturalistic paradigm is holistic in its orientation, seeking to study reality as a whole, without dividing it artificially into parts and segments to suit the convenience of the evaluator. Unlike the rationalistic evaluator, the naturalistic evaluator seeks to first describe the phenomena and then search for regularities and patterns. In naturalistic inquiry, the methods used are those of the anthropologist and the ethnographer.

Scope of Evaluation

Various categorizations of evaluation are based on the information needs of the programme. Some common evaluation categories are as follows (Bhola, 1990):

- *Internal and external evaluation:* The distinction between internal and external evaluation is in terms of who conducts the evaluation. In general, *internal evaluation* is conducted by the programme staff themselves. In instances when they use the services of evaluation specialists, they are in control of the process of evaluation, from the planning stage up to the dissemination and use of evaluation results.

  External evaluation is conducted by evaluators who do not belong to the programme. The services of an outside evaluation group are engaged by the programme to help ensure objectivity in evaluation.
- *Formative and summative evaluation:* The concepts of formative and summative evaluation are primarily based on process. Formative evaluation is the evaluation of the programme and its various components in the very process of their formation. The information generated can be used to improve the programme services,

structure, systems, schedule of activities and other elements. The emphasis is on the process.

Summative evaluation is normally designed to 'sum things up'. It is conducted at the end of the programme in order to ascertain whether the objectives have been achieved and its impact on the clients, as well as its cost-effectiveness. The results of summative evaluation provide the basis for the decisions that should be taken by programme planners and managers.

- *Evaluation based on the units of analysis* such as learner evaluation, programme evaluation, group evaluation and community impact evaluation.

MONITORING AND EVALUATION IN INDIAN ADULT EDUCATION

How M&E is viewed in Indian adult education and how different adult education programmes used M&E methods to improve the performance is an important point for analysis. M&E systems followed in major adult education programme in India are discussed in brief here.

National Adult Education Programme

NAEP is the first adult education programme in India to place major emphasis on monitoring, evaluation and research. Recognizing the importance of M&E and research, NAEP document clearly stated,

> A mass education programme, inevitably, faces the risk of considerable wastage and misreporting. In this connection the importance of systematic monitoring cannot be exaggerated. It must permeate the entire programme and provide feedback for introducing necessary correctives from time to time. It is also important to have inbuilt arrangements for applied and coordinated research so that the experience of NAEP is systematically analysed and provides guidelines for future action. (Ministry of Education and Social Welfare, 1978, p. 16)

True to its policy statement, GoI conducted a series of workshops in collaboration with the Council for Social Development to prepare a manual, 'Monitoring in NAEP' in the early 1979. The book covered a wide range of issues concerning M&E of NAEP and presented formats for collection and compilation of data for the monitoring system at different levels. It covered not only the literacy component but functionality and social awareness aspects of the programme at both the conceptual and operational levels. It was really a great contribution to the understanding of monitoring system in multidimensional adult education programme.

At the practical level, monitoring was done at four levels, that is, AEC at the village level, project level, state and national level. At the beginning of the programme in a centre, the adult education organizer would give a report—Instructor's Initial Report—on the number of learners enrolled, their demographic details, venue of the centre, instruction time and teaching and learning material supplied. From then on, s/he was expected to give monthly reports pertaining to details of dropouts, day-to-day functioning of the centre, receipt of honoraria, supervisor's visits to the centres, talk-cum-discussions arranged, syllabus covered and other information and problems relating to the centre. The reports of all the 300 centres in a project were consolidated at the project level and sent to the DAE. In addition to the initial and monthly reports, detailed quarterly and annual reports are sent from the project. These reports consist of details of the number of personnel in the project, teaching and learning material supplied, training and orientation programmes conducted, expenditure incurred, difficulties and problems encountered. These project reports are consolidated at the state level and sent to DAE, GoI, New Delhi.

Internal evaluation was done by the project staff based on the learners' progress. This consists mainly of assessment of learners by supervisors in three stages: after three months, after six months and after eight months of enrolment. One of the problems is the DAE gave only guidelines for the assessment of learners. It is up to the individual supervisors to operationalize the criteria. This resulted in lack of uniformity in the test. Individual projects have not been evaluated. Only macro-level evaluations were conducted by various institutes such as the Tata Institute of Social Sciences, IIM Ahmedabad, Madras Institute of Development Studies and Sardar Patel Institute of Economic & Social Research. They followed a rationalistic paradigm and are focused on the outcomes of the projects. Studies in naturalistic paradigm are very rare.

No doubt that monitoring reports are sent promptly but the contents of the reports are limited to quantitative data. This data was seldom verified by officers. As regards quality, there is no mention at all. Data audit of any kind was hardly ever undertaken. The weakness of monitoring in NAEP was identified by NLM (MHRD, 1988, p. 13), which mentioned, 'Monitoring lacks credibility, there was considerable misreporting'. Monitoring is confined to traditional methods and the main trust of monitoring quantitative parameters included not only literacy but also functionality and awareness aspects of learners' achievements.

Total Literacy Campaign

NLM, which was envisaged based on the strengths and weaknesses of NAEP, discussed the establishment of a detailed monitoring system and computerized management information system (MIS). The policy document mentioned (MHRD, 1988, p. 46) that 'a computerized Management Information System will be instituted to ensure reliable steady flow of information needed for improvement in management at all levels'. It proposed steps for collection of data at various levels and computerization at the district level. It also suggested extensive analysis of data down to the individual learner or instructor.

Even in its inception, NLM envisaged 'concurrent external evaluation and impact studies' to be an integral part of the programme. The mission document proposed that 'institutions of social science research, universities and voluntary organizations will be invited to undertake concurrent data audit and formative as well as summative evaluation'. It also stated that 'impact studies will be undertaken to assess the results of the Mission on incidence of illiteracy, and the extent to which the specific objectives are achieved' (MHRD, 1988, p. 48).

However, the monitoring system of TLC continued in the same model as was done in NAEP. In fact, it was somewhat diluted than

NAEP. Since TLC is a voluntary programme, the reporting of data at the village level was entrusted to the village committees which were constituted for TLC. The main reporting work was done by the conveners of village committees, who are mostly government functionaries at the village level. Most of the monitoring formats developed in NAEP were followed in TLC also. The reporting is mostly confined to the quantitative data of number of volunteers and learners enrolled and some demographic details. So, naturally, the same problems of NAEP such as lack of credibility of data or misreporting continued in TLC.

In terms of evaluation, TLC adopted a better system of internal and external assessment system for evaluation. IPCL primers adopted in TLC had in built assessment tests after three or four lessons in the primer. These are very useful to assess the learner's progress and prepare internal evaluation report. Moreover, detailed guidelines were given during the TLC for conducting internal and external evaluation of the programme. External evaluation of each project by reputed and empanelled academic institutions was mandatory and became the basis for the sanction of PL&CE to the project district. Arun Ghosh Committee, while critical about some of the earlier methods of evaluation, gave further inputs for the improvement of the evaluation system in TLC. However, there was a lot of criticism on the methodology adopted by some of the external agencies and the rate of success given by them to districts. Sometimes these agencies gave high rate of success, much above the internal evaluation which created problems. Most of the external agencies adopted a rationalistic evaluation paradigm and focused on the quantitative data.

MONITORING AND EVALUATION IN SAAKSHAR BHARAT

SB continued the policy of TLCs in regard to M&E. However, more stress was given to the computerization of learner information. The SB document (MHRD, 2009) mentioned that the objective performance parameters would be prescribed for each agency involved in the implementation of the scheme. A web-based MIS would be put in place for real-time monitoring, which would be critical for optimizing the outreach and impact of the programmes. NLMA, state literacy mission authority (SLMA) and district bodies would review the progress at their respective levels. It was proposed to place the name and progress of each learner in the public domain. Monitoring would not be unidirectional but a two-way communication process.

With regard to evaluation the document indicated that high quality evaluations would be carried out to facilitate detailed analysis, including cost-benefit analysis and future planning. Elaborate procedures for concurrent, summative and impact evaluation would be laid down. Literacy data would also be supplemented through field research. Reputed agencies with an impeccable track record, expertise and experience will be commissioned to carry out evaluations. The evaluation process will be a tool of correction through participation. Total openness and transparency will be the watchwords in the entire evaluation process (MHRD, 2009).

WEB-BASED PLANNING AND MONITORING INFORMATION SYSTEM (WePMIS)

For the first time in the Indian adult education programme, online monitoring through Web-based Planning and Monitoring Information System (WePMIS), which was developed by National Informatics Centre (NIC, 2011), was introduced in SBP. The main objective of this system is to monitor physical and financial progress in real time.

The application has been designed to be used by the MHRD, state education department officials (or SLMA), the district panchayats, block-level officials like the BDOs and block pramukhs, gram panchayat officials like the gram pradhan and preraks (coordinators). The relevant data is to be made available in the public domain. The data has to be fed at various levels, mainly at the gram panchayat level. It has all the components of a scheme including microplanning from the grassroots to monitoring at the national level.

Notwithstanding the intentions, the monitoring system in SB continued to be as in the earlier TLC model except uploading data on non-literates and learners on the website created by NLM. The common perception in the field is that computerized monitoring system without providing computers at the block and panchayat levels created more problems in monitoring than improving the effectiveness of the monitoring system. The mission's entire energy is diverted to uploading huge survey data on the website. The village coordinators have been asked to upload the data on the website, but no data input devices have been given to them. Most of these coordinators are not digital-literate and most of the villages have no access to computers. They spent their energies on collecting the information on a written form, going to mandal/taluk/block headquarters or nearest town getting it uploaded with the help of local computer training centres. This to an outsider seems a simple task, but to someone living in a village and travelling many times to get the data converted to digital form is a gigantic task. Further, Internet connectivity in these small towns is very poor and entering huge data online takes a long time and energy for the village-level workers. Entry of huge amounts of data on the website from different parts of the country has made the website very slow and sometimes the website does not open at all. If there is any problem in uploading, the village-level people have to complain to the mandal coordinator who in turn has to send the complaint to different levels until it is sorted out at the national level.

The website maintained at the national level does not provide any monitoring tools at the state or district or block levels, but they can only view the data. It has become unidirectional without any feedback or analysis to the field functionaries. After getting UNESCO King Sejong Literacy Prize in 2013, showcasing the system, NLM abandoned the computerized monitoring system, although this was not officially announced.

MONITORING SYSTEM USING TABLETS: ANDHRA PRADESH EXPERIENCE

After the unofficial closure of web-based monitoring system at the national level or, to put it in a simple way, after the transfer of the key official responsible for the introduction of web-based monitoring system at the national level, the Government of Andhra Pradesh introduced its own online monitoring system. It designed a web portal and an App with twin objectives of (a) providing information on SB and adult education programmes to the public and (b) online monitoring and review of the programme and performance of the functionaries. Thus, the state literacy mission gets first-hand reports directly from the field. It gives both qualitative and quantitative reports in respect of various indicators. It is also helpful in monitoring the visits of various functionaries. Each of the functionaries at mandal, division and district level is provided with 7" tablets along with a 10 GB data card to upload reports and data. This is the first time that tablets or some gadget is provided to the functionaries for monitoring. Two reports—one on AEC and the other on basic literacy—were designed to upload on the tablet. Besides this, one visit report with details and a photo of the centre at the time of visit is to be uploaded from the field itself along with a photo of the centre at the time of visit. Over a period of time, this system also became dysfunctional and manual reports with earlier formats are being used in the monitoring of SBP.

In evaluation of the programme, SB followed TLC system in getting external evaluation of the programme. But, instead of taking district as a unit, as in the case of TLC, it took the state as a unit and got evaluation done by IIM. The same problems that occurred in earlier evaluations continued in SB in terms of approach and methodology.

DISCUSSION ON MONITORING AND EVALUATION IN INDIAN ADULT EDUCATION

As seen from the discussion on M&E in Indian adult education, there are a number of grey areas which have not been addressed properly. This resulted in the monitoring system becoming weak and lacking credibility. Some of the grey areas of M&E are discussed here in brief.

Gap between Policy and Implementation

There is a wide gap between policy and implementation in M&E of literacy programmes in India. Policy documents clearly highlighted the importance of systematic M&E, but, in practice, sufficient importance is not given to M&E. Monitoring framework and indicators have not been developed systematically before launching the programme. Even if they are developed at the national level, they have not been communicated to the field level. Monitoring is considered a simple task of reporting from a lower level to a higher level. Monitoring formats have been supplied to the field functionaries, which they filled and sent to higher levels. The perception that monitoring in adult and NFE did not require systematic monitoring plan pervaded both at the policy level and the field level.

Rationalistic and State Perspective

The entire monitoring is confined to traditional monitoring perspective based on rationalistic perspective. Community-based participatory methods of monitoring and naturalistic evaluations are essential to improve M&E methods in adult education which is a non-formal system of education. But M&E in adult literacy has not given importance to this aspect. Participatory monitoring, involving local beneficiaries in measuring, recording, collecting, processing and communicating information to assist local functionaries and local group members in decision-making, is very much necessary in view of the uniqueness of literacy programmes.

Uniqueness of Adult Literacy Not Considered

The uniqueness of literacy programmes and difficulty in collecting reliable data during functioning of centres in the night have not been recognized in the monitoring system. It is very difficult to verify or validate data as most of the literacy classes are conducted between 7:00 PM and 10:00 PM in rural areas. It is almost impossible for an outsider to go and verify the data during actual functioning of the literacy classes. Further, there is no reliable baseline data on the literacy level of enrolled learners. So, the huge data produced is not considered authentic and credible. Participatory monitoring is effective in such circumstances. But this system has not been adopted in any programme.

Confined to Quantitative Data

M&E in adult education collected only quantitative data based on the monthly periodical reports furnished from the field. Qualitative data has not been given the importance it deserves. The tour diaries and other qualitative reports of field functionaries do not give any clarity on functioning of the centres. Other types of data on inputs and processes are not included in the monitoring system. Unlike formal school education, there is no MIS for adult education in India, and all the data is compiled on an ad hoc basis.

Focused on Literacy Skills

Although Indian literacy programmes always claimed that they adopted the task-based functional literacy concept, the monitoring is mostly confined to skill-based literacy component, and other components such as awareness and functionality are not included in the monitoring system. Further, evaluation focused narrowly on literacy achievement and literacy rates. Other critical aspects of the literacy movement—environment building and its contribution for enrolment of children, especially girls, and neo-literates changed behaviour, paying attention to their children's education, the formation of SHGs, and awareness created against deprivation and the organization on common social issues were set aside from weightage and scores (Rao & Govinda, 2000).

Lack of Credibility

One major problem of M&E system in Indian adult education programmes is lack of credibility of data. NLM itself mentioned this point in its policy documents (MHRD, 1988, 2009). There is no authenticity to internal assessment and evaluation as it is again reported by the same instructor or volunteer who enrolled and conducted the classes. The external evaluation reports are also imbibed with lots of problems. Many of the weaknesses pointed out by the Arun Ghosh Committee have not been sorted out. External evaluation by external agencies is a kind of lottery as it is based on sampling. It is very difficult for the external agencies to get reliable data in the field. In many cases, there is no correlation between external and internal evaluation reports.

UNESCO highlighted the importance of M&E and developed a model MIS for an NFE programme as EFA Global Monitoring System and piloted it in a few countries. The experience of the pilot project conducted by UNESCO in Andhra Pradesh is relevant to the monitoring of adult education programmes in India, although the pilot project was on NFE. The experience is presented here in brief as a model.

EXPERIENCE OF UNESCO PILOT PROJECT IN ANDHRA PRADESH

Between 2004 and 2006, I worked as a coordinator for a UNESCO pilot project of MIS for NFE programmes and also worked as a consultant to UNESCO on the same project. UNESCO took the initiative to establish internationally comparable monitoring information system for NFE to provide feedback on provisions, efficiency and effectiveness of NFE in pursuing EFA goals. As a first step towards building non-formal education management information system (NFEMIS), UNESCO initiated pilot projects in different countries to develop, test and use a normative set of NFE M&E methodologies. The primary objective of this initiative was to build a sound information base to strengthen policies, planning, delivery and management of NFE at all levels. As a part of this exercise, one pilot project has been undertaken in Andhra Pradesh. In the first phase project, prototype developed by the UNESCO was tested in two districts in Andhra Pradesh—Warangal and West Godavari. Based on the experience and deliberations, UNESCO revised the guidelines and tools and developed a handbook and software for NFEMIS.

CONCEPTUAL FRAMEWORK OF NFE

Despite some definitional differences peculiar to the Indian context, the study in Andhra Pradesh, as a starting point, has adapted the conceptual framework of NFE as outlined in the UNESCO prototype, wherein NFE includes any organized, systematic educational activity carried out outside the framework of the formal system to provide selected types of learning to particular subgroups in the population, adults as well as children.

The premises of NFE adopted in Andhra Pradesh are as follows: (a) NFE is planned and provided by diverse governmental and non-governmental agencies, (b) NFE is cross-sectoral—taking place within and between different development sectors and (c) NFE is meant for a wide range of children, youth and adults, from different social and economic backgrounds, who have not had the opportunity to benefit from formal basic education.

DIAGNOSTIC STUDY

As a part of planning, a diagnostic study was conducted in Warangal and West Godavari districts to identify the NFE activities, providing agencies and beneficiaries. The findings emerged from the diagnostic study revealed a very diversified picture (Table 7.1).

It is found that 25–30 agencies are providing NFE at the grassroots level. As far as the monitoring system is concerned, no directory or database for NFE providers is available at the district or lower level. There is also no coordination or exchange of information among the agencies providing NFE. Every agency has its own monitoring and data analysis system, which is hierarchically structured. Government organizations and NGOs have different system of monitoring, and there is no cross flow of data. Most of the government departments have computerized databases. It became evident that all the NFE agencies do collect information regarding their NFE programmes and maintain their database. The data flow is mainly upward and is used mainly to monitor the programmes in relation to its objectives as set up by different agencies. There is very little sharing of the information across different agencies. There is no authentic directory of the different NFE agencies.

One thing that emerged clearly during the study is that there is huge potential for creating a NFEMIS at the district level using the indicators. Indicator development is a complex process having a dynamic

Table 7.1 *NFE Opportunities Identified in the Diagnostic Study Conducted in Andhra Pradesh*

NFE Activity	Provider/Implementing Agency	Beneficiaries
Literacy	–	–
Basic literacy	SG (ZSS)	Non-literates
Post-literacy	CG/SG(ZSS)	Neo-literates
Continuing education[a]	CG (ZSS)	General public
Non-Formal Basic Education for Out of School Children and Youth/Equivalency Schooling		
Alternative education	–	–
Equivalency programme (open school)	CG/SG (open school society)	Out of school children
Bridge schools[a]	CG/SG (DPEP)	Out of school children
Child labour schools[a]	DPEP/NCLP	Out of school children
Training to school committees[a]	DPEP	School committee members
Life Skills/Quality of Life Improvement Training		
Health & hygiene	CG/SG (M&H Dept.)	General public
Family planning	CG/SG (M&H Dept.)	General public
HIV/AIDS prevention education	CG (AIDS control project)	General public
Leadership & management development	CG/SG (NYK, DYWO)	Youth
Environmental conservation	CG/SG (forest Dept.)	General public

(Continued)

Table 7.1 *Continued*

NFE Activity	Provider/Implementing Agency	Beneficiaries
Pre- & post-natal care[a]	CG/SG (WD&CW Dept.)	Pregnant women
Immunization[a]	CG/SG (M&H Dept.)	Infants/children
Sanitation[a]	CG/SG (RWW Dept.)	General public
Individual Promotion Programmes		
Fine arts schools[a]	Fine arts colleges/NGOs	General public
Pre-school Education		
Pre-school education	CG/SG (ICDS Projects)	Children (3–5)
Early childhood education[a]	CG/SG (DPEP)	Children (3–5)
Urban Development[b]		
Trainings to NDCs[a]	CG/SG (municipalities/CBOs)	General public
DWCUA[a]	CG/SG (municipalities/CBOs)	Women
Tribal Development[b]		
Trainings to VTDs[a]	CG/SG (ITDA)	VTD members

Source: DAE (2003b).

Notes: [a]Other sub-categories; [b]Additional main categories; CG: Central Government; SG: State Government relation with monitoring information system. Development of suitable indicator is not possible without an effective monitoring information system whereas systematic monitoring information system is difficult without a correct set of indicators. Taking this into consideration, model indicators have been developed using diagnostic study as reference point. The details of variables and indicators proposed for NFEMIS are given in Annexure 8.

Based on the pilot projects, UNESCO developed a manual and software for monitoring NFE which is available at UNESCO website (http://unesdoc.unesco.org/images/0014/001457/145791e.pdf). But NFEMIS has not been implemented in India because of various reasons. UNESCO expected that the national government would take the lead and implement the monitoring system as it would be beneficial in policy-making at the national level, but NFE dealt with many subjects which do not come under one department or ministry. There is no coordination mechanism to collect and compile data proposed in NFEMIS and no ministry or department took the initiative to establish the monitoring system. So this is another failed story of monitoring system in India.

This kind of effort needs to be done for adult education programmes in India so that convergence between various agencies imparting adult education can be established and an indicator-based monitoring system can give a clear picture of adult education opportunities and progress at the local level.

Overall, M&E in Indian adult education adopted a rationalistic perspective and neglected community-level participatory methods. M&E is considered as a simple issue and equated with reporting. International experiences have not been taken into consideration while designing M&E. No systematic MIS has been established. Effective MIS requires permanent organizational set-up. The types of institutional set-ups created for implementation of literacy programmes in India are discussed in the next chapter.

Delivery Mechanisms

International Literacy Day is celebrated every year on 8 September by the State Literacy Missions. I attended many such functions. Speakers, mostly political executives or policy-makers in bureaucracy, talk at length on the importance of literacy and claim that adult literacy has been given the highest priority in government policy. They speak of grand plans to eradicate adult illiteracy in the next two or three years. After the meetings, it is common to see volunteers or preraks, who either work voluntarily or for small honorarium, mobilized for the meeting, submitting to the chief guest a representation pleading for permanence in the job or enhancement of honoraria. The chief guest or the senior officer present in the meeting says that they would look into the matter and solve their problems shortly. Later in informal discussions, some of the speakers ask how long the adult education programmes would continue. Some of them say that it is unfortunate that adult education programmes are continuing even after 70 years of Independence. It should be temporary for one or two years to improve the literacy rate and be closed. Some question the need for a regular department and permanent staff for adult education programmes. On the other side, volunteers and preraks who have been working for more than a decade are expecting some kind of job security and increase in remuneration. They compare adult education programmes with the Integrated Child Development Services (ICDS). The two programmes started at the same time, but the functionaries of the ICDS programmes are given a different treatment. Village-level functionaries of ICDS got improved service conditions and enhanced remuneration, whereas for adult education functionaries both remained stagnant. They say adult education should be a permanent scheme like school education and there should be better remuneration.

There is constant debate on whether adult education should be temporary or permanent. Who should run the programme—the government or civil society? Should it be planned at the national or local level? Does it require professionals to implement the programme? If so, what type of capacity-building/training is required? These are some of the critical and unresolved issues in adult education. There has been wide debate on these issues at international and national levels, and there is constant tension between various options available for them. Different options are followed in different programmes in different countries, depending on the perspective and context of the programme. Some of the policy options available and options selected in India on each of these areas are discussed here.

INSTITUTIONALIZATION VERSUS AD HOC OR TEMPORARY

A major dilemma in policy discourse of adult education is whether it should be institutionalized or conducted on an ad hoc basis. The decision depends on how adult education is perceived in a particular society. If it is viewed from a lifelong learning perspective, institutional arrangements needed to be made on a permanent and sustained basis. On the other hand, if adult education is viewed as a temporary short-term literacy project, then temporary organizational set-up has to be established.

CENTRALIZATION VERSUS DECENTRALIZATION

Policy on central planning or decentralized planning is very critical for adult education in any country. It also reflects national objectives versus local objectives. Both have advantages and disadvantages. Planning at the national level provides clear leadership at the national level and gives direction to the programme. It becomes part of the national policy-making and facilitates M&E. Contrary to this, planning at the local level gives flexibility in terms of objectives and content of the programme. Effective programmes can be designed based on the needs and interests of the people. It encourages local initiatives and people's participation.

GOVERNMENT VERSUS COMMUNITY

The most important decision on adult education is who should own and run the programme. Is it the government or community or civil society groups and non-government organizations? There are arguments, both in support of government ownership and against it. In most of the developing countries, adult education programmes are owned and run by national governments. In fact, in developing countries, where poverty and illiteracy go hand in hand, governments cannot abandon financial responsibility. On the other hand, community or civil society groups organize adult education programmes in some of the developed countries. Here, resources are mobilized locally, mostly by the community and run by an informal agency.

INSTITUTIONAL LOCATION

In most countries, adult literacy is located within some branch or sub-branch of the Ministry of Education, but there are countries where it is located within a more generalized department or within the Ministry of Labour, Women's Affairs, Social Development and so on. It depends on the national perspective of adult education. If adult education is viewed from the broad perspective of development, it is to be located in the development department rather than the education department. If adult education is viewed as education, then it is to be located in the education department/ministry. Both have advantages and disadvantages as discussed in Chapter 3.

PROFESSIONAL VERSUS PART-TIMERS

A major policy issue that has a great bearing on adult education is appointment of full-time professionals or part-time personnel to implement the programme. It has direct relevance on institutionalization of adult education programmes and is influenced by many factors such as finances earmarked for the programmes. Only institutionalized programmes can recruit full-time professionals to deal with various aspects of adult education. Against this view is the belief that adult education programmes can be implemented by part-time people who are appointed for short duration or deputed to adult education programmes on a temporary basis. Most of the developing countries adopted the latter model in the implementation of adult education programmes.

PERMANENT VERSUS TEMPORARY STAFF

Related to it is employing regular permanent staff or temporary contract employees to run the programme at higher levels. There are arguments in favour of both. Some view that professional full-time staff are essential for effective planning and execution of adult education programme. They will have sufficient theoretical knowledge to understand various options in the programme. On the other hand, some believe that there is no need for regular permanent staff for adult education as it is a temporary programme. Further, they argue that permanent staff will bureaucratize the programme.

PAID WORKERS OR VOLUNTARY WORKERS

Another contentious issue that has a bearing on human resources in adult education is payment of remuneration for the instructor/teachers who conduct literacy classes. Some argue that adult education, especially the literacy programme, has to be conducted as a voluntary programme without financial incentives to the volunteers/instructors. They point out the difficulties in mobilizing large financial resources required for payment to instructors and also in generating commitment through payment. There are two sections within the group who oppose payment. One group opposes because financial resources are limited and the other group opposes payment on moral grounds.

The others advocate some monetary incentive to the instructors because nowadays nobody is willing to work without any benefit. Further, it is difficult to sustain voluntarism over long periods. They assert that there will be no accountability on the part of voluntary workers to complete the course and see that the learners become literate. Moreover, it is very difficult to motivate educated persons for voluntary work in the present times of capitalist and consumerist culture in society.

CAPACITY-BUILDING VERSUS TRAINING

Whether adult education programmes needed capacity-building or training has become a subject of a keen debate. The two terms are often confused and used interchangeably. Capacity-building encompasses a whole range of activities designed to empower individuals and institutions. The basic idea is to improve effectiveness, often both at organizational and individual levels. On the other hand, training is used to refer to teaching a person a particular skill or behaviour. It includes knowledge, skills and attitudes. Training is just one element of capacity-building. It usually focuses on providing skills for a specific problem and benefit individuals without strengthening the capacities of institutions.

In policy-making, it is argued that capacity-building is required for conducting activities or schemes that are permanent in nature and not required or possible for short-term projects or programmes. Since adult education is perceived as a short-term programme, it is believed that capacity-building is not required. Further, capacity-building requires huge human and financial resources which are not available for adult education. Simple training is sufficient to execute adult education programmes. That is why the term capacity-building is not used frequently in the adult education sector. There are two approaches to training of functionaries of adult education. One is the direct method of training where participants are directly trained by the experts/resource persons. The other one is the cascading method of training, where training is conducted at various levels.

Let us examine which one of these options is adopted in Indian adult education with reference to organizational structure, human resources and training for delivery.

ORGANIZATIONAL SET-UP AND
HUMAN RESOURCES IN ADULT EDUCATION IN INDIA

Since Independence, there have been three major models of organizational set-up for adult education in India. One is the direct implementation by the government ministry/department, another is implementation through autonomous agencies specially constituted for this purpose, and the third is implementation through convergence with PRIs. NAEP, TLCs and SB represent the three models respectively. Let us discuss each of them in detail.

National Adult Education Programme

NAEP is the first adult education programme in India, which has institutionalized adult education in the country. The GoI provided leadership at the national level and took joint responsibility with state governments for financing and management of the programme. It identified various agencies and constituted appropriate administrative and managerial structures.

NAEP was implemented in the project mode. A project was an administrative unit responsible for the organization of the programme in a compact and contiguous area with more or less common environmental background and learning needs. The number of centres in a project varied with the organization that implemented the programme. The Rural Functional Literacy Project (RFLP) was a centrally sponsored project, implemented through the state government, consisting of 300 AECs, headed by a project officer, with a supervisor for every 30 AECs. AECs conducted adult education activities and enrolled 30 learners in the 15–35-age group.

Education departments at national and state levels were given the responsibility of implementation. Permanent structures—adult education departments and SRCs—have been established for the implementation of the programme at the state level. A similar structure was created at the district level as well. However, no permanent institutions were established at the village level. The programme was very structured and little flexibility was given at the state or district or project levels. The role of the advisory committees, which were constituted at all levels, involving local elected representatives, was limited to participation in the committee meetings conducted once or twice a year and make suggestions for improvement of the programme.

Human Resources

NAEP recruited full-time staff for programme delivery and academic support. It established regular adult education departments in many states and generated a cadre of adult educators. NAEP also established SRCs for adult education under the NGO sector, and they also recruited many people from universities and created a pool of academicians for adult education. Many of them continue in adult education even now.

Four categories of people worked in NAEP in the government sector. They are (a) policy-makers and administrators at national and state levels, (b) middle-level officers at district and taluk levels, (c) academicians working in university departments and SRCs of adult education and (d) functionaries and instructors at the village level. Of the four categories, the first three were full-time employees, either recruited directly or taken on deputation from various agencies by the state governments. The third category was of academicians working in SRCs. Most of them have good academic qualifications and worked in SRCs run by NGOs on a regular or contract basis. Their service conditions are not as attractive as those of the first category. The last category was of part-time organizers, who received a paltry honorarium of ₹50 per month, which was subsequently enhanced to ₹100. These functionaries were often unemployed youths with varied educational background, ranging from seventh pass to post-graduation.

Training

While planning NAEP, it was envisaged that training of senior-level personnel in the administration, as well as among the implementation agencies, was the responsibility of the DAE, New Delhi. The responsibility of training other functionaries rested with SRCs.

The report of the review committee on NAEP, 1980, spelt out that no instructor should be permitted to start a centre without initial training of at least three weeks. This training should be supplemented by a refresher course of about 10 days after three or four months. The third training programme of two weeks should be organized before the start of the second year and a similar programme each year thereafter.

Compared to the other programmes, training was more systematic and a lot of groundwork was done before the conduct of trainings in NAEP.

The direct method of training was used in imparting training to the field functionaries. Organizers were trained for 21 days in two spells (11 days in the first spell and 10 days in the second spell). The aim of the training programme is to equip the organizer with necessary skills in performing the functions or roles as organizer of the centre, evaluator, teacher of literacy, post-literacy worker, generator of awareness and disseminator of functional information. Training was conducted for all 300 organizers in a project in three camps simultaneously. The training programme gave a lot of importance to the teaching of primers. Resource persons from developmental departments were invited to give lectures on the functional aspects of the programme.

Total Literacy Campaign

In 1988, National Literacy Mission Authority (NLMA) was established as an autonomous nodal agency at the national level, in charge of adult education and joint secretary (adult education) designated as the director general. NLMA consists of a general body and an executive committee, the former headed by the MHRD and the executive committee by the secretary, elementary education and literacy. The counterpart of NLMA at the state level was SLMA, a registered society, headed by chief minister/education minister of the state. NLMA managed all the institutions at state (for example, SRCs) and district levels and took major policy decisions concerning sanction and management of the programmes which are mostly implemented through district agencies. The state government's role was limited to forwarding proposals and review of implementation.

In TLCs, the district was taken as the unit for implementation of the campaign and the GoI directly selected the district based on their preparedness to take up mass campaign. In each TLC, one society is registered, commonly named as ZSS, for organizing the campaign. In most of the states, the district collector/district magistrate headed the ZSS. However, in a few states such as West Bengal, the district panchayat president presided over the body. A ZSS consists of the general council and executive committee with members from different sections of society and officials of different agencies. A team of full-timers assisted the ZSS in implementing the programme. A three-pillared structure was created in TLC for effective implementation.

Village Campaign Committees, consisting of village elders, women, activists, voluntary workers and prospective beneficiaries, were constituted at the village level to organize the campaign. NGOs and community-based organizations (CBOs) were included in these committees. However, the main responsibility of implementation of the programme lay with ZSS.

During the TLC, the programme was regarded as a temporary short-term initiative for one or two years. So, as a matter of policy, neither permanent structures were established nor was any infrastructure created. There was a good deal of decentralization in planning and implementation of the programme. District-level committee, that is, ZSS, played a decision-making role in running the programme. The district collector/magistrate and district administration played a key role and provided all the resources for the programme. Village-level committees facilitated community mobilization and participation.

Human Resources

As TLC was conceived as a short-term single effort, it mobilized a large number of persons from different sectors for implementation of the programme. The services of these people were taken mostly on deputation or secondment, which means that they worked in the literacy programme but their salaries were paid by the parent department or agency. This was possible because autonomous bodies (NLMA and SLMA) were created at national and state levels for implementing the programme. On the suggestion of the GoI, many state governments issued orders for such secondment work for people interested in literacy. Many state governments also wound up adult education departments and used the services of people from other development departments and agencies. SRCs established during NAEP period in the NGO sector continued and provided academic support during TLC.

TLC adopted voluntary approach at the field level. Teaching activity was conducted by the volunteers who worked without any financial incentives. They were motivated by a sense of patriotism. This approach is totally different from the one that was adopted during NAEP under which part-time workers were paid. This has its advantages and disadvantages. This approach enabled the workers to reach more people in a short period. It considered adult education as a simple activity that could be imparted by any individual who has minimum education. All available human resources were mobilized for a specific period and TLC did not consider long-term human resource policy.

Trainings

In TLC, the number of people involved was large, the cascading method of training strategy was adopted for training volunteers, master trainers (MTs) and resource persons. Key resource persons (KRPs) were selected from among interested teachers and trained at the district level. KRPs, in turn, trained MTs at the taluk level, who trained volunteers at the mandal or village level. Resource persons were identified from locally available social workers, teachers and activists.

Training was visualized not as a one-time activity, but organized in repeated rounds of 4 + 2 + 2 + 1 days' duration. The initial training of four days was to concentrate on the overall objectives of the TLC and on the transaction of Primer 1. The second and third rounds of 2-day training each were to coincide with the start and the actual transaction of Primers 2 and 3 respectively. The final round of 1-day training laid emphasis on the learner evaluation and the organization of post-literacy programmes. But, in practice, training was not effective in many districts in TLC (informal discussion with SRC people). Training was conducted on an ad hoc basis for a short duration, in most cases, of one or two days. There was huge transmission loss in the cascading mode of training.

Saakshar Bharat

The SB model is a mix of NAEP and TLC models. While launching SBP, it was decided that PRIs will be the fulcrum of adult literacy and skill development programmes in compliance with the 73rd Constitutional Amendment. Therefore, the implementation of SBP has been entrusted to gram panchayats and each gram panchayat is asked to constitute a panchayat Lok Shiksha Samiti (LSK), which will be responsible for the implementation of the programme. Similar types of committees are formed at block and district levels also. Accordingly, committees have been constituted at the panchayat, block and district levels in all the districts where SBP has been implemented.

A lok shiksha kendra (or AEC) is established in each gram pan-chayat. It was envisaged that LSK would be the nerve centre of the adult education programme. It will be the venue for the registration of learners for a variety of teaching activities, such as basic literacy, basic education, skill development and CEPs. It will provide institutional, managerial and resource support to the literacy campaign.

Although NLMA and SLMA continued at the national and state levels, new committees at the district, block and village levels were formed. Instead of depending on government department/agency or creating autonomous agencies, it depended on PRIs for community involvement and ownership of the programme. SB is planned for a specific period and no permanent structures were created for adult education at the grassroots level. Theoretically, the committees at dis-trict and lower levels were given lots of powers, but, in reality, there is very limited flexibility in terms of programme strategies, content and resources. Everything is fixed at the national level and detailed guidelines were issued on finances and monitoring. Thus, it became a centralized programme. In terms of community participation, SB visualized local PRIs representing communities and their involvement would automatically lead to community participation. But, in reality, PRIs did not own the programme to the extent it was expected and the subtle gap between the PRIs and the local community is not well understood in the programme. Panchayati Raj officials, who were expected to supervise the programme, did not own up the programme, mainly because it was administered by the education department at the state and central levels.

Human Resources

SB adopted a mixed approach in human resource. The staffing pattern of NLMA and SLMAs at the national and state levels, constituted during TLC, continued in SBP. It employed full-timers on a contractual basis at a remuneration of ₹6,000 per month for district and block/mandal. Similarly, two paid workers, called village coordinators or preraks are employed in each village with an honorarium of ₹2,000 per month. One of the village coordinators had to be a woman. The selection of prerak is done by panchayat LSK.

But, in the case of basic literacy, it followed the TLC strategy of employing volunteers to teach non-literates. The village committee with the help of a prerak has to identify the volunteers and ensure that literacy classes are conducted for the learners. This strategy of employing partial payment mode and partial voluntary mode has created many problems at the field level. Further, the policy on voluntarism is not based on any ideological or theoretical understanding of voluntarism but simple logic of limited finances. Thus, it gave flexibility to states to give remuneration if states or other agencies provide funds. Since it is not a major campaign like TLC, it has become very difficult to motivate persons with patriotic appeal.

Training

SBP recognized the importance of training, and its policy document mentioned

> Teaching adults is an art that requires a specialized set of skills. Quality instructors are, therefore, a prerequisite for the success of the programme. Since the programme does not engage professional teachers, but relies mainly on volunteers with little or no previous teaching experience, they will be given intensive high-quality training in andragogy in local language both at the time of induction and during the course of the literacy programme. As the key focus of the programme is on women and other disadvantaged groups, the literacy educators will be especially sensitized on gender, social, and cultural issues. Special attention will be given to training in numeracy. (MHRD, 2009)

SBP basically adopted the cascading method of training which was followed in TLC. KRPs, who are trained at the state level, trained MTs at the district level. They, in turn, trained volunteers at the panchayat level. The training schedule, curriculum and the Trainer's Guide Book are provided by SRC. SBP trainings are modelled on the lines of TLC, so deficiencies of trainings in TLC flowed into SBP's training system.

Although the three major programmes adopted different approaches in delivery mechanism, there are certain underlying assumptions that are common among them. Some of the assumptions and problems in terms of organizational setup, human resources and training in Indian adult education are discussed below.

DISCUSSION ON DELIVERY MECHANISM

In India, adult education has been institutionalized to some extent at national and state levels, but it has never been institutionalized at the field level. As pointed out by Mathew (2012) in India, formal education, especially at the school level, was always seen as a system with a regular and permanent institutional set-up, whereas adult education was seen as a programme co-terminus with the particular five-year plan. Further, the constitution directed the state to provide free and compulsory education to all the children up to the age of 14. However, it was never considered as an obligation on the part of the state to provide education to all adults who missed schooling.

Short-term Perspective

In India, adult education programmes are always presented in the short-term perspective. Plans are made to achieve total literacy in the short period of five years. This can be seen from the short duration of initial programme plans of different adult education programmes. For example, NAEP was planned from 1978 to 1984, TLCs for a period of 2–3 years, and SBP for a period of five years from 2009 to 2012. All these programmes are extended for some more time, depending on the political situation in the country.

The main reason for this is that adult education or adult literacy has always been regarded as a short-term programme to achieve specific targets. Shah (2012) makes two important observations in relation to the pre-NLM programmes: One, that adult education programmes were seen as short-term interventions tied to target fulfilment. He points out that the history of adult education bears testimony to the development and dismantling and infrastructures at different periods. During the 1950s, a national-level institution called National Fundamental Education Centre, several regional training centres for social education officers and a number of Janata Colleges were set up only to be closed within a decade due to the change in the GoI's policy (Shah, 2012). The same is the case with the National Institute of Adult Education which was established in 1990 and was closed in 1996. Similarly, different institutions opened and closed for PL&CE at different levels, which was discussed earlier, is the best testimony to this perception.

GAP BETWEEN POLICY AND IMPLEMENTATION ON DECENTRALIZATION

Almost all the policy documents of adult education highlighted the importance of decentralization in adult education programmes. Since the adult education programme is implemented as a centrally sponsored scheme, and guidelines and funding are mostly provided by the national government, it has led to centralization of the programme to a large extent. Except in TLC, there is no flexibility in the implementation of programmes at the grassroots level. This has been pointed out in SBP document. The Planning Commission's policy paper (Planning Commission, 2008) is particularly critical of NLM's pan-Indian approach. In fact, the SBP's policy document gave option for different modes of implementation of literacy activities, depending on local circumstances. According to the document, basic literacy programme can be implemented through (a) volunteer-based campaign, (b) centre-based resident instructor, (c) residential camps and (d) part residential and part volunteer based. It appears that the concerned state can decide the policy regarding the mode of implementation. But in practice, the strategy to be adopted in a particular state is not left to the decision of the concerned state but is decided by NLM. Funding rather than viability was the deciding factor in such circumstances.

WEAK COMMUNITY PARTICIPATION

Village-level community participation is also very weak in adult education programmes in India. No systematic effort has been made to make adult education institutions in villages as long-run sustainable model. In NAEP and TLC, village-level committees had been constituted by official. SB envisages involvement of PRIs as a remedy for community participation. But the PRIs have not owned the programme.

The role of NGOs in organizing adult education programmes is very limited except that of BGVS, which partnered with the government and facilitated mass mobilization for literacy campaign through kala jathas. Civil society groups and local CBOs also participated in adult education to a limited extent. They mainly contributed for community mobilization during the TLC period. Although SRCs and Jan Shikshan Sansthans are established in the NGO sector, they are considered more as government organizations as they are totally funded by the government.

As Bhola (1991b) rightly pointed out, establishing AECs right within communities—as twins to the primary school—has been a pertinent hope of adult educators and community development people. However, the history of adult education is full of dashed hopes. AECs within communities, with different names, have been attempted and then abandoned because of resources to run them dried up or because communities showed no interest and made no use of the centres. Based on his international experience, he commented, 'Seen in an international perspective the reality of the organization of adult education can be seen to be at the same time marked by organizational pluralism and institutional fragmentation. Overall, the organization of adult education is not commensurate with the real needs' (Bhola, 1991b, p. 20). The same is the case with Indian adult education.

LACK OF HUMAN RESOURCE POLICY

There is no human resource policy in adult education. Notwithstanding the implementation of a variety of adult and lifelong learning programmes in India, not much attention has been paid to the preparation of human resources or professional manpower, specially teachers and trainers. It is argued that one of the reasons for the slow progress of literacy in the country is the poor quality of trainers and teachers in this field (Shah, 1999).

Further, Shah (2009) pointed out that there is no training system to develop competent manpower. The present tendency in adult education in India is to conceive the programmes as short-term projects, assuming that such brief programmes could be operationalized without professionally trained staff, regular pay and perks. Hence, there has been hardly any serious thinking on professionalization of adult education. Unlike lawyers, doctors, engineers and social workers, the majority of practitioners of adult education do not have a homogeneous professional background. There are no qualifying examinations for a person to become an adult educator. Due to the voluntary nature of programme, adult education as a profession is neither well established nor well understood.

At the national and state levels, regular officers headed the programme. There is no system to select and post interested and committed officers to head the programme. The postings are routine in nature. Further, at the state level, the tenure is very short. In programmes like adult education, the personality of the officers plays a dominant role in designing approach and strategies. So, the selection of officers who have commitment for literacy and understanding of its intricacies is very important for the success of the programme. Adult education functionaries at the grassroots level have generally been either ill-paid local workers or volunteers with some degree of social commitment. Some of them have done extremely good work in literacy campaigns. There is no policy to use their services in a continuous manner in adult education or in other areas of development.

WEAK TRAINING

Almost all policy documents identified training as the weakest area in adult education (MHRD, 1988, 2009). The report of the evaluation of the literacy campaign in India by an expert group under the aegis of NLM was of the view that the quality of training of the functionaries was poor. The training of the adult education functionaries at all levels lacked participatory and communicative techniques.

Mohankumar (2009) mentioned some major assumptions in traditional training methodology adopted in adult education programmes in India. They are as follows:

- Acquisition of subject knowledge by learners will automatically lead to action or change in behaviour.
- The trainer 'owns' the knowledge and can therefore transmit or impart it as 'instructor'.
- Learning depends essentially on the trainers' teaching capacity and the learners' learning capacity.
- Teaching is the responsibility of the trainer as also of the training institution.
- Knowledge and training are value-neutral and 'objective'.

Many research studies have identified deficiencies in the training programme. Among them are a training plan, the perfunctory nature of training, transmission loss in training and lack of training resources (Shah, 1998). It is observed that the method of training was not geared to meet the needs of adolescents and women learners, who constituted the bulk of the learners. This was mainly due to the short duration of the training and the absence of follow-up training (Shah, 1999).

Research and evaluation of adult educator training programmes is a neglected area. As a result, very little is known about the effectiveness of training programmes or the impact they have had. It is necessary to understand not only the outcome but also the processes involved in training so that corrective action may be taken whenever needed. Research and evaluation of training programmes, using participatory and action research methodologies, would help to improve the quality of training (Dighe, 2005b).

GAP BETWEEN STATE AND USER PERSPECTIVE

In India, adult education programmes are looked at from the state perspective as a short-term programme to achieve particular goals of literacy and never been institutionalized in lifelong learning perspective. There are two reasons for transitory nature of adult education. One is the perception of policy-makers that it is short intervention confined to adult literacy. Once literacy is achieved, there is no need for adult education. The other one is the fear that through institutionalization adult education will lose its capacity to be responsive to the real ever-changing needs of adults in communities and ultimately adult education will become a shadow of the formal primary education. On this Bhola (1991a) says that these fears are real. But the solution seems to be in being organizationally and programmatically vigilant rather than remaining or ever ad hoc and transient.

Here, it is relevant to mention ASPBAE (2006) which highlighted that adult education, like the education of children, has to be seen as a permanent business of the nation. While the targets and objectives may change but adult education needs will never be finished. Insights from past programmes indicate that the institutionalized systems have long-term value, as compared with one that is programme based.

On the whole, adult education in India is viewed as a short-term intervention without any human resource policy. Training was very weak, and there was no effort to develop professional training institutions. However, some efforts have been made at the field level to give effective training to functionaries within the limitations. Experiences of the training in West Godavari district are presented here.

TRAINING: FIELD EXPERIENCES

As the district officer of adult education, I visited a training class on continuing education in Tanuku, West Godavari, on 22 May 2000. About 40 preraks of Tanuku, Undrajavaram and Peravali mandals attended the class which was conducted in municipal office meeting hall. At the time of my visit at 10:00 AM, two mandal literacy organizers (MLOs), who were in charge of the training, and about 30 preraks were present, and training timetable and training notes were being distributed. Three resource persons were also present—one from a noted NGO, another a lecturer in a local degree college and a mandal development officer of a nearby mandal. All of them, well versed with CEP, participated in the district-level orientation class conducted before the commencement of training of preraks. Notes of their lecture were circulated to the participants. Immediately, one of the MLOs, who was acting as the coordinator of the training started the programme and introduced guests and resource persons who were going to cover different topics. Then I, as the district officer, addressed the class and explained the objectives and contents of the training and its relevance to their day-to-day work. In the first session, the lecturer who had been closely associated with CEP, explained the four objectives of continuing education in detail and how it was being implemented in the district with people's participation. In Q&A session after the lecture, preraks raised some administrative issues, such as release of funds and constitution committees. The MLO clarified the issues and mentioned the difference between academic understanding of the issue and administrative problems in implementation and how to overcome the hurdles. After lunch break, the next session on community and people's participation was conducted by the resource person from the NGO, who has vast experience in community mobilization. He elaborated various techniques for community participation with examples. The class was very interesting and the participants followed the lecture with rapt attention. The next on role of literacy in rural development was taken up by the MDO. He explained how literacy and rural development were mutually beneficial and reinforce each other. He explained the difficulties in linking literacy and development in practice and the role of development agencies and preraks in achieving the convergence. He suggested that the CEC to act as the resource centre for development information. In the next class, the other MLO briefed on the monitoring system in continuing education and formats to be filled by the preraks at regular intervals using the formats supplied in the training notes. Next, he mentioned activities to be taken up by preraks in their villages. After the Q&A, the training concluded with a vote of thanks and a song by one of the preraks.

The next year, a team from NLM headed by a deputy secretary of GoI, which visited the district to study the CEP, commented that they had never come across such indoctrination of preraks. In other districts, they had seen good centres and bad centres, but, in West Godavari, they had found clarity and uniformity in thinking and acting in all functionaries. This was mainly because of the intensive training given to the preraks.

On another occasion, I visited a volunteers training camp of Akshara Mahila in Undi Mandal in West Godavari district. The volunteers were educated members identified by WSHGs, and they were given 7 days training in three spells—3 + 2 + 2 days. Training was conducted in small batches of 10–20 people. This was one such camp. All the resource persons were adult education department staff, well versed with the teaching methodology for adults. No outside resource persons were invited. The focus of the training was on impartation of literacy skills to the non-literates and emphasis was on practice at the training session. I visited the class on the second day of the camp. In the first session, the class started with a SHG song. MLOs then asked the volunteers for a recap of the first day's discussion and the lessons completed. Then all members were asked to repeat the core principles of adult pedagogy—call the learners before coming to the literacy class, treat them all as equals, learners are illiterate but not ignorant, teaching should be learner-oriented and focus on activity-based learning. In the process of repetition, all members were able to tell core principles without looking into the book or any prompting. Then they started the fifth lesson which combined vowels and consonants. After explaining the basis for combining two types of letters for forming new letters, the MLO showed different words and asked them to tell new words that could be formed with the letters they had already learnt in the previous lessons and this lesson. Each member was given an opportunity to state the new words. The class was conducted in activity mode and no lectures were given by the resource person. After completing the lesson, members were given an opportunity to speak for five minutes on any of the topic relating to SHGs. The next lesson started with a song by one of the members. They had been taught with demonstration how to prepare teaching aids and games with low-cost material. This was one of the most interesting training classes in which I have participated.

There are different options for the delivery of adult education. India opted for national-level centralized programmes and perceived them as short-term interventions. Consequently, the programme has not been institutionalized at the village level and services of part-time paid workers or volunteers are used for implementation of the literacy programme. There is no clear-cut human resource policy, and the delivery mechanism depends on financial support from the government. The funding pattern of adult education programmes in India is discussed in the next chapter.

Funding for Literacy

Every year, before the state budget for the next year is finalized, various departments are called for a meeting with the finance department to discuss the budget proposals. Normally, the discussion is very serious, the finance people propose cutting of allocations in view of the state's difficult financial position and the departments asking for additional funding for new initiatives. When the subject of adult education comes up for discussion, the atmosphere becomes light and non-serious. Finance officials say that the programmes are not effective as they had not achieved total literacy even after so many years of programme. They suggest that the department should try to mobilize more volunteers instead of paid workers to expand the programme. Without much discussion on the subject, they would agree to provide the same level of funding as had been provided in previous years as the state's share. If the department people ask for additional allocation, they are asked to submit a separate proposal to GoI with proper justification and the state would give its share. Generally, the separate proposals are never approved by the GoI, as it would be beyond its funding pattern. The underlying assumption is that huge amounts are spent on the adult education programmes, and they are not cost effective.

I had the opportunity to hear an interesting argument between a senior bureaucrat from the state government and an activist working with an NGO in one of the workshops organized by the Andhra Pradesh State Literacy Mission in Hyderabad. The senior officer of the education department said that the government had allotted ₹35 crore for Akshara Sankranti, a state-run adult education programme in the budget, and that it would be possible to achieve total literacy in the state utilizing the funds. The NGO representative pointed out that the budget was very meagre and that the cost per learner in the state was less than ₹35, and it would not be possible to provide good quality literacy programme with this amount. He said that with this meagre funding, the government would expect total literacy in the state by making all the adult learners achieve 3rd standard. The state official replied that though the per learner cost may be small, adult literacy programme is a voluntary programme and the amount is more than sufficient if spent judiciously. He added that there had been huge unspent balances in the districts as they were not able to spend the amounts allotted to them and it was not the funds but commitment of the functionaries that was more important. The discussion reflects the different perspectives of funding to the literacy programmes in India, one is state's perspective and other is people's perspective.

What is the funding policy on literacy programmes in India? Who are the funding agencies? What has been the experience of allocations and utilization of funds for adult education programmes? How much funding is required for implementing an effective adult education programme? These are the critical questions for the success of any adult literacy education programme. The budgetary allocations show the commitment and seriousness of the policy-makers towards a particular programme. Naturally, funding depends on the value society, and political system gets out of spending resources on a particular programme. The same is true in the case of adult education.

HUMAN CAPITAL VERSUS HUMAN RIGHTS

There are two perspectives in which policy-makers look at education or literacy. One is human capital framework and the other is human rights framework. In human capital framework, developed by Becker (1964), and others, education is viewed primarily as an investment wherein individuals and families forgo current earnings and incur costs in return for higher future income. It considers education relevant in acquiring skills and knowledge that serves as an investment in the productivity of the human being. Thus, education is important because it makes workers more productive, thereby being able to earn a higher wage. By regarding skills and knowledge as an investment in one's labour productivity, economists can estimate the economic returns on education for different education levels, types of education, etc. (Robeyns, 2006). Here education has instrumental value, both at individual and societal level. In this, the value of education can be measured by either the input method and/or the output method. The input method looks into the resources spent on education by individuals, families and the state. By contrast, the output method assesses the outcome or impact of education, such as a higher standard of living enjoyed by the more educated vis-à-vis the less educated and improved productivity in society (Psacharopoulos, 2006).

On the other hand, human rights framework propounded mainly by international agencies such as UNESCO and UNICEF views education as a human right. Every human being, including every child, is entitled to decent education, even when one cannot be sure that education will pay off in human capital terms. The rights-based discourse clearly focuses on the intrinsic importance of education. Education is not seen simply as a 'good thing' to be pursued if and when some funds are available, but rather as the right of every child, implying that the governments need to mobilize the resources needed to offer a quality education (UNICEF, 2003).

Viewing education as a right is the conceptual opposite of viewing education as human capital. The latter stresses efficiency considerations, the former focuses on justice, as right considerations. There are limitations in both the frameworks. Human capital framework excessively focuses on the economic benefits of education and does not take into consideration the intrinsic value of education to the individual and society. In the case of human rights framework, its main emphasis would be only on the legal right to education. Some countries give legal right to education and still many children are outside the education system. To overcome the limitations of both frameworks, Amartya Sen and others proposed the capabilities approach. Education is important in capabilities approach for both its intrinsic and instrumental reasons.

FUNDING AGENCIES

Now let us see who are the funding agencies that provide resources for adult education. In any educational activity, costs can be classified into two categories, based on who is bearing it. One is the cost of education incurred by the learners and the other one is the cost of education incurred by the institutional level. If the institutional costs are borne by the government, they are called public costs. In adult education, the costs are borne using different sources of funding, depending on the socio-economic development and cultural context of the country or region where it is organized. Different sources of funding for adult education across the countries are discussed here.

Government/The State

In most of the countries, the government is a major source of financing of adult literacy and adult education (UNESCO Institute of Lifelong Learning [UIL], 2013). In some countries, the central government directly funds the programme or supports NGOs that organize adult education programmes. In some other countries, it is the responsibility of provisional or local governments which conduct adult education programmes in their region. In developed countries, the local governments and municipal councils coordinate adult education programmes.

Individuals/Participants

In this case, government or agency organizes the programme and collects a fee from the participants. This model is mainly adopted in developed countries for complementary programmes like life skills and income-generating programmes. In some developing countries, a nominal fee is collected from the participants, especially in courses conducted by NGOs.

Group of People/Community

In some cases, community or CBOs fund adult education programmes conducted in their communities. Community learning centres established in countries like Thailand are the best examples of community funding. Similarly, CBOs organizing adult education for their members and WSHGs conducting literacy classes for non-literate members of their group are worthy of mention.

Private Organizations/NGOs

Another major source of finance for adult education is private organizations, especially, NGOs, including voluntary associations, charitable trust and foundations. In many countries, corporate houses have established trusts as a part of their CSR and are providing funds for various adult education and literacy programmes. Some educational institutions are offering adult education courses free of cost before or after normal school hours as a community service.

International Organizations

International organizations such as UNESCO, World Bank, the Department for International Development, and Action Aid support adult education and literacy programmes in some developing countries. There are many bilateral and multilateral agencies providing funds for adult education in other countries.

The funding to the programme, especially government funding, whether at national, regional or local level, operates in two broad ways: supply-side or demand-side. Supply-side policies subsidize the cost of providing learning, while demand-side approaches contribute to the individual's ability to pay (UIL, 2013). In the former case, the financial means flow directly from the financier or sponsor to the educational institution. In the latter case, money flows directly from the financier to the learner and from there to the institution. The former is more common in developing countries, and the latter is the prevalent mode in developed countries.

FINANCING ADULT EDUCATION IN INDIA

In India, adult education is viewed neither in the human capital framework nor in the human rights framework. These frameworks do not apply directly to adult education. Human capital framework applies partially to adult education, not as fully as in the case of the formal education system. This is mainly because adult literacy education programmes are conducted mostly in non-formal mode and does not require full-time attendance. Here, the individual does not completely forego current earnings for the benefit of future income, but loses leisure time and incurs opportunity costs. Further, the rate of economic returns to the individual is not directly proportional to the investment as is the case with formal education. However, other social benefits of such investment exceed the economic benefits in the immediate day-to-day life compared to school education. Similarly, human rights framework also is not applicable to adult education as it is not included in the Right to Education Act of Government of India, and it is not recognized as a basic human right. It is not pure economic perspective, nor the human rights perspective that guides budget allocation for adult education.

Adult education is seen more in the development perspective and perceived as a social welfare measure to ameliorate illiteracy and poverty among disadvantaged sections of the population. As pointed out by Balasubramanian (2005), literacy programmes in India have for long been treated as a part of welfare programmes. So, the budget for adult education is allotted based on the availability of funds, not as an investment or fulfilment of human rights. As far as source funding is concerned, Shah (2008) mentioned that the agencies discussed in the following sub-sections provide financial resources for adult education programmes in India.

Government of India

In India, the main source of finance for adult literacy programmes is the GoI, which not only formulates adult education policies and develops programmes but also provides substantial funds for their implementation through administrative and academic infrastructure that has been developed over the years (NLM, 2008). However, the funding pattern varied from programme to programme. In some programmes, like NAEP, it was 50 per cent, and, in TLC, it was two-thirds of the total programme cost. In the case of academic institutions like SRCs and Jan Shikshan Sansthans, GoI provides 100 per cent grant-in-aid.

Similarly, GoI has been providing funds to several NGOs under the grant-in-aid scheme for field programmes.

Funds by State Governments

Generally, state governments provide matching share of funds provided by the GoI as per the norms of the schemes. It varies from scheme to scheme. For example, in NAEP, adult education projects were launched by the central and state governments in equal ratio, and, in TLC, state governments shared one-third of central funding. In SB, it was one-fourth of the central funding, which was later changed to 40 per cent of the total cost. Besides share in funding, state governments bear the expenses on salaries and other contingencies of supervisory officers working in adult education programmes at state and district levels. Some state governments initiated their own literacy programmes and fully funded them, for example, Padhana Badhana programme in Madhya Pradesh and Akshara Sankranti/Bharati in Andhra Pradesh.

Contributions from Other Sectors/Ministries for Literacy

In some cases, other sectors/departments also provide some resource support for adult literacy/education. Their contributions range from earmarking of funds, as part of their own programmes, for awareness and knowledge dissemination to sparing the services of their personnel to work for literacy and CEP on deputation or secondment basis. Many ministries, such as Women and Child Development and Youth Welfare, have a literacy component in some of their programmes. Other agencies, including universities, colleges and schoolteachers under central and state governments, also participate in literacy and CEPs in various capacities.

Support from Local Bodies' Budget

As per the 73rd and 74th Constitutional Amendments, a large number of social sector and infrastructure-related subjects are devolved to the elected local self-government bodies, both in urban and rural areas. Adult education, like formal school education, is one of them.

In many cases, they have not directly contributed from their own funds but from funds provided by the central and state governments are channelized through them. However, the extent of devolution of resources to panchayats varies from state to state. Some states such as Kerala, Karnataka and West Bengal not only devolve funds directly to panchayats in respect of literacy and CEPs but also accord a great deal of priority for the panchayats and urban local bodies to effectively utilize the funds. In SBP, as a policy, funds are released directly to the committees headed by the panchayat chairperson.

Foreign Bilateral/Multilateral Agencies

There has not been any significant external funding to adult literacy, unlike primary education, where substantial external funding was received from many bilateral and multilateral agencies. UNESCO has been involved in encouraging and giving awards for innovations and best practices in programmes. It has also been involved in promoting research and documentation of innovations and best practices.

Involvement of NGOs

Many NGOs participate in the literacy programme at the local level. But the involvement of major NGOs on a large scale is very limited, except BGVS which played a major role during TLCs in motivation and mobilization by conducting kala jathas. Generally, local NGOs run literacy classes in villages or urban slums for a particular period of time or take up literacy activity as a part of their other activities such as skill development programmes or livelihood skill trainings. It is difficult to assess the contribution of NGOs at the local level because there is no mechanism at government level to monitor their contributions or activities at the national or state level.

Support from Private/Corporate Sector

There has been no tradition of private and corporate sector involvement in literacy programmes, as can be seen in the case of formal education system from pre-primary to higher and professional levels.

There have been a few cases of corporates entering the adult literacy sector using ICTs, especially computers for literacy. One example is computer-based literacy programme conducted by TCS on an experimental basis in many states.

Civil Society and Individuals' Support

Civil society contribution to adult literacy programmes in India is considerable when literacy campaigns are conducted. It is estimated that during the TLC phase, NLM mobilized nearly 150 million non-literates and 12–15 million literacy volunteers. At least another 2 million academic resource persons provided training and other academic and managerial support on a voluntary basis. Even at a conservative estimate of ₹1,000 per volunteer, and reckoning the average TLC duration to be 10 months (i.e., ₹10,000 per volunteer), the cost to the government on 12 million volunteers alone would have been ₹12,000 crore, if payments were made (NLM, 2008).

Learners'/Individuals' Contribution

Learners'/individuals' contribution to literacy programmes is limited in the Indian context because most of the learners are people from below the poverty line and their capacity to support their education is limited. The maximum they can do is give their time for literacy and participate in literacy-related functions and events. However, when the organizers approach the community for contribution, it is the learners whom they approach with greater liberty and expectation. And it is the learners who contribute whatever they can, sometimes in kind, in the form of time and labour, etc.

It is difficult to assess the share of contribution of each of the above agencies in adult education as no agency has compiled such data. Similarly, any attempt to calculate the overall financial support for literacy is complicated. Central government funds may go to multiple ministries, and the responsibility for resource mobilization may be devolved to lower tiers of government. Moreover, it is almost impossible to aggregate funds from NGOs, employers and donors (UNESCO,

2005). The data available is of allocations made by the government in five-year plans and budgetary allocations at central and state levels.

LITERACY FUNDING IN FIVE-YEAR PLANS

Allocations for adult education programmes in five-year plans give some clarity on the importance given to adult education by the government and help understand the funding pattern to literacy in India. Plan-wise outlay and expenditure to education and adult education in five-year plans is given in the Tables 9.1 and 9.2.

As can be seen from Table 9.1, there has been a significant increase in total plan outlay, education outlay and adult education outlay over a period of time. The outlay for adult education has increased from mere 50 million in the first plan to 60,000 million in the eleventh plan. However, when adult education outlay is seen as a percentage of total plan outlay, it ranged from 0.005 to 0.36 in different plans. Similarly, if it is seen as a percentage of the total education outlay, it varied from less than 1 per cent in the fourth plan to 8.6 per cent in the seventh plan. This reflects a lack of consistency in plan allocations.

Table 9.2 shows that the percentage of expenditure out of total outlay for adult education ranged from 30.5 per cent to 127.7 per cent in different plans. Here also, there is no consistency in expenditure, which shows that the programmes are planned on an ad hoc basis. In his paper, 'Funding Adult Education Programmes in India', presented for the Paulo Friere Memorial Lecture, Shah (2008) pointed out that the expenditure on adult education as percentage of total budgeted expenditure of Central and state governments, including plan and non-plan, brings out the dismal picture of adult education both at the Centre and in the states. The percentage of total adult education expenditure to total budgeted expenditure varied from 0.42 to 0.06 during the period 1951–1952 to 1999–2000. In fact, decline in (in terms of percentage) the case of states has been very steep, that is, 0.79–0.06 during the last fifty years, notwithstanding the increase in absolute expenditure. He inferred that while there was consistency in the Central policy, there was a lot of fluctuation in states with regard to adult education.

Table 9.1 Plan-wise Percentage of Education and Adult Education Outlay to Total Plan (₹ Millions)

| Five-Year Plan | Total | Outlay on Education | | Total Education to Total Plan | Percentage of | |
		Total Education (Outlay)	Adult Education (Outlay)		Adult Education to Total Plan	Adult Education to Total Education
First Plan (1951–1956)	20,690	1,690	50	8.17	0.24	2.96
Second Plan (1956–1961)	48,000	2,770	50	5.77	0.10	1.81
Third Plan (1961–1966)	75,000	5,600	60	7.35	0.08	1.07
Fourth Plan (1969–1974)	159,022	8,220	80	5.17	0.05	0.97
Firth Plan (1974–1979)	388,532	12,850	180	3.31	0.05	1.40
Sixth Plan (1980–1985)	975,000	25,240	1,280	2.59	0.13	5.07
Seventh Plan (1985–1990)	1,800,000	63,830	5,490	3.55	0.31	8.60
Eighth Plan (1992–1997)	4,341,000	212,180	15,550	4.89	0.36	7.33
Ninth Plan (1997–2002)	8,592,000	535,250	11,020	6.23	0.13	2.06
Tenth Plan (2002–2007)	15,256,390	922,754	17,734	6.05	0.12	1.98
Eleventh Plan (2008–2012)	26,987,300	1,935,700	60,000	7.17	0.22	3.01

Table 9.2 Plan-wise Education and Adult Education Outlay and Expenditure (₹ Millions)

Plan	Total Education Outlay	Total Education Expenditure	Percentage of Expenditure	Adult Education Outlay	Adult Education Expenditure	Percentage of Expenditure
First Plan	1,690	1,530	90.5	50	50	100
Second Plan	2,770	2,700	97.4	50	40	80
Third Plan	5,600	5,820	103.9	60	20	33.3
Fourth Plan	8,220	7,740	94.1	80	60	75
Fifth Plan	12,850	8,840	68.7	180	230	127.7
Sixth Plan	25,240	27,740	109.9	1,280	1,534	119.8
Seventh Plan	63,830	76,050	119.1	5,490	6,098	111
Eighth Plan	212,180	254,140	119.7	15,550	11,707	75.2
Ninth Plan	535,250	493,750	92.2	11,020	8905	80.8
Tenth Plan	922,754	965,672	104.6	17,734	14,037	79.1
Eleventh Plan	1,935,700	1,768,000	91.3	60,000	18,320	30.5

Tilak (2016), analysing the expenditure on adult education with reference to GDP in 2013–2014, mentioned that the share of public expenditure on education as GDP percentage reported during 2013–2014 was 4.4 per cent in entire education sector, whereas the expenditure on the adult education sector was only 0.01per cent. He pointed out that while the share of the education sector is gradually rising, the share of adult education has remained constant. In terms of share of adult education in total expenditure in plan and non-plan schemes, he observed that plan expenditure in the adult education sector during 2013–2014 was 0.36 per cent, with plan expenditure of 0.82 per cent and non-plan expenditure of 0.12 per cent. As regards the sharing of Centre and states share in terms of expenditure in the adult education sector, the Central share was 0.87 per cent and the state share was 0.22 per cent during the same financial year.

Tilak (2016) made a similar analysis of expenditure in the adult education sector among the states, which shows that most of the states spent less than 1 per cent of their total education budget on adult education. However, some of the states such as Tripura (2.78%), Delhi (2.57%) and Bihar (1.42%) reported higher expenditure on the adult education sector. States such as Punjab (0.01%), Haryana (0.02%), Himachal Pradesh (0.03%) and Andhra Pradesh (0.17%) reflected lower expenditure during 2012–2013.

Further, Tilak analysed the expenditure on SB. The total allocation and expenditure on SB in the Eleventh Five Year Plan indicated that of the outlay of ₹4,343 crore allocated for 3 years during 2009–2012, an expenditure of only ₹1,180 crore was incurred, which is only 27 per cent of the total allocated amount. Similarly, against the outlay of ₹3,000 crore allocated for the Twelfth Five-Year Plan, an expenditure of ₹1,387 crore (46%) was incurred during the 4-year period. However, the overall expenditure of SB during Eleventh and Twelfth Five-Year Plans was around 24 per cent.

UNIT COST OF ADULT EDUCATION

Another way to analyse the funding pattern is looking at unit cost or per learner of adult education programmes. This is a bit complicated because different programmes use different yardsticks to measure the per learner cost depending on the model whether the programme engaged volunteers or paid workers for teaching. Let us look at the per learner cost in major adult education programmes in India.

National Adult Education Programme

Under NAEP, the GoI and state governments have to open equal number of projects in a state. There was no focus on the unit cost, and the total grant for a project was generally around nine lakh rupees per year. There is a wide disparity between the amount sanctioned and the amount released to the project and the actual expenditure incurred. The unit cost of a typical RFLP under NAEP in West Godavari district (Rao, 1988) is given in Table 9.3 as an example to calculate the unit cost.

As per Table 9.3, the cost per learner is ₹100 and the cost per successful learner or literate is around ₹290. This is in spite of the fact that NAEP is not a voluntary-based scheme and honoraria to the organizers were included in the cost estimation. In the initial years, ₹50 was paid to the organizers, but the amount was increased to ₹100 from 1986 onwards. Honoraria were not dependent on the rate of success or number of people made literate. Similarly, there were no incentives to the learners except that the enrolled learners were given books and other material free of cost and classes were taught at the convenience of the learners. All the supervisory staff were regular

Table 9.3 *Unit Cost under NAEP in West Godavari District of Andhra Pradesh*

	1985–1986	1986–1987	1987–1988
Expenditure	833,288.85	873,347.10	900,077.70
Enrolment	8,850	9,000	9,000
No. of Successful Learners	2,846	2,519	3,133
Cost per Learner	94.16	97.04	100.01
Cost per Successful Learner	292.79	346.70	287.29

Source: Rao (1988).

government employees who received their salary directly from the State government treasury. Their salaries were not included in the per learner cost.

Cost Estimation in TLC

In TLC, the GoI and state governments shared the cost of the project in the ratio of 2:1 and the grant was released directly to ZSS in the form of grant-in-aid. The cost of TLC ranged from 3 to 5 crore rupees in each district. For example, in West Godavari district TLC, the total enrolment was 792,362. Of them, 635,196 successfully completed the course. The total expenditure was ₹32,772,000 (*NIRD Evaluation Report*). Based on this, the per learner cost in West Godavari district was ₹41.35 for enrolled learners and ₹52 for successful learners. In TLC, there were no incentives for the volunteers, and all of them worked voluntarily without any salary or honorarium.

As pointed out by Varghese (2013), estimating the real costs of the TLC programmes is a difficult task for at least two reasons: (a) non-availability of established methodologies and (b) inadequacy of information base. He suggested two ways of arriving at cost estimates of TLC programmes. One is using direct monetary expenditure of the programme, and the second one is based on the total human effort that has gone into the programme. Based on the direct monetary expenditure on TLC programme, per learner and per literate expenditure calculated by him for some TLC districts are given in Table 9.4.

Table 9.4 *Cost Estimate per Learner and per Literate*

District	Cost per Learner	Cost per Literate
Wardha	56.1	73.6
Sindhudurg	113.6	199.8
Burdwan	40.2	48.1
Midnapore[a]	35.9	56.0
Ernakulam	38.0	52.0

Source: Varghese (2013).

Note: [a] Bifurcated into Purba Medinipur and Paschim Medinipur in 2002.

Cost Estimate Based on Human Inputs

Further, Varghese (2013) made cost estimation of TLC using the second method, that is, the human effort or labour. In TLCs, the programme was run in a voluntary mode and the labour is the most significant input, but unlike in the formal system, in the TLCs, labour constitutes an unpaid input. It does not, therefore, enter into the cost estimation made in financial terms. Since it is necessary to cost' all inputs in order to arrive at an estimate of actual social costs, unpaid inputs have also to be assigned their input value.

Table 9.5 *Total Man Hours of Work on TLC: Midnapore and Ernakulam (Million Man Hours)*

S. No.	Item	Midnapore	%	Ernakulam	%
1	Training Time	9.6	14.5	0.8	15.2
2	Instructional Time	49.0	73.5	4.0	72.3
3	Programme Management	8.0	12.0	0.7	12.5

Source: Varghese (2013).

Most of the volunteers were teachers, students or unemployed youths. In the case of programme management, persons holding higher positions were also involved. Assuming the starting salary of a primary schoolteacher (say ₹1,800 per month) as the basis, Varghese estimated following unit costs in Midnapore and Ernakulum districts:

- Per learner expenditure in Midnapore: ₹352
- Per literate expenditure in Midnapore: ₹559
- Per learner expenditure in Ernakulam: ₹225
- Per literate expenditure in Ernakulam: ₹308

Adding up cost on account of other inputs like teaching–learning material, campaign expenditure administrative and travel expenses, which are included in the direct financial allocation of the programme, per learner expenditure is estimated as follows:

- Per learner expenditure in Midnapore: ₹388
- Per literate expenditure in Midnapore: ₹615

- Per learner expenditure in Ernakulam: ₹256
- Per literate expenditure in Ernakulam: ₹352

Per learner or per literate expenditure depends on the number of learners per literacy centre, and those two move in opposite directions. The difference between per learner and per literate cost is due to stagnation and dropout. Some persons drop out; there are others who continue to attend the literacy classes but fail to reach NLM norm.

It is seen that the major difference between the two patterns of expenditure lies in honorarium which stands for salaries under NAEP. A substantial share of the total costs under NAEP went to this item, while no expenditure was incurred on this item in the TLCs. But the TLCs spent a fairly large proportion of the total costs on environment building with a view to generating demand. More than two-fifths of the total TLC cost was spent on teaching–learning material. In fact, nearly three-fourths of the expenditure of the TLCs had been on teaching and learning materials, management and environment building.

Saakshar Bharat Programme

Like earlier literacy programmes, SB is a centrally sponsored programme with the expenditure sharing ratio of 75:25 between the Centre and state governments. In 2016, the ratio changed to 60:40. The funding pattern of SB is slightly different from the earlier pattern in that it combined different components of adult education, such as basic literacy, continuing education, skill development and equivalency, into a single programme. In basic literacy, it has different funding pattern for different models, for example, per learner cost is ₹5,625 for resident camp of 45 days, ₹1,333 per resident instructor for 30 people for one year. These two models are applicable only in specific hill and forest terrains and northeastern states. In all other places, it is ₹230 per learner in volunteer mode (MHRD, 2009). This includes the cost of teaching and learning material, training of volunteers and resource persons, assessment and certification.

The unit cost of basic literacy in SBP in different states during TLC is given in Annexure 9. The per learner cost in this programme varied widely from state to state, depending on the number of people made literate. For example, in Assam, it was ₹753 and ₹33 in Tamil Nadu. On an average, the all-India level was ₹113. The expenses of the programme on continuing education and other activities such as honoraria paid to the coordinators at various levels, management cost, etc., are not included in the cost of basic literacy.

Besides the differences in the perspectives of plan allocations and unit cost, there are many problems in funding of adult education programmes in India ranging from inadequate funding to irregular flow of funds. Some of these problems and their impact on the adult education programmes are discussed here.

FLOW OF FUNDS

There are two steps in resource support for any programme: one is allocation of funds and the other is timely release of funds—even flow of funds as per the programme requirements. A major problem in Indian adult education programmes is not only the low allocation of funds but also the irregular and partial release of funds. This can be seen in all adult education programmes since Independence. Any field functionary of the programme will vouch that irregular release of funds is a major hurdle in the implementation of adult education programmes in India.

One major reason for irregular flow of funds is the lengthy and complicated procedures adopted for the release of funds. Since inception, adult education programmes are centrally sponsored schemes and funding has to be shared between Central and state governments. The Central government releases its share to the state government or to the implementing agency as per the policy of the programme, and the state has to release its corresponding share to the agency. Funds are released in the form of grant-in-aid, as it has been a temporary plan scheme. Grants are released in instalments and accounts and utilization certificates have to be submitted for every instalment for release of further grants. Whenever the state failed to release its share of grant for some reason or other, the central grants were stopped. Since it is considered a temporary programme, regular full-timers have not been appointed in many states and proper infrastructure has not been created, settlement of accounts for every instalment has become very difficult. As a result, submission of accounts and utilization certificates got delayed which in turn led to delays in the release of further grants and payment of honoraria or salaries to the field functionaries. The delay ranged from 12 to 36 months in CEP and, in some cases, payments were avoided in the name of 'programme years'. Payments were made for five years though the programme ran for more than 7 years. Preraks have gone to court and the cases are still pending.

The same financial procedures continued even in SBP. In this programme, there was an inordinate delay of 12–24 months in the payment of honoraria to the preraks. This dented the credibility of the programme at the grassroots level. Generally, the Central government blames the state government and the latter blames district level or implementing agencies for delay in the submission of accounts; however, people working at the field level are not interested in knowing the level at which it is pending but feel that they have not been receiving their remuneration in time. This has very badly affected the morale of the functionaries of the programme. Consequently, whatever expenditure has been incurred does not yield the desired results. Moreover, there is a lot of scope for corruption whenever arrears payments are made.

So, some alternative financial procedures have to be adopted in adult literacy programmes as was done to some extent in TLCs, where lump sum grants were given to the districts in advance. The other alternative is following the same procedure as has been adopted for permanent schemes in school education or higher education for components like salaries of teachers and cost of food, etc. Otherwise, the limited resources spent on adult education will not be fruitful.

LACK OF POLICY ON PAYMENT TO FACILITATORS

Lack of clear policy on two important issues, which have a bearing on financial resources, has created problems in the implementation of adult education programmes. One is the payment of remuneration to the volunteers/instructors, and the other is the creation of infrastructure for implementation. Pay for facilitators is one of the most sensitive issues in the whole adult literacy sector. Volunteerism is successful for a short duration in a major campaign with patriotic appeal. The TLCs have celebrated the volunteer spirit and other programmes such as Akshara Sankranti in Andhra Pradesh tried to replicate the model. But, over a period of time, volunteerism has become an economic necessity for under-funded literacy programmes. Generally, pressure is put on poor people to volunteer as facilitators. For instance, in SBP, documents show that the volunteer model of basic literacy programme has been adopted in many states (except in northeastern states). This is not because of the policy, but only because of difficulty in providing funds for payment to volunteers. In other words, funding problems led to this decision not out of policy consideration of volunteerism. Over a period of time, preraks—village-level functionaries—are pressurized to get volunteers to conduct basic literacy programme, and they in turn request their relatives and friends to work as volunteers to protect their jobs. NLMA document (MHRD, 2009, p. 12) says, 'Payment of honorarium to Literacy Educators may also be considered by the State governments, Gram Panchayat or NLMA through any funding source, including donations or public-private partnership, but not from budgetary support of the Government of India'.

In the same way, policy on funding to create an infrastructure for implementation of adult education programmes is very vague. In most of the programmes, central grants are provided for programme cost and states are expected to give resources for infrastructure and management costs. States have to give these funds in addition to their share for programme costs. Most of the states are reluctant to give this additional funding because of resource crunch. They neither reject nor provide funds, but simply keep quiet, and the implementing agencies have to manage infrastructure in one way or the other. This results in the diversion of funds. For example, in the SB funding pattern, ₹25,000 can be spent on running the district office and payment of honoraria to district coordinators. It is common knowledge that this amount is insufficient to run the programme at the district level. But neither the Centre nor the states are willing to provide additional grant.

Our experience in creating infrastructure for adult education in West Godavari reflects the ground level.

CREATING INFRASTRUCTURE: WEST GODAVARI EXPERIENCE

After a major literacy campaign in West Godavari district, we wanted to construct a building by name 'Saaksharata Bhavan' (Literacy Building) in Eluru, which would be a symbol of literacy achievements in the district and serve as an office building and meeting hall for adult education programmes. Since the adult education department has no funds for the construction of any such building, we thought we could approach members of Parliament and the state assembly, who have some funds earmarked for such activities. We approached the senior most official of the district, who was very supportive of literacy programmes, to use her good offices to request the political leaders and business houses to give donations for the building. The officer, in an informal chat, said that the political leaders give their funds if they get votes or some money out of the construction and business people give money only if it is useful for their business or get wide publicity for their charity. Adult literacy programmes can do neither. So, it is very difficult to get sponsorship for the building. However, she agreed to put in a word. We realized the truth in her words only when we started the construction of the building. Of course, we completed it with great difficulty with the support of one MP and some district officials. We inaugurated it with all fanfare and arranged a permanent literacy exhibition. Five years later, I visited the building and found it in a dilapidated condition because there were no funds for its maintenance and no one is willing to give a donation for it. The fate of the adult education programme seems to be the same.

INADEQUATE FUNDING

There are two contradicting views on funding of adult education in India; some believe that huge funds are allotted to adult education programmes, compared to its importance at the cost of other sectors in education. They argue that adult education has not shown much impact in all these years and better results in improving literacy rates can be achieved if this amount is diverted to the primary education sector. They look at the programme at the macro level. The other side argues that very meagre amounts have been allotted for adult education all these years and never exceeded 2 per cent of the total education budget in the country. It is as low as ₹90–180 per learner, making the cost in India the lowest in the world. They look at adult education from the micro-level unit cost.

It would be difficult to make a general statement on costs because financial requirements of a programme depend on many factors, such as the approach followed, the components and activities included in the programme. For example, financial requirement would be less if it is a voluntary programme supported by the community as is the case with AMP, whereas huge budget is required for a government programme run through qualified teachers and paid workers. Compensatory type programmes such as basic literacy or basic education require less funding compared to the complementary type, which includes training and continuing vocational education.

Whatever the arguments, funding of adult education programmes in India does not correspond to its targets. This problem is not confined to India. Among the number of challenges identified by the United Nations Literacy Decree Mid-Decade Review submitted to the UN General Assembly in October 2008, inadequate financial resources was identified as one of the major challenges to achieving 'Literacy for All'. A benchmark of 3 per cent educational budget for adult literacy was recommended. In India too, the Working Group on Adult Education and Literacy under the Eleventh Five Year Plan indicated that one of the major constraints in preventing NLM from making required headway was a severe resource crunch (Shamsu, 2012).

As per the *EFA Global Monitoring Report 2006* (UNESCO, 2005), the estimated average cost per learner is US$47 in sub-Saharan Africa, US$30 in Asia and US$61 in Latin America. When the cost is computed for 'successful' learners or completers, the respective averages are US$68, US$32 and US$83. The cost for an enrolled learner ranged from US$16–167 and per successful learner from US$18–199.

(However, caution should be exercised in comparing figures from country to country as purchasing power levels and programme types differ). The report mentioned, 'It should be assumed that a good-quality literacy programme that respects benchmarks will cost between $50 and $100 per learner per year for at least three years (two years of initial learning and ensuring that further learning opportunities are available to all)' (UNESCO, 2005, p. 238). There are no such benchmarks for adult education in India.

As suggested in ASPBAE (2006) report, we need not only more resources but also better quality of resources, and quality comes at a cost. There is no point in having more of poor quality resources—more instructors who are inadequately trained or who lack confidence to deal with adult learners, more supervisors who have no training or experience of what they are supervising and no commitment to the task. So, for each of the resources, we need to try to assess both the quantity and the quality of the resources required to make the programme really successful. The World Bank reports commenting on this says:

> A vicious circle may be created whereby cheap but ineffective programs disappoint financiers and preclude more expenditure that might make them more efficient. Countries that decide to engage in adult literacy should consider their long-term commitment and determine the extent to which they are willing to fund more effective but also more expensive programs. (Abadzi, 2003a, p. 28)

As suggested by Tilak (2016), there is a need for adoption of proper cost norms for minimum quality along with a comprehensive long-term approach ensuring steady/sustained growth in allocation. Further, realistic norms on Centre–state shares for adult education programmes need to be adopted and relative priorities are to be decided within the adult education budget.

Adult literacy programmes are meant for the poorest of the poor sections of society because the poverty map and illiteracy map always overlap. These people have little awareness of their rights and their capacity to influence funding policy practically nil. The other sections, especially, corporate and vocal sections of society, which dominate the policy-making process, do not show much interest in social development programmes including literacy. Political parties cannot afford to ignore poorer sections in policy documents as it reflects badly on their ideologies. So, they include literacy and other social development programmes in policy papers. But they make little effort to implement the programmes effectively through sufficient funding. Further, if there is any financial crunch in government the first causality would be adult education programmes. This is because there is no clear policy on funding. A qualitative programme requires sufficient funding equivalent to formal education. The next chapter suggests the way forward for designing and implementing literacy programmes in India.

Conclusion and the Way Forward

In this book, an attempt has been made to analyse Indian adult education programmes from different perspectives prevailing in the field, which include (a) state versus user perspectives, (b) individual dimension versus social dimension of literacy, (c) literacy as education versus literacy as development and (d) policy versus implementation. It examined how these perspectives influenced the programmes both at policy and practice levels. Policy assumptions of major adult education programmes—NAEP, TLC and SB—and their operational problems for each of the critical areas are discussed in detail.

One thing that emerged from the discussion is that adult education is not an isolated social problem that can be tackled through simple and short-term interventions, but a complex activity involving a wide range of factors from national policies to classroom interactions. Each of these factors has divergent perspectives that are bundled together in the formulation and application of adult education programmes in India. This resulted in internal contradiction and lack of cohesiveness.

The analysis might look pessimistic and present totally negative picture of the programme. But, at the field level, there are many instances where excellent programmes are conducted by the activists in trying circumstances. People really committed to the cause of literacy working as instructors and enthusiastic learners did good work against many odds. Take for example a literacy centre in Gutala village, located on the banks of the Godavari River in West Godavari district of Andhra Pradesh. I visited the centre in 1986. About 25 male learners, all in the age group of 18–25 years, were actively participating in the learning process. The centre, being conducted in the house of the instructor, John, aged about 65, a retired schoolteacher, was buzzing with activity—learners playing games using flash cards. The instructor was encouraging each learner to participate in the recognition of words using the flash cards. Even the flash cards had been prepared by the learners themselves. He asked some learners and some educated youths who had gathered there to prepare cards or paper cuttings (headings in old newspapers) for using as teaching learning material. I was told that John was running the third batch in the village and nearly 50 learners of the two earlier batches had become literate. He asked one learner to sing a song in my presence. All the learners encouraged that person to sing and vigorously clapped when he completed the song. The atmosphere in the centre was lively and motivating. I was told that they regularly discuss various issues in the centre including their problems in the village.

The same was the case with the literacy centre in Gangadivipally village in Geesugonda Mandal of Warangal district, which I visited in 2011. Rajamouli, former Sarpanch of the village, who was instrumental in mobilizing people for literacy, accompanied us to the literacy centre located near the panchayat office. It had all the facilities for a literacy centre and the support of the villagers. Around 30 women, most of them members of SHGs, gathered there to acquire literacy skills. They were discussing issues relating to SHGs and economic development programmes in the centre. Support of the village community and linking literacy with SHGs played a dominant role in the effective functioning of the centre. It was heartening to see the zeal and enthusiasm of the activists and villagers at the many centres I visited.

How to make such centres a normal phenomenon in adult education? This is the fundamental issue. Based on the discussion in the preceding chapters, some conclusions and suggestions for the way forward are discussed here.

CONCEPT OF LITERACY

Conceptual clarity is the most essential prerequisite for the success of any literacy programme. Literacy is not a simple concept that any person without any understanding can conduct a literacy class and make it a success. In our experience, we find that only people with a clear understanding of literacy and its methodology have conducted literacy programmes successfully. This can be seen in the success rate of literacy classes conducted by well-trained teachers and experts.

Adult education programmes in India viewed literacy from the state perspective in the individual dimension. The user perspective in social dimension is completely neglected in the programmes. Within individual dimension, literacy is viewed as a skill in population census and as a task in adult literacy programmes. These conceptual problems have created a lot of confusion among field functionaries and beneficiaries and each one has used his own definition of literacy. Literacy programmes have to overcome the conceptual problems by defining literacy in the Indian context. This has to be done from the user perspective rather than the state perspective and has to move from the traditional stereotyped assumption that literacy is an individual skill to a broader view of social practice. Therefore, literacy has to be defined to include both individual and social dimensions in terms of the skills required, tasks that can be conducted and activities that can be performed as a social practice. Literacy should be viewed as a process rather than as a product, especially the socio-technical process. Once literacy is perceived as a process rather than as an end product, the binary classification of literates and illiterates stands ignored and literacy will be viewed from the perspective of learning continuum.

LITERACY AND DEVELOPMENT

Understanding the relationship between literacy and development is very important. Indian adult education programmes in government sector are, to a large extent, focused on the educational perspective and ignore the development perspective. Literacy is seen primarily in terms of measurable literacy skills to be attained after a course. It is very important that literacy should be part of overall development of an individual and inseparable from the living, working and learning of the people in an integrated whole. So, the focus of adult literacy programmes should be not on the improvement of literacy rate but on development-oriented literacy that is essential for improving people's quality of life. The benefits of literacy are not automatic but depend on the social context in which it is located and ensue only when broader rights and development frameworks are in place. For this, a suitable institutional and social framework has to be created.

CONTENT AND PEDAGOGY

In India, primer development is considered a task of experts, and it is mostly developed based on their assumptions. They highlighted the state perspective of literacy in individual dimension. For the literacy programme to be effective, the content of the primers should be based on the user perspective, taking into consideration the felt needs of the learners instead of purely on development needs as perceived by the state. In other words, the content should strike a balance between the felt needs of the users and the development needs proposed by the policy-makers, that is, between the state perspective and user perspective. Primers should desist from presenting a negative image of illiterates as lazy and empty minded responsible for their own problems but take into consideration their life experience and circumstantial problems. Primers have to be designed at the local level for each group/category of learners relevant to their life based on their needs and interests. The curriculum should link locally relevant content to core national values through integrating the two—start with local issue and proceed to identify broad national values. For example, a local issue like infant and maternal mortality can be the starting point for discussion on the small family norm.

The uniqueness of local language and culture has to be taken into consideration while developing primers and the methods should be suitable for the language. Each Indian language, especially South Indian languages has its uniqueness and needs separate treatment. Primer development has to be based on proper research and not on the basis of assumptions made by a few experts. The NCFAE, which is long overdue, should be finalized and approved to give states clear guidance on content and pedagogy for adult education programmes. The contradictions between the content and pedagogy are to be reconciled, that is, if the content is imparting literacy skills, then the pedagogy has to be confined to that only.

MOTIVATION AND MOBILIZATION

In most of the adult education programmes, motivation is considered as an easy task. It is either confined to individual motivation strategy in which illiterates are approached directly by volunteer/instructor or through social mobilization using multimedia to reach the message to the public as a whole. Motivation is both an individual and a social activity, which requires a multidimensional approach using a combination of individual and social motivations. That kind of motivational and advocacy strategy has to be evolved. Uniform motivational strategy for all sections of population is not effective, and it should be based on the needs and interests of potential learners, and cater to different groups. A clear motivational plan aimed at different sections of population has to be worked out as has been done in the case of AIDS control, water and sanitation programmes.

Sustaining motivation is another major issue that requires serious attention while designing motivational strategy. The gap between motivation policy envisioned in policy documents and actual implementation needs to be bridged. Community mobilization has to be an integral part of the motivational strategy as adopted in many countries for the effective implementation of the programmes. It helps not only people's participation but also community ownership of the programmes.

POST-LITERACY AND CONTINUING EDUCATION

PL&CE is one of the neglected areas in Indian adult education. This is mainly because of the perception that literacy is a static concept, which assumes that once a person becomes literate, s/he will continue to be literate throughout her/his life. It should be recognized that literacy is only the foundation and there is no point in laying the foundation without constructing a building. PL&CE is such building. Both literacy and post-literacy are integral parts of a whole that is lifelong learning.

Lifelong education/learning is very important in India, where more than one-third of the population is non-literate, and another one-third has less than eight years of schooling. There are lifelong learning opportunities for persons who have completed secondary education, but there are no such opportunities for people below that level. PL&CE is the only opportunity for improving their knowledge and skills. So, our country needs to develop a new culture of lifelong learning for all and create an institutional framework for that.

MONITORING AND EVALUATION

M&E in adult education is considered weak, and it lacks credibility. It is mainly based on rationalistic approach in the state perspective. Further, there is a wide gap between policy and implementation. Policy documents highlight the importance of an effective monitoring system, but at the field level, it is confined to routine reporting.

Adult education, which is unique in terms of time and locale and operates in non-formal mode, requires M&E quite different from the traditional system. M&E system requires a paradigm shift from traditional quantitative system to an alternative participatory M&E in naturalistic paradigm. Community-based participatory method of monitoring stakeholders' involvement is critical for improving the credibility and quality of M&E.

DELIVERY MECHANISM

Adult education in India has always been considered as a short-term scheme to improve the literacy rate among adults. It requires a long-term vision and plan at national and local levels. It has to be implemented in a decentralized manner. The national government should give only broad policy guidelines; state governments should evolve a framework of implementation; and districts should implement the programmes as was done in TLCs. AEC/CEC should be seen in social perspective as a permanent institution like a school or a hospital and a mechanism has to be evolved for the convergence of all adult education and NFE at the AEC level. A local institution, either an NGO, CBO or local committee, should own the programme at the village level and facilitated by the government, which partners with various development agencies.

A clear human resource policy has to be evolved for adult education. It should have adult education professionals at the top level and people with qualification in adult education to be appointed at the middle and lower levels. The instructors should have good academic qualifications or received intensive training in dealing with adults and methods of teaching. They should be paid reasonable remuneration for the work as is done in other sectors such as ICDS and rural development. The staff at each level should have an opportunity for upward mobility. Volunteerism can be encouraged in the NGO sector for short-duration programmes.

Capacity-building, not mere training, should be introduced in adult education at both institutional and individual levels for the success of the programme. It is necessary to have a different category of trainings to different categories of people in the programme. Senior level people, who are responsible for the administration of the programme at national, state and district levels, need to be trained at higher levels in administrative institutes on both academic and administrative aspects before they are posted in adult education. Various institutions/ agencies like the Department of Personnel and Training and some academic institutions have developed systematic training methodologies for effective training of government functionaries. Services of these institutions have to be used and systematic training methodologies adopted in adult education programmes.

FUNDING

Divergent perceptions prevail on funding of adult education. Some look at adult education funding from macro-level figures in plan documents, and others see it from micro level per learner cost. In the former perspective, huge funds are being provided to the adult education, whereas in the latter view point the funding is meagre and one of the lowest in the world. Whatever it may be, the funding for literacy should be in tune with the literacy policy. Ambitious policy with huge targets without corresponding funding may result in ineffective programmes. There is a wide gap between funding policy of the State and actual funding. The huge budget recommended in international reports may not be possible in the Indian context. In such a case, the programme has to adopt an approach that is suitable to the local conditions within the budget provision. Irregular flow of funds is a major constraint in the implementation of adult education programmes. This needs to be resolved. An institutionalized framework for release of funds would be efficient and cost effective. Literacy funding should be seen from a long-term perspective and not as a short-term temporary project as is the case now. A clear policy has to be evolved on payment of remuneration to the functionaries and creation of infrastructure.

On the whole, imparting literacy has to be regarded as a serious activity and a clear perspective on each of the issues involved is essential for the success of the programme.

ANNEXURES

ANNEXURE 1. PRESCRIBED LITERACY SKILLS UNDER NAEP

1. **Reading skills**
   a. The learner should, at the end of the programme, be able to read orally—pronouncing correctly a simple passage of about 5–6 sentences in a minute. Such a passage may be from the reading material, used at the centre, and should be preferably in the same letter type.
   b. The learner should be able to read approximately 10–20 words, of hand-written (bold) material, per minute.
   c. The learner should be able to read with understanding road signs, posters, simple instructions and some headlines of newspapers for neo-literates.
   d. The learner should be able to comprehend the material noted in items, i, ii and iii above, and should be able to answer questions relating to it.
2. **Writing skills**
   a. The learner should be able to copy a minimum of 10 words per minute from a small passage. The words in the passage may be of not more than four letters. They should also be able to understand what is written.
   b. The learner should be able to take down dictation at the speed of at least seven words per minute.

   c. The learner should be able to write on a straight line with proper spacing on ruled paper.

3. **Computational skills**

   a. The learner should be able to make minor calculation of up to three digit figures, involving simple addition, subtraction, multiplication and division; the divisor in case of division and multiplier in case of multiplication should be one digit.

   b. At the end of the course, the learner should be in a position to gain a practical knowledge of metric weights and measures.

   c. The learner should be able to know tables up to 10.

4. **Application of literacy skills**

   a. The learner should be able to read captions, signboards (written road signs), posters, newspaper headlines and other communications that come to him in legible and bold handwritten papers.

   b. The learner should be able to write simple letters and simple applications, and fill up forms such a money orders and loan and bank forms.

   c. The learner should be able to keep account of the day-to-day expenditure and savings and be able to check entries in their post office or bank passbook.

   d. The learner should be able to follow and act upon instructions given on bags of fertilizers, pesticides, seeds, medicines, etc.

ANNEXURE 2. PRESCRIBED LEVELS IN 3Rs UNDER NLM

1. **Reading**

   a. Reading *aloud* with normal accent simple passages on a topic related to the interest of the learners at a speed of 30 words per minute.

   b. Reading *silently* small paragraphs in simple language at a speed of 35 words per minute.

   c. Reading *with understanding* road signs, posters, simple instructions and newspapers for neo-literates, etc.

   d. Ability to follow simple written messages relating to one's working and living environment.

2. **Writing**
   a. Copying with understanding at a speed of seven words per minute.
   b. Taking dictation at a speed of seven words per minute.
   c. Writing with proper spacing and alignment.
   d. Writing independently short letters and applications and forms of day-to-day use to the learners.

3. **Numeracy**
   a. To read and write 1–1,000.
   b. Doing simple calculations without fractions, involving addition, subtraction up to three digits and multiplication and division by a single digit number.
   c. Working knowledge of metric units of weights, measures, currency, distance and units of time.
   d. Broad idea of proportions and interest, without involving fractions and their use in working and living conditions.

The NLM norms in 3Rs have been divided into three levels; these are as follows:

1. **Level I:** Ability to
   - Read and write words and sentences having most frequent letters and vowel signs;
   - Read and write numbers up to 50;
   - Do simple sums and problems of addition and subtraction up to 50 without 'carry over' or 'borrowing' respectively; and
   - Write one's name.

2. **Level II:** Ability to
   - Read and write words and sentences having almost all the letters, all vowel signs and some conjunct letters;
   - Read and write numbers up to 1,000;
   - Do simple sums and solve problems involving addition and subtraction up to 100 with 'carry over' and 'borrowing' respectively;
   - Do small sums in currency, weights and measures of decimal system; and
   - Write name of family members and own address.

3. **Level III:** Ability to
   - Read and write words and sentences, having any of the letters, vowel signs and conjunct letters;
   - Comprehend a simple and small unknown passage or text, newspaper headings, road signs, etc.;
   - Read and write numbers up to 1,000;
   - Do sums and compute simple problems involving multiplication and division within 1,000; and
   - Apply skills of reading, writing and numeracy in day-to-day activities, that is, read letters, sign boards; write letters; keep household accounts, etc.

ANNEXURE 3. LITERACY LEVELS USED UNDER LAMP

LAMP used five levels of literacy in its assessment (UIS. 2005).

Level 1 indicates persons with very poor skills, where the individual may, for example, be unable to determine the correct amount of medicine to give a child from information printed on a package.

Level 2 respondents can deal only with material that is simple, clearly laid out and in which the tasks involved are not too complex. It denotes a weak level of skill, but more hidden than Level 1. It identifies people who can read, but test poorly. They may have developed coping skills to manage everyday literacy demands, but their low level of proficiency makes it difficult for them to face novel demands, such as learning new job skills.

Level 3 is considered a suitable minimum for coping with the demands of everyday life and work in a complex, advanced society. It denotes roughly the skill level required for successful secondary school completion and college entry. Like higher levels, it requires the ability to integrate several sources of information and solve more complex problems.

Levels 4 and 5 describe respondents who demonstrate command of higher-order information processing skills.

ANNEXURE 4. TABLE SHOWING LITERACY LEVELS IN WEST GODAVARI LITERACY SURVEY

(2A)	Reading
2A1	Can recognize all letters of Telugu and also numbers up to 10, but cannot read combing the letters and words.
2A2	Can read words with conjunctions, and also, numbers up to 100.
2A3	Can read simple sentences with conjunctions; able to do additions and deductions up to 100.
2B	Writing
2B1	Can write letters and also numbers up to 10, but cannot write combining the letters and words.
2B2	Can write words with conjunctions, and also, numbers up to 100.
2B3	Can write simple sentences but not the level of literate and can do simple calculations.

ANNEXURE 5. LIST OF SUBJECTS COVERED IN *JANAVACHAKAM* PRIMER USED IN NAEP IN ANDHRA PRADESH

Lesson No.	Subject
0.	Signature to give confidence to the learner and see own name in letters
1.	Numbers
2.	We can read
3.	We can write
4.	Education for All
5.	Population education
6.	Cooperative movement
7.	Agriculture encouraging manures and pesticides
8.	Agriculture on multi-cropping
9.	Loans and credit

(Continued)

(Continued)

Lesson No.	Subject
10.	Motherland
11.	Small family norm
12.	Environment and social forestry
13.	Understanding society
14.	Inflation
15.	Child-rearing and parenting
16.	Patriotism
17.	India and Andhra Pradesh
18.	Details of our country and people
19.	Revision

ANNEXURE 6. LESSONS IN TLC PRIMERS DEVELOPED BY SRC, HYDERABAD (USED IN MAJORITY OF DISTRICTS IN ANDHRA PRADESH)

Primer I
1. Individual needs and satisfying them through hard work
2. Income generation
3. Education for all
4. Minimum wages
5. How improve income
6. Small family norm
7. Savings
8. Team work
9. Village development

Primer II
1. Child marriages
2. Over expenditure for social functions
3. Gender equity
4. Immunization
5. Home remedies
6. Child-rearing

7. Personal and environment hygiene
8. Green trees and environment
9. Over population
10. Comic story

Primer III
1. Improved production through agriculture methods
2. Adulteration
3. Cooperative movement
4. Using government schemes
5. Selling votes for money (voter awareness)
6. Community development through unity
7. Rivers in the state
8. India is our country
9. Application form and promissory note

ANNEXURE 7. LIST OF SUBJECTS COVERED IN SAAKSHAR BHARAT PROGRAMME PRIMERS DEVELOPED BY SRC, HYDERABAD

Primer I
1. Individual needs and satisfying them through hard work
2. Income generation
3. Education for all
4. Minimum wages
5. How to improve income
6. Small family norm
7. Savings
8. Team work
9. Village development

Primer II
1. Child marriages
2. Over expenditure for social functions
3. Gender equity
4. Immunization
5. Home remedies

6. Child-rearing
7. Personal and environment hygiene
8. Green trees and environment
9. Over population
10. Comic story

Primer III

1. Improved production through agriculture methods
2. Adulteration
3. Cooperative movement
4. Using government schemes
5. Selling votes for money (voter awareness)
6. Community development through unity
7. Rivers in the state
8. India is our country
9. Application form and promissory note

ANNEXURE 8. NON-FORMAL EDUCATION MONITORING INFORMATION SYSTEM VARIABLES AND INDICATORS

Variable	Indicator
NFE Providers	Number of NFE Providers by type of agency and type of programme
Target Group	% of target group on total population by gender and age
Educators	Number of educators by gender, age, level of skills and education
	% of instructors by level of education
Village/Habitations Covered	% of villages/habitations covered by NFE
Enrolment	% of learners enrolled by gender and age in target population
	Proportion of learners by type of NFE programme

Variable	Indicator
Environment Building	Number of publicity programmes/awareness activities regarding NFE programmes for demand creation
	% of targeted habitations covered
Infrastructure	% of units having infrastructure facilities for conduct of NFE
Teaching Learning Material	% of learners provided with TLM by type of programme
Curriculum	Type of curriculum adopted in the courses
Training	Duration of training to instructors by type of programme and level of education
Incentive	% of instructors provided incentives by range
Contact Hours	Number of contact hours by type of programme
	Proportion of actual contact hours on planned contact hours
Teaching Methods	Type of teaching methods followed during the course
Attendance	% of learners in different ranges of attendance
Course Completion	% of participants who completed the course
Level of Equivalency	% of participants who appear for the exam in equivalency programmes by grade in formal system.
Knowledge/Skills Level	% of learners by level of knowledge or skills acquired
Budget	% of resources/budget earmarked for NFE of total budget by type of programme, by agency
Learner Cost	Per learner cost by type of programme
Linkages Established	% of participants established linkage with formal education/development agencies
Dropout/Retention	Dropout rate/retention rate
Use of Skills Acquired	% of completers who applied skills/knowledge acquired in NFE in their day to day life
Demand for Upgradation of Skills	% of completers taking action for upgradation of skills/knowledge
Improvement in Socio-Economic Matters	% of completers who have got improvement of their income, productivity or quality of life, etc.

ANNEXURE 9. EXPENDITURE ON BASIC LITERACY IN SAAKSHAR BHARAT AND PER LEARNER COST

S. No.	State/UT	Expenditure under Basic Literacy (in ₹ crores)	Committed Liability under Basic Literacy (in ₹ crores)	Total Certified March 15 (in ₹ crores)	Per Learner Cost (in ₹)
1	Assam	9.69	14.02	0.0313	757.51
2	Jharkhand	4.42	18.5	0.0531	431.64
3	Maharashtra	2.97	2.97	0.016	371.25
4	Telangana	34.5	2.12	0.1	366.2
5	Nagaland	2.74	0.73	0.0097	357.73
6	Meghalaya	0.49	0.01	0.0014	357.14
7	Arunachal Pradesh	2.83	0.7	0.0115	306.96
8	Himachal Pradesh	1	0	0.0041	243.9
9	Manipur	1.98	0	0.0095	208.42
10	Sikkim	0.3	0.006	0.0016	191.25
11	Karnataka	42.87	8	0.2714	187.44
12	Dadra and Nagar Haveli	0.16	0.17	0.0018	183.33
13	Tripura	0.65	0.18	0.0047	176.6
14	Uttarakhand	5.92	0.34	0.0366	171.04
15	Odisha	6.33	0	0.0383	165.27
16	Haryana	2.79	0	0.0189	147.62
17	Chhattisgarh	34.68	0	0.2706	128.16
18	West Bengal	28.72	0	0.2385	120.42
19	Rajasthan	48.7	2	0.4269	118.76
20	Bihar	68.87	12.28	0.8127	99.85
21	Andhra Pradesh	41.9	0	0.421	99.52
22	Madhya Pradesh	5.68	0	0.0714	79.55

S. No.	State/UT	Expenditure under Basic Literacy (in ₹ crores)	Committed Liability under Basic Literacy (in ₹ crores)	Total Certified March 15 (in ₹ crores)	Per Learner Cost (in ₹)
23	Uttar Pradesh	27.47	0	0.6141	44.73
24	Gujarat	2.17	0	0.0596	36.41
25	Tamil Nadu	7.06	0	0.2159	32.7
26	Jammu and Kashmir	0	0	0.0146	0
27	Punjab	0	0	0.0031	0
	Total	**375.2**	**48.01**	**3.73**	**113.55**

Source: Quarterly Review Meeting of State Literacy Missions, held on 9 June 15.

REFERENCES

Abadzi, H. (2003a). *Adult literacy: A review of implementation experiences.* Washington, DC: The World Bank.

———. (2003b). *Improving adult literacy outcome: Lessons from cognitive research in developing countries.* Washington, DC: The World Bank.

Ahl, H. (2006). Motivation in adult education: A problem solver or a euphemism for direction and control? *International Journal of Lifelong Education, 25*(5), 385–405.

Andhra Pradesh Directorate of Adult Education. (APDAE 2003). *Diagnostic study reportflNFEMIS pilot project.* Andhra Pradesh, India.

ASPBAE. (2006). Resourcing for quality: Adult literacy learning. Background paper prepared for the *Education for All Global Monitoring Report 2006,* Paris, UNESCO. Retrieved from http://unesdoc.unesco.org/images/0014/001459/145938e.pdf

Athreya, V. B., & Chunkath, S. R. (1996). *Literacy and empowerment.* New Delhi: SAGE Publications.

Balasubramanian, K. (2005). Country paper–India. In *Literacy and livelihoods: Learning for life in a changing world.* Proceedings of International Expert Meeting, Vancouver, Canada, Commonwealth of Learning. Retrieved from http://oasis.col.org/handle/11599/139

Becker, G. S. (1964). *Human capital: A theoretical and empirical analysis, with special reference to education.* Chicago, IL: The University of Chicago Press.

BGVS. (1993). *Grey areas in post-literacy.* New Delhi: Author.

Bhola, H. S. (1988). A policy analysis of adult literacy education in India: Across the two national policy reviews of 1968 and 1986. Paper presented at the *32nd Annual Conference of the Comparative and International Education Society,* Atlanta, GA, 17–20 March. Retrieved from https://files.eric.ed.gov/fulltext/ED290909.pdf

———. (1990). *Evaluating ‡literacy for development· projects, prgrams and campaigns: Evaluation planning, design and implementation, and utilization of evaluation results.* Unesco Institute for Education and German Foundation for International Development, Hamburg Germany. Retrieved from https://unesdoc.unesco.org/ark:/48223/pf0000087728

Bhola, H. S. (1991a). Literacy as a social process: Literacy as social intervention. *ASPBAE Courier 47*, 6–14. Retrieved from https://files.eric.ed.gov/fulltext/ED340261.pdf

———. (1991b). Organizing adult education for all. Background document for the International symposium on the question of organizational and institutional arrangements for delivery of adult education, UNESCO, Paris, and Osaka University of Economic and Law, Osaka, Japan. Retrieved from https://files.eric.ed.gov/fulltext/ED332043.pdf

——— (2006). Approaches to monitoring and evaluation in literacy programmes. Paper commissioned for Literacy for Life, the *Education for All Global Monitoring Report 2006*, Paris, UNESCO Institute of Education.

———. (2008). Adult literacy for sustainable development: Creating a knowledge-based discourse for action. In *Signposts to literacy for sustainable development*, Hamburg, Germany, UNESCO Institute for Lifelong Learning.

———. (2010). Literacy. *Indian Journal of Adult Education*, 71(2, April–June), 5–29.

Bordia, A. (1980). The national adult education programme: Background and prospects. In A. B. Shah & S. Bhan (Eds.), *Non-formal education and the NAEP*. New Delhi: Oxford University Press.

———. (1982). *Planning and administration of national literacy programmes: The Indian experience*. Paris: IIEP (mimeo).

———. (1999). Agenda for adult education research: The South Asian perspective. In W. Mauch (Ed.), *World trends in adult education research,* Hamburg, Germany, UNESCO Institute for Education.

Carlsen, A. (2010). Adult education and lifelong learning: International developments. In *Compendium on literacy and inclusive development*. New Delhi: NLM.

Census of India. (2011). *Provisional population totals: India datasheet 2011*. New Delhi: Office of the Registrar General Census Commissioner.

Chakrabarti, V. (2012). Planning and management of continuing education programme. In *Two decades of national literacy mission: Some perspectives*. New Delhi: Indian Adult Education Association.

DAE. (2003a). *Handbook for developing IPCL material*. New Delhi: Ministry of Education and Social Welfare, GoI.

———. (2003b). *Diagnostic study report, NFEMIS pilot project*. Andhra Pradesh, India.

Daniel, J. (2005). Keynote address of expert meeting on literacy. In *Literacy and livelihoods: Learning for Life in a changing world*. Proceedings of International Expert Meeting, Vancouver, Canada, Commonwealth of Learning. Retrieved from http://www.paddle.usp.ac.fj/collect/paddle/index/assoc/col007.dir/doc.pdf

Daswani, C. J. (2000). Total literacy campaigns in India: Status and issues. In C. J. Daswani & S. Y. Shah (Eds.), *Adult education in India: Selected papers*. New Delhi: UNESCO.

Dave, R. H. (1976). Foundations of lifelong education: Some methodological aspects. In R. H. Dave (Ed.), *Foundation of lifelong education*. Hamburg, Germany: UNESCO Institute for Education.

Dighe, A. (1996). The impact of literacy on women in India. In Carolyn Medel-Anonuevo (Ed.), *Women reading the world: Policies and practices of literacy in Asia*. Hamburg, Germany: UNESCO Institute for Education.

Dighe, A. (2000). *Social mobilization and total literacy campaigns: Year 2000 Assessment, Education for All*. New Delhi: MHRD and NIEPA.

———. (2005a). Pedagogical approaches to literacy acquisition. Background paper commissioned for the *EFA Global Monitoring Report 2006*, Literacy for Life, Paris, UNESCO.

———. (2005b). Improving the quality of training of adult education practitioners in the South Asian region: Some considerations. In F. Youngman & M. Singh (Eds.), *Strengthening the training of adult educators*. Hamburg: UNESCO Institute for Education. Retrieved from http://unesdoc.Org/images/0013/001398/139862eo.pdf

Dumont, B. (1990). Post-literacy: A prerequisite for literacy. In *Literacy lessons series*. Paris: UNESCO.

Dutta, S. C. (1986). *History of adult education in India*. New Delhi: Indian Adult Education Association.

Facilicom Consult. (2003). *Steps and methods to mobilize the community*. Retrieved from http://siteresources.worldbank.org/INTECAREGTOPCOMDRIDEV/34004326-1113591395520/20451886/smallgrantshighlight1.pdf

Faure, E., Herrera, F., Kaddoura, A. R., Lopes, H., Petrovsky, A. V., Rahnema, M., ... Ward, F. C. (1972). *Learning to be: The world of education today and tomorrow*. Paris: UNESCO.

Freire, P. (1972). *Pedagogy of the oppressed*. New York, NY: Penguin Books.

George, A. (2000). Beyond literacy: The adult literacy movement in Nellore and its impact. In M. Karlekar (Ed.), *Reading the word: Understanding the literacy campaigns in India*. Mumbai: Asian South Pacific Bureau of Adult Education.

GoI. (1966). *Report of the education commission 1964fi66*. New Delhi: Ministry of Education.

Gomez, S. V. (2008). Luggage for journey: From literacy and development to integral literacy and sustainable development. In *Signposts to literacy for sustainable development*. Hamburg, Germany: UNESCO Institute for Lifelong Learning.

Hamadache, A., & Martin, D. (1986). *Theory and practice of literacy work: Policies, strategies and examples*. Paris: UNESCO.

Illich, I. (1971). *Deschooling society*. New York, NY: Penguin Books.

Jarvis, P. (1985). *The sociology of adult and continuing education*. Beckenham: Croom Helm.

Kak, K. K. (2000). Planning and non-literate Indian. In C. J. Daswani & S. Y. Shah (Eds.), *Adult education in India: Selected papers*. New Delhi: UNESCO.

Knowles, M. (1980). *The modern practice of adult education: From pedagogy to andragogy*. Cambridge: The Adult Education Company.

Kumar, K. (1989). *Social character of learning*. New Delhi: SAGE Publications. Retrieved from http://www.arvindguptatoys.com/arvindgupta/socialcharacter.pdf

Kumar, K. K. (2010). Strengthening India's adult education policy in the context of the Belem framework. In *Compendium on literacy and inclusive development*. New Delhi: NLM.

Maslow, A. A. (1987). *Motivation and personality*. New York, NY: Addison Wesley Longman.

Mathew, A. (1990). *Ministry of education: An organisational history*. New Delhi: NIEPA.

———. (2012). India's new perspective of adult education. In *Compendium on literacy & inclusive development*. New Delhi: NLM.

———. (2013). Conceptual evolution of adult education in India and correspondence with global trends. *Journal of Educational Planning and Administration*, 27(2), 179–201.

———. (2014). Indian adult education in the context of global scenario: A critical and comparative appreciation. In *Literacy and adult education: Selected readings*. New Delhi: NUEPA.

Mathew, A., & Rao, C. K. M. (1994, 22 January). Divergent perceptions of literacy campaigns: Towards a balanced view. *Mainstream*, pp. 15–23.

McCaffery, J., Merrifield, J., & Millican, J. (2007). *Developing adult literacy: Approaches to planning, implementing, and delivering literacy initiatives*. Oxford, UK: Oxfam.

Mercy Corps. (2009). *Guide to community mobilisation programming*. Retrieved from https://www.mercycorps.org/sites/default/files/CoMobProgrammingGd.pdf

Merh-Ashraf, S. (2004). *Adult education in India: Search for a paradigm*. New Delhi: Sunrise Publishers.

MHRD. (1988). *National literacy mission*. New Delhi: Department of Education.

———. (1992). *Total literacy campaigns: Guidelines for project formulation*. New Delhi: Department of Education.

———. (2009). *Centrally sponsored scheme: Saakshar Bharat*. New Delhi: Department of School Education and Literacy.

Ministry of Education and Social Welfare. (1978). *National adult education programme: An outline*. New Delhi: GoI.

Mohankumar, V. (2009). Training: Meaning, functions and methods. *Indian Journal of Adult Education*, 70(2), 46–70.

Mohankumar. V., & Dua, S. C. (2012). List of external evaluation reports on total literacy campaigns. In *Two decades of national literacy mission: Some perspectives*. New Delhi: Indian Adult Education Association.

NIC. (2011). *Web-based planning and monitoring information system (WePMIS): User manual*. New Delhi: NLM and NIC.

NICHD. (2000). *National reading panelflTeaching children to read: An evidence-based assessment of the scientific research literature on reading and its implications for reading instruction.* Retrieved from https://www1.nichd.nih.gov/publications/pubs/nrp/Documents/report.pdf

NLM. (1988). *Jana Shikshan Nilayam.* New Delhi: MHRD, Department of Education.

———. (1994). *Evaluation of literacy campaign in India: Report of expert group.* New Delhi: MHRD, GoI.

———. (1998). *Scheme of continuing education for neo-literates.* New Delhi: MHRD, Department of Education.

———. (2008). *National report for CONFINTEA VI.* New Delhi: Department of School Education & Literacy, MHRD, GoI of India.

Oxenham. J., Dialllo, A. H., Katahoire, A. R., Petkova-Mwangi, A., & Sall, O. (2002). *Skills and literacy training for better livelihood: A review of approaches and experiences* (Working Paper Series). African Region Human Development, World Bank Africa Region.

Patel, I. (1994). *Trends in adult education research in India.* New Delhi: National Institute of Adult Education (mimeo).

———. (1996). Analysis of total literacy campaign primers. In Carolyn Medel-Anonuevo (ed.), *Women reading and the world: Policies and practices of literacy in Asia.* Hamburg, Germany: UNESCO Institute for Education.

———. (2000). India: Adult education—Legislative and policy environment. In Daswani C. J. and Shah, S. Y. (eds), *Adult education in India: Selected papers.* New Delhi, UNESCO.

Perfetti, C. A., & Marron, M. A. (1995). *Learning to read: Literacy acquisition by children and adults.* Philadelphia: National Centre on Adult Literacy. Retrieved from https://files.eric.ed.gov/fulltext/ED396155.pdf

PGAS. (1998). *Continuing education programme in West Godavari District.* Eluru, Andhra Pradesh, India.

———. (2000a). *Akshara anubhavalu* [literacy experiences] (Telugu). Eluru, Andhra Pradesh: Author.

———. (2000b). *Literacy survey.* Eluru, Andhra Pradesh (mimeo).

Planning Commission. (2008). *Eleventh Five Year Plan, 2007fi2012.* Social Sector Volume II. New Delhi: GoI, Oxford University Press.

Premchand. (2014). Impact of adult literacy programmes on literacy—A study. *Indian Journal of Adult Education*, 75(3), 28–32.

Prinsloo, M. (2005). Connections between child and adult literacy regarding learning, skill levels and practice. Paper commissioned for the *EFA Global Monitoring Report 2006*, Literacy for Life, Paris, UNESCO. Retrieved from https://pdfs.semanticscholar.org/4cda/5aeaa2a5425e594dadf7120c022c68 52723f.pdf

Psacharopoulos, G. (2006). The value of investment in education: Theory, evidence, and policy, *Journal of Education Finance*, 32(2), 113–136. Retrieved from http://www.jstor.org/stable/40704288

Quigley, B. A. (1997). *Rethinking literacy education: The critical need for practice-based change*. San Francisco: Jossey-Bass Publishers.

Ranganayakamma. (1995). *Telugu narpadam ela?* Vijayawada: Aruna Publishing House.

Rao, C. K. M. (1988). *Factors influencing adult education programmes: Their differential impact in tribal and non-tribal areas* (PhD Thesis). Visakhapatnam, Andhra University.

Rao, N., & Govinda, R. (2000). Evaluating literacy campaigns: Issues and prospects. In M. Karlekar (Ed.), *Reading the word: Understanding the literacy campaigns in India* (pp. 337–348). Sydney, Australia: Asian South Pacific Bureau of Adult Education.

Robeyns, I. (2006). Three models of education: Rights, capabilities and human capital. *Theory and Research in Education, 4*(1), 69–84.

Rogers, A. (2004a). Adult literacy—Adult Motivation. *Journal AEDfIAdult Education and Development, 61*. Retrieved from http://www.iiz-dvv.de/index. php?article_id=342&clang=1

———. (2004b). The world of adult literacy today. In G. M. Farrell (Ed.), *ICT and literacy: Who benefits? Experiences from India and Zambia*. Vancouver: Commonwealth of Learning.

———. (2005). Literacy and productive skills training: Embedded literacies. *Journal AEDfIAdult Education and Development, 65*. Retrieved from http://www. dvv-international.de/adult-education-and-development/editions/aed-652005

Scottish Executive. (2003). *An adult literacy and numeracy curriculum framework for Scotland*. Edinburgh: Learning Connection, Communities Scotland.

Scribner, S., & Cole, M. (1981). *The psychology of literacy*. Cambridge: Harvard University Press.

Selvaraj, M. S. (1986). *Adult learning theories*. New Delhi: Directorate of Adult Education, MHRD, Department of Education, GoI.

Shah, S. Y. (1998). Professionalization of Indian adult education. Paper presented at *Second Asia Regional Literacy Forum*, 9–13 February 1998, New Delhi. Retrieved from http://files.eric.ed.gov/fulltext/ED443949.pdf

———. (1999). *An encyclopaedia of Indian adult education*. New Delhi: NLM, MHRD, Department of Education, GoI.

———. (2008). Funding adult education programmes in India: A study of policy, process, pattern and problems. Paper presented as *Paulo Friere Memorial Lecture 2008*. Retrieved from *http://www.academia.edu/3424810/ Funding_Adult_Education_Programmes_in_India_A_Study_of_Policy_Process_ Pattern_and_Problems*

———. (2009). Mapping the field of training in adult and lifelong learning India. Paper presented in *Teachers and Trainers in Adult Education and Lifelong Learning: Professional Development in Asia and Europe*, 29–30 June 2009, Bergisch Gladbach. Retrieved from http://www.die-bonn.de/asem/ asem0921.pdf

Shah, S. Y. (2012). Adult education in India: Historical perspective. In *Two decades of national literacy mission: Some perspectives*. New Delhi: Indian Adult Education Association.

Shamsu, S. (2012). Allocation of budgetary resource for adult education. In *Compendium on literacy and adult education*. New Delhi: NLM.

Spratt, J. E. (2004). *Alternatives for literacy assessment* (Working Papers 2005–001). SIL International. Retrieved from https://www.Sil.org/resources/publications/entry/7844

Street, B. V. (1984). *Literacy in theory and practice*. Cambridge University Press.

Tilak, J. B. G. (2016). Providing adequate financial resources for adult education sector. Paper presented in national conference *Towards Literate India: Prospects & Strategies*, 28 June 2016, NLM, MHRD, Department of School Education and Literacy, GoI, New Delhi.

Torres, R. M. (2002). Lifelong learning in the North and educational for all in the South. In Carolyn Medel-Anonuevo (Ed.), *Integrating lifelong learning perspective*. Hamburg: Germany, UNESCO Institute for Education.

UIL. (2013). *2nd global report on adult learning and education: Rethinking literacy*. Hamburg, Germany: UIL.

UIS. (2005). *Literacy assessment and monitoring programme (LAMP)*. Montreal, Canada. Retrieved from www.uis.unesco.org

UNESCO. (1956). *Working paper on the definition of fundamental education*. Administrative Committee on Co-ordination Working Group, UNESCO, Paris. Retrieved from http://unesdoc.unesco.org/images/0014/001448/144817eb.pdf

———. (1993a). *Continuing education: New policies and directions*. APPEAL Training Material for Continuing Education Personal, Bangkok, UNESCO Principal Regional Office for Asia and the Pacific.

———. (1993b). *Post-literacy programmes*. APPEAL Training Material for Continuing Education Personnel, Bangkok, UNESCO Principal Regional Office for Asia and the Pacific.

———. (1998). *Monitoring and evaluation of literacy and continuing education programmes: Practitioners„ manual*. APPEAL, Bangkok, UNESCO Principal Regional Office for Asia and the Pacific.

———. (2004). *Plurality of literacy and its implications for policies and programmes* (Position Paper). Paris: Author.

———. (2005). *Education for all: Literacy for life/EFA Global Monitoring Report 2006*. Paris: Author.

———. (2006). *Handbook for literacy and non-formal education facilitators in Africa*. Paris: UNLD–LIFE Publication.

———. (2015). *EFA global monitoring report, education for all 2000fi2015: Achievements and challenge*. Paris: Author.

———. (2017). *Reading the past and writing the future: Fifty years of promoting literacy*. Paris: Author.

UNESCO Institute of Education. (1997). Final report of fifth International Conference on Adult Education—CONFINTEA V. 14–18 July 1997, Hamburg. Retrieved from https://unesdoc.unesco.org/ark:/48223/pf0000110364

UNICEF. (2003). *The state of the world„s children 2004: Girls, education and development*. New York. Retrieved from https://www.unicef.org/sowc04/files/SOWC_O4_eng.pdf

Varghese, N. V. (2013). Total literacy campaigns in India: A study of their organisation and cost-effectiveness. In A. Mathew & J. B. Tilak (Eds.), *Literacy and adult education: Selected readings*. New Delhi: NUPEA and Shipra Publications.

Varma, D. V. V. S. (1999). *Chaduvu vachakam* (Telugu). Eluru, Andhra Pradesh: Paschima Godavari Akshara Samiti.

Venkatanarayana, M., & Chaganti, R. (2012). *Achieving universal literacy in Andhra Pradesh: Status and prospects* (MPRA Paper No. 48061). Munich Personal RePec Archive, Munich University Library. Retrieved from http://mpra.ub.uni-muenchen.de/48061/1/MPRA_paper_48061.pdf

Wagner, D. A. (1993). *Literacy and development: Rationales, assessment, and innovation*. National Centre for Adult Literacy International Paper IP93–1, Philadelphia, University of Pennsylvania. Retrieved from http://citeseerx.ist.psu.edu/viewdoc/download?doi=10.1.1.20.4825&rep=rep1&type=pdf

World Bank. (n.d.). *Participatory monitoring and evaluation*. Retrieved from http://go.worldbank org/G966Z73P30

INDEX

ABOUT THE AUTHOR

C. Krishna Mohan Rao, who has a doctorate in sociology, has worked in the literacy, adult and non-formal education sectors for over three decades at state, national and international levels in various organizations, including the Government of Andhra Pradesh, the National Institute of Adult Education and UNESCO. During his tenure as the Deputy Director of Adult Education in West Godavari, the district received National Award from the Prime Minister for commendable performance in literacy during the decade 1991–2001. His innovative group-based literacy programme, Akshara Mahila, was recognized as one of the best literacy programmes in the world by UNESCO, and he was invited to address the first White House Conference on Global Literacy in New York in September 2006. He was also selected as a member of the international delegation for literacy advocacy, headed by Mrs Laura Bush, the then First Lady of the United States.

He has many honours and awards to his credit, including Telugu Vishisht Seva Patram from the Government of Andhra Pradesh and Gadicharla Harisarvothama Rao Award by the Potti Sreeramulu Telugu University, Hyderabad. He has published many papers on literacy and development in both English and Telugu. In 2017, he took voluntary retirement from government services and is now working with an NGO on education and development issues.